Video Analysis: Methodology and Methods

Hubert Knoblauch/Bernt Schnettler
Jürgen Raab/Hans-Georg Soeffner
(eds.)

Video Analysis: Methodology and Methods

Qualitative Audiovisual Data Analysis in Sociology

3rd, revised edition

PETER LANG
Frankfurt am Main · Berlin · Bern · Bruxelles · New York · Oxford · Wien

Bibliographic Information published by the Deutsche Nationalbibliothek
The Deutsche Nationalbibliothek lists this publication in the
Deutsche Nationalbibliografie; detailed bibliographic data is
available in the internet at http://dnb.d-nb.de.

Cover Image by Bernardo Fernández.
Reproduces with kind permission by the artist.

ISBN 978-3-631-62041-0
© Peter Lang GmbH
Internationaler Verlag der Wissenschaften
Frankfurt am Main 2012
All rights reserved.

All parts of this publication are protected by copyright. Any
utilisation outside the strict limits of the copyright law, without
the permission of the publisher, is forbidden and liable to
prosecution. This applies in particular to reproductions,
translations, microfilming, and storage and processing in
electronic retrieval systems.

www.peterlang.de

Contents

Introduction

Hubert Knoblauch, Bernt Schnettler & Jürgen Raab
Video-Analysis. Methodological Aspects of Interpretive Audiovisual
Analysis in Social Research 9

Methodologies of Video Analysis

Thomas Luckmann
Some Remarks on Scores in Multimodal Sequential Analysis 29

Christian Heath & Paul Luff
Video Analysis and Organisational Practice 35

Lorenza Mondada
Video Recording as the Reflexive Preservation and Configuration of
Phenomenal Features for Analysis 51

Hubert Knoblauch
Videography. Focused Ethnography and Video Analysis 69

Jürgen Raab & Dirk Tänzler
Video Hermeneutics 85

Research Fields of Video Analysis

Dirk vom Lehn & Christian Heath
Discovering Exhibits: Video-Based Studies of Interaction in Museums and
Science Centres 101

Cornelius Schubert
Video Analysis of Practice and the Practice of Video Analysis. Selecting
field and focus in videography 115

Anssi Peräkylä & Johanna Ruusuvuori
Facial Expression in an Assessment 127

Monika Wagner-Willi
On the Multidimensional Analysis of Video-Data. Documentary
Interpretation of Interaction in Schools 143

Bernt Schnettler
Orchestrating Bullet Lists and Commentaries. A Video Performance Analysis of Computer Supported Presentations 155

Practices of Video Analysis

Elisabeth Mohn
Permanent Work on Gazes. Video Ethnography as an Alternative Methodology 173

Eric Laurier & Chris Philo
Natural Problems of Naturalistic Video Data 183

Sigrid Schmid
Video Analysis in Qualitative Market Research – from Viscous Reality to Catchy Footage 193

Epilogue

Hans-Georg Soeffner
Visual Sociology on the Basis of 'Visual Concentration' 209

Contributors to this volume 219

Introduction to the third edition

Methods for analyzing social interaction with audio-visual data have improved significantly over the past few years. It is only a slight exaggeration to say that this research area has been expanding enormously in the last few years, and the interest in qualitative video analysis is growing at dizzy speed. This rapid development was not anticipated at the time when the first edition of this book was prepared and published. A second edition is already sold out. The editors, as well as the contributors, are pleasantly surprised by the widespread attention this book and the papers included have received. Unusual enough for an edited book of this type, it is therefore living to see a third edition.

One of the reasons for this widespread interest may lie in the fact that it was probably the first book published in English to address the methodology of interpretive video analysis in the Social Sciences. As a collected volume, it, secondly, includes a number of excellent contributions which are grounded in decades of experience with video analysis, particularly in the ethnomethodological tradition. Represented by authors like Christian Heath, this mostly anglo-saxon strand has, undoubtedly, set the international standards for qualitative video analysis in this area (for a historical overview cf. Erickson 2011). A third reason for the interest in this book is to be seen in its methodological pluralism. When we first published this collection, it was our firm intention to open the methodological debate between different theoretical traditions within the field of qualitative social research using video data. Therefore, the book at hand includes contributions representing forms of video analysis more entrenched in the 'continental' tradition of interpretive social research, like communicative genre analysis, sociological hermeneutics or documentary analysis.

As broad as the range of approaches represented in this book may be, the texts are generally committed to what is increasingly called videography. The notion of videography highlights the fact that video is not only used as a technology for analyzing audiovisual data made available by different media, such as film, television or the internet. The notion of videography underlines the fact that the audiovisual data have been recorded by the researchers themselves in a more or less naturalistic social situation (cf. Knoblauch, Schnettler, Tuma, in print).

In the face of the rapid changes in the field, the reader should be aware of some publications which give insights in more recent developments of methods of video analysis in various fields, such as education (Goldman et al. 2009; Dinkelaker & Herrle 2009), and on specific issues, such as the analysis of films (Reichertz & Englert 2011). The most prominent and encompassing publication on qualitative video analysis is, without doubt, the monograph by Heath, Hindmarsh & Luff (2010). This book will be a useful reference for everyone looking for a thoroughly developed methodology and for practical advice when conducting own research with video data. In addition, the journal *Qualitative Research* recently devoted a special issue (2012) on the question of qualitative video analysis.

Regardless of the increasing number of publications on the methodology of interpretive video analysis, there are still a number of problems and tasks pending to be resolved in the nearer future, which cannot be addressed here (cf. Knoblauch 2012). It is still too early to consider the field as settled. Therefore, the temptation to update the articles in this book was high. For reasons of feasibility as well as time and costs we had to dismiss the idea of an updated version. We remit the interested reader to another book in preparation in which we discuss in detail recent developments in video analysis (Tuma, Schnettler & Knoblauch 2012). It also includes examples from our own research and provides practical instructions.

Particularly with respect to the methods of collecting and analyzing audiovisual recordings, books, however, are of limited help when seeking to enhance ones methodological skills and expertise. For video analysis, as in many other qualitative methods, the old boy scout's aphorism "Learning by Doing" applies. Fortunately enough, there are now numerous workshops and special training courses on how to conduct video data analysis.

With the present third edition, we make available once again what has resulted as an important milestone in the development of interpretive video analysis. We wish to express our gratitude to Dr. Kloss from the editing company Lang for his patience and solidarity with which he accompanied this project.

Bayreuth, Berlin, Bonn & Magdeburg
Summer 2012

The editors

References

Dinkelaker, J. & Herrle, M. 2009: *Erziehungswissenschaftliche Videographie.* Wiesbaden: VS Verlag für Sozialwissenschaften

Erickson, F. 2011: Uses of video in social research: a brief history. *International Journal of Social Research Methodology* 14, 3, 179–189

Goldman, R., Pea, R., Barron, B. & Denny, S.J. (eds.) 2009: *Video Research in the Learning Sciences.* New York: Routledge & Kegan Paul

Heath, C., Hindmarsh, J. & Luff, P., 2010: *Video in Qualitative Research.* London: Sage

Knoblauch, H., Schnettler, B. & Tuma, R. (in print): Videography, in: Flick, U. (ed.): *Handbook of Qualitative Research*, London: Sage

Knoblauch, H. 2012: Introduction to the special issue of Qualitative Research: Video Analysis and Videography. *Qualitative Research* 12,3: 251-254

Reichertz, J. & Englert, C.J. 2010: *Einführung in die qualitative Videoanalyse. Eine hermeneutisch-wissenssoziologische Fallanalyse.* Wiesbaden: VS

Tuma, R., Knoblauch, H. & Schnettler, B. 2012: *Videographie. Einführung in die Video-Analyse sozialer Situationen.* Wiesbaden: VS (in preparation. An English version of this book will be published by Lang)

Hubert Knoblauch, Bernt Schnettler & Jürgen Raab

Video-Analysis
Methodological Aspects of Interpretive Audiovisual Analysis in Social Research

I

In recent years, we have witnessed the proliferation of an increasingly sophisticated new instrument of data collection: Video camcorders. Camcorders do not only allow for a rich recording of social processes. They also provide and produce a new kind of data for sociology. In fact, some authors believe to be able to discern a "video revolution": the effects of this "microscope of interaction" are expected to be as profound as was the invention of the tape recorder, which gave rise to new research disciplines such as conversation analysis.

In fact, video is much more widely used nowadays in the most diverse branches of society than the tape recorder ever was. Video-art, wedding videos, holiday videos and the huge variety of usages of video on the internet demonstrate to anyone and everyone that video has become a medium that pervades our everyday life. An ever-increasing role is played by video-mediated forms of communication, such as video-conferences (Finn, Sellen & Wilbur 1997). It is quite likely that the dissemination of UMTS will also lead to a more wide-spread use of mobile video mediated communication and video-messaging. Finally, video surveillance technologies have become an accepted part of our daily lives (Fyfe 1999, Fiske 1998).

As accepted and broadly used as camcorders and video records may be in all institutional spheres as well as in private life, the methodological discussion of their use in scholarly studies is greatly underdeveloped. As a medium used by the people themselves, video deserve much closer attention than we are able to pay them in this book. If we, however, look at the science of society – sociology (and, for that matter, other social scientific disciplines) – we discern a wide disregard for video. Whereas text-centred approaches have been subject to innumerable methodological reflections and methodical designs, video has neither as a method of data collection nor as a medium used by the members of our society been able to attract much attention from sociologists and other students of society and culture.

It is for this reason that we would like to take this opportunity to tackle the task of presenting methodologies for the analysis of video. By this we do not mean methodologies for the use of visual data, for this has already been the subject of many books (cf. Banks & Murphy 1997, Davies 1999, Emmison & Smith 2000, Pink 2001).

Instead, we are interested in methodologies that address questions related specifically to analytical work with video recordings.

Very early on, the advantages of video as an observational technique proved to be quite obvious (cf. Gottdiener 1979, Grimshaw 1982, Heath 1986). Compared to observations made by the naked human eye, video recordings appear more detailed, more complete and more accurate. In a technical sense, they are more reliable since they allow data analysis independent of the person who collected the data. However, despite the fact that video now is widely used in sociology and the social sciences, there have been but very few attempts to discuss the methodology of working with this medium as an instrument of data collection and analysis. No doubt, debates on visuality, visual culture and visualisation abound – also in the social sciences. Nowadays, there is a huge amount of criticism at the level of epistemology. Anyone interested in the field will discover flourishing debates on the cultural meaning of videoclips of Madonna's pop songs or the epistemological question as to the hows and whys of the picture's betrayal of the viewer. However, few are the scholars who actually address the question of what to do in case one dares not just to talk about epistemology, but instead to use the medium and work empirically with the data produced within its various forms (Jordan & Henderson 1995, Heath 1986, Lomax & Casey 1998, Heath 1997, for classroom interaction cf. Aufschnaiter & Welzel 2001).

By publishing this volume, we wish to change this situation, at least to some degree. The goal of this book is to provide ways in which videos can be analysed sociologically. The book, then, is an attempt to gather a number of researchers familiar with video analysis in order to focus on, scrutinise and clarify the crucial methodological issues in doing video analysis. The questions we would like to tackle are: what are the central features of video data; what kinds of video data can be distinguished; and particularly how should we analyse and interpret video data? In trying to answer these questions, the book will provide support for all those who are planning to use video as an instrument of data collection and analysis.

II

When we speak of video analysis, it should be stressed that we are not referring to any and all kinds of work with video. To the contrary, there are a number of qualifications to the kind of studies represented in this volume which must be named in addition to all those features mentioned in the papers. First, it will become quite obvious that we have limited the range of studies presented *to social scientific analyses* of video data. People, their actions and the structures constructed by these actions lie at the heart of what is of interest to these studies. Within the social science framework, a variety of disciplines will be represented: sociology, anthropology, linguistics and education – as well as a number of researchers who would locate themselves across these disciplines or in fields in which their studies are being applied (such as architecture, city planning or design). For the sake of brevity and for other contingent reasons, we have to concede that a number of disciplines are not represented in which video analysis has gained some importance, such as the psychology of perception or the visual arts.

The range of disciplines and the kind of video analysis portrayed in this volume share a second feature. Whoever scans the contributions in this book will soon discover that they seem to share a similar topic. Across the variety of fields, most of the studies focus on what one would call activities and interaction. Be they studies of the use of high technology and workplace settings, be they studies of people visiting museum, science studies or classroom investigations etc. – all of them to focus on *visual conduct* in general and on *interaction* in particular. It is the focus on the *audiovisual aspects of people in action* which constitutes the central subject of these video analyses. In more theoretical terms, one could say that the field of video studies is circumscribed by what Erving Goffman called the 'interaction order', i.e. the area of action in which people act in visual co-presence – a co-presence which can be captured by the camera. And since what people do covers a huge range of areas, the potential topics of video analysis is almost endless.

As varied as the topics may be, the manners in which the authors approach their topics are just as distinct. Although video analysis initially privileged experimental settings and studios, the kinds of analyses included here turn to what has come to be called "*natural data*". Of course, natural data does not resemble the data found by natural scientists; since all video analysts agree in the interpretive character of their data, there should be no misunderstanding of natural data in this sense. Instead, by natural data we mean that the recordings are made in situations affected as little as possible by the researchers (Silverman 2005). Natural data refers to data collected when the people studied act, behave and go about their business as they would if there were no social scientists observing or taping them. There is no doubt that the very presence of video technology may exert some influence on the situation that is being recorded, an influence commonly labelled 'reactivity'. In fact, this issue is addressed in this volume. Nevertheless, many studies show that the effect of video becomes negligible in most situations after a certain phase of habituation. The stress on the naturalness of data should, however, not be understood as a total neglect of other kind of situations. Interviews or even experiments may also be subjected to video analyses, the general assumption being that they are not as a result taken to represent something else (i.e. what is talked about in the interview), but only as what they are: interviews or experiments. In general, however, video analyses turn to more profane situations: people at work, people in the museum, people sitting in a café etc. It is, by the way, this orientation towards "natural situations" that leads video analysts to sympathise strongly with ethnography, particularly the kind of ethnography which turns towards encounters, social situations and performances as championed by Erving Goffman (1961, 1967, 1971). In order to distinguish this ethnographically oriented video analysis from other standardised forms of video analysis, it seems therefore quite reasonable to apply to it the term 'videography' (cf. Knoblauch, this volume).

However, although the "naturalness" of the data is a goal towards which video analysts in general strive, it would be misleading to assume that there is only one sort of data for video analysis. Rather, there is a whole array of what may be called "data sorts" produced by video data collection. There are two reasons for this variety: first, because people in "natural situations" may themselves use video recording technology, they provide video researchers with various sorts of videos, such as weddings videos, videos from other festive occasions or bits and pieces of their everyday life. Second, researchers may produce videos in differing ways. They may, for example, ask the actors themselves to portray their everyday life by means of the video, e.g. by producing video diaries[1]; they may actively use the camera as an instrument of visual construction of data or they may edit the video data in various ways which are now much more readily accessible. On these grounds, we would suggest distinguishing between various sorts of video data. By sorts of video data, we refer to the ways in which the data are constructed (cf. Knoblauch 2003: chap. III). Some sorts of video data are sketched on the diagram below. The ways in which data is constructed may be distinguished in two dimensions: on the one hand, the data are manipulated through various technical procedures. No doubt, the technical recording itself may be considered a decisive form of manipulation. However, whereas different technologies (Super 8, V 8, digital video etc.) produce almost the same results, the differing technologies allow for an additional set of manipulations: beginning with repeating, slow motion and single frame, these include ways of selection, highlighting, enlargements etc. We subsume all these forms under the label "record". Secondly, videos may be distinguished by the way they address the situation. Whereas some just try to "copy" what has been visualised, others attempt to make something seen which is not happening without their influence. Wedding guests wish to see the newlyweds kissing each other in front of the camera; the experimenter wishes that the subjects shake hands, the film maker wishes the actors to hit each other. This level of manipulating the situation for the sake of what may be seen on the video by the recipients we call 'recipient design'. Within these two dimensions we can locate a number of data sorts: video-diaries, weddings videos, "natural videos" etc.

The studies represented in this volume share an additional common feature. Whereas in a number of fields, e.g. in psychology or in engineering, we find a strong tendency to standardise, even automatise data analysis (Mittenecker 1987, Koch & Zumbach 2002), the contributors of this volume propose a rather different methodology. It is not that they oppose standardisation or automatisation in general. However, they all share the conviction that it is definitely premature to approach audiovisually

---

[1] Thus Holliday (2000) asked subjects to produce 'auto-ethnographic' videos in order to show how they organize their daily lives. In a similar way, in Anthropology, for example, indigenous people have been asked to use the video in order to preserve their "native" perspective (cf. Ruby 2000).

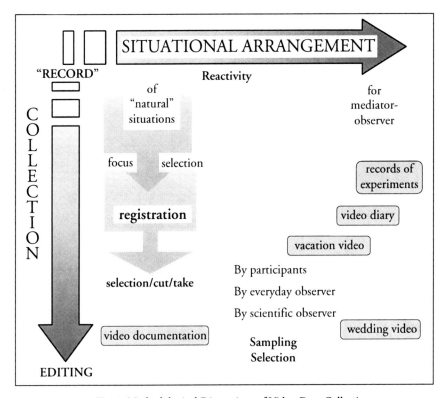

Fig. 1: Methodological Dimensions of Video-Data Collection

recorded data by means of standardised coding procedures. Instead, all of the methods suggested here can be said to relate to what is commonly called *non-standardised, qualitative* or, to be more exact, *interpretive social research*.[2] They share the assumption that the world in which people act is a world of meanings and that, therefore, research on people in action must account for the meaning of these actions. Yet it would be utterly misleading to assume that the volume's methodological orientation is monolithic. Within the field of interpretive or qualitative video analysis, there is still quite a variety of approaches. The volume tries to collect at least the most prominent of them. Ethnomethodology and conversation analysis represent, of course, major fields, as do genre analysis, grounded theory and sociological hermeneutics.

---

2 To Pink (2001), reflexivity is the major feature of visual anthropology in general and video studies in particular. In our view, reflexivity is subordinated to the demand for interpretation – a demand which goes back to founding fathers of interpretive social sciences such as Weber and Schutz.

Thus, the papers as a group share a series of topics which are crucial for the current state of video analysis. In addition to the common orientation as social scientific, naturalistic and interpretive studies of social interaction, all papers stress that *sequentiality* is fundamental to video analysis. Although sequentiality can mean various things, (particularly between the hermeneutic notion and the rather conversation-analytical one), the parallel between the sequentiality of the medium and the sequentiality of social activities is fundamental to video analysis. Since all approaches are interpretive, the analyses build in one way or the other on what may be called "ethno-hermeneutics". They also share the methodological conviction that interpretive analysis of video-data requires more than "visual empathy" combined with a mainly descriptive "structured microanalysis" as Denzin (2000) suggests.

III

There is no doubt that the book cannot at once solve all the problems of video analysis. To the contrary, the papers presented here permit us to identify a series of issues that urgently need to be tackled. First, the problem of *complexity:* the relative neglect of video in the social sciences is sometimes attributed to its complexity and abundance. A few minutes of recording produce a large quantity of visual, kinaesthetic, and acoustic data that must be transcribed and prepared for analysis. Video data is certainly among the most complex data in social scientific empirical research. It is multi-sensual and sequentially ordered, enclosing both diachronic and synchronic elements, e.g. speech and visual conduct, gesture, mimic expressions, representation of artefacts and the structure of the environment, as well as signs and symbols. Moreover, it represents aspects related to recording activity itself, such as the angle and the focus of the camera, the cuts, and other elements pertaining to the activity of filming and editing. Hence, video recording generates an extraordinary abundance of data, confronting the researcher with the problems of data management, retrieval and selection. This may not only cause the problem of data overload, but also raises the question of how to select sequences appropriate for further scrutiny. It might also be the case that the quality of the recordings may be detrimental to analytic purposes. There may be interesting parts of video that can not be selected for further scrutiny due to, for example, recording problems (wrong perspective, defect in recording, people running through the image, etc.). Beyond such obvious practical restrictions, the methodological problem of what constitutes the unit of analysis and how to assure a balance between time-consuming microanalysis and an overview over the whole data corpus remain open questions for future methodological debates.

The second problem to be tackled urgently is the *technological challenge*. The role of technology should be taken into consideration to a much stronger degree than we can do here. The very fact that the methodology is heavily based on a technology subjects it to future technological developments. This does not only raise the question mentioned above of what impact the technology may have on social scientific video analysis (and *vice versa*). Video confronts the researcher with a number of technical and material challenges. Some of them concern the implementation of camera, microphones, software etc. This technical part is still underestimated in the methodological discussion. Even if technology may not be considered an "autonomous actor" (Rammert & Schulz-Schaeffer 2002), the employed artefacts definitely exert at least some influence upon the course of action in the research process. Without doubt, the instruments change the way in which we collect, construct, analyse and interpret our data. Methodological considerations rarely reflect this material issue because we are used to discussing methodology in much more abstract terms. Hence, we may ask in which ways the instruments interfere with our analytical work. This question is especially pertinent for video analysis, which, compared to other qualitative methods, requires quite a lot of technology. Indeed, it may represent one of the most expensive and intricate ways to conduct qualitative research. Fortunately, equipment has become much cheaper and easier to handle in the last few years. Today, filming does not cost us 30,000 German Marks as it did when social psychologist Kurt Lewin started using films in the 1930's (Thiel 2003). Nonetheless, researchers still must purchase camcorders, tapes, tripods, microphones, etc. for the purpose of recording videos. In addition, analysing video data requires intelligent storage and cataloguing systems for raw data, powerful computer hardware and a series of software tools to digitalize, transcribe and analyze data and to present research results. Due to miniaturization and popularization, a very basic version of video equipment has even become accessible for students. Nevertheless, expenses entailed for basic research equipment (somewhere between equipment available for popular use and that used by television professionals) easily may amount to tens of thousands of Euros – in addition to the space, time and patience required to select the appropriate apparatus and software. Its handling requires also novel technical skills, quite unprecedented in qualitative inquiry. And, unlike other, more conventional forms of qualitative research, e.g. participant observation or interviews, preliminaries and preparation take considerably more time in qualitative video analysis. This may cause a certain delay in the analytical work, as quite extended portions of time are consumed by mere "craftsmanship". (As a result, qualitative inquiry may become more similar to quantitative research. As in surveys, much work is invested in preparation, providing skills to the coders, handling the data-collections etc.).

Third, the relation between text and image must be clarified. No doubt, the relation between the spoken and the visual is of general epistemological importance. In the case of video analysis, however, this issue exhibits a very practical aspect: the *transcription* of data inscribes in its particular way how the visual is accounted for by the analysis, so that any further development of video analysis will also depend on the way in which data are being transcribed or otherwise made accessible for analysis. Analysis will increasingly be able to draw on visual representation, with the result that written transcripts may lose their importance to such a degree as to possibly open the way for a "visual mentality" in analysis – a mode of analysing that depends less on the written word than on visualisation and imagination. The ongoing technological changes may also affect the way (and are already now affecting the ways) in which studies are being presented (cf. for example Büscher 2005). However, for the time being, we still rely on the rather conventional forms of transcriptions and frame grabs which are used in this book.[3] Consider that transcribing data is not just a preliminary phase of analysis. It forms an essential part of analysis. Transcribing generates observations that are fundamental to analytical inferences. As in research based on natural communicative activities or interviews, the transcription of video data is simply indispensable.

Conversation analysts and linguists have developed a wide array of transcription systems that transform the analytically important aspects of spoken language into textual representations (cf. Dittmar 2002 for a comprehensive overview). Nevertheless, transcription systems for video data still remain in an experimental stage. "There is no general orthography used for the transcription of visual and tactile conduct". However, "over the years researchers have developed *ad hoc* solutions to locating and characterizing action" (Heath & Hindmarsh 2002: 20?). In this volume, readers will find a variety of approaches for transcribing the visual aspect which, nevertheless, may all be characterized as relatively preliminary. These "ad hoc solutions" are comprised of transcripts consisting basically of detailed description of what occurs in the video. There are also types of transcriptions for the non-verbal aspects and their relation to the verbal behaviour of the participants, 'conduct score', and sketches of action sequences or 'thick interpretative descriptions' in addition to representations of data that attempt to make use of the visual potential of video data.

Finally, one of the most salient problems is the *legal implications* of video-recording. Like any other form of research, video analysis is subject to legal and ethical restrictions. This concerns questions such as: where are video analysts permitted to film, who is permitted to record social interactions for analytical purposes, which of these images may be stored, analyzed or even used for publication and thereby disclosed to a wider audience. Although there have been intense debates on issues related to video recording in public places, their focus has been primarily on security issues and the questions of infringement on individuals' right to privacy. To our knowledge, there is no specific regulation for scientific video recordings at the moment.[4] To assure that some kind of 'informed consent' exists seems to be, in the meantime, the most reasonable practical solution, although there may be cases in which this is virtually impossible (e.g. for each single pedestrian in wide-angle shots of public places). In addition,

---

3 In addition, some of the video recordings analyzed in the different contributions to this book are available at http://www.tu-berlin.de/fb7/ifs/soziologie/AllgSoz/publikationen.htm.
4 We are grateful to Prof. Dr. Hansjürgen Garstka, the German federal government's Secretary for Data Security, for his comment on the legal situation in Europe.

unlike for example the case of interview transcripts, anonymisation of moving images is a technically much more demanding task. Consequently, respecting the right to privacy in video analysis is a difficult and as yet unresolved problem, in addition to the legal implications of possible infringements on copy-rights and other rights that may be touched by capturing, recording, analysing, storing or publishing video data of some sort (i.e. the fine distinction the legal systems draws in the field of data protection in general). Legally, the use of video for scholarly purposes of the kind described above oscillates between the individual freedom, which puts particular restrictions on "natural recording" practices, on the one hand, and the freedom of research, which puts no limits on the potential subjects of video recording to the extent that these may be of scientific relevance. Because of the tension between these two extremes, researchers often find themselves caught in a dilemma. We hope that this dilemma will soon find a legal solution.

IV

As mentioned above, the different directions of video research represented in this volume share a number of features: they are social scientific, naturalistic, interpretive studies of visual conduct. As such, they refer, of course, to the long tradition of sociological thinking in general as well as to the study of social action and interaction in particular. In focusing on the realm of the visual, they also draw on the history of visual anthropology and sociology. The era of visual studies was opened at the turn of the last century, when photography and film started to be used within the social sciences (for an example see Breckindrige & Aboth 1910, MacLean 1903, Walker 1915, Woodhead 1904). By means of visual technologies, anthropology developed a visual branch (Collier 1979, cf. Bateson & Mead 1942, Mead 1975, Collier 1967, Collier & Collier 1986). In the form of the much more tenacious development termed visual sociology (Curry 1984, Curry & Clarke 1978, Henney 1986), it focused mainly on photography, and film was used primarily as a means of presenting results than as a datum to be analysed. Famous early examples are A. C. Haddon, Baldwin Spencer or Robert Flaherty who, starting at the turn of the 19th century, used film in order to analyse human conduct. Flaherty, for example, became familiar with the language and culture of the Inuit Eskimo and involved them in the making of his film studies. Another example is "The Ax Fight" by Asch und Chagnon, in which a short, violent fight among the Yanomamo Indians, filmed from a certain distance, is portrayed. The text of the film consists of the comments made by both researcher during the situation filmed (cf. Marks 1995). No doubt, anthropology developed an unprecedented collection of film data which was, as mentioned, mostly used to document reality instead of analysing it (Heider 1976).

The analysis of films as data took another route. As one of the first to use film as a datum for the study of behaviour, Kurt Lewin filmed a behavioural sequence as early as 1923/1924. Lewin analysed this sequence as an example for a behavioural conflict.

Building on Lewin, in 1935 Gesell published a book on "cinema analysis" as a "method for Behavior Study" in which he used frame-to-frame analysis (for more details cf. Thiel 2003). One could consider the famous analyses of Bali dance by Margaret Mead and Gregory Bateson (1942) as a continuation of these studies. In a later study, Bateson and the so called "Palo Alto group" used film in order to analyse interaction between family members. Again, psychologists were included (such as Frieda Fromm-Reichmann and Paul Watzlawick) because the main goal was to investigate if it is interaction that produces the "psychological disturbance" of individual family members. It was also Fromm-Reichmann who initiated the famous project on the "History of the Interview" in which the various modes of interaction were analysed for the very first time (Bateson 1958). Whereas the use of video in psychology increasingly came to focus on what was called "non-verbal behaviour" (cf. the seminal studies by Ekman & Friesen 1969), a parallel development saw the establishment of a marginal stream of studies with employed films to attempt to capture behaviour in a more encompassing and meaningful way. Among these were the studies of Ray Birdwhistell (1952, 1970), who analysed the interplay between nonverbal and verbal behaviour in minute detail, coining the notion of kinesics. (Birdwhistell also has the distinction of being one of Erving Goffman's teachers, who was to become so important for the study of interaction). In a similar vein, Albert Scheflen (1965) analysed the role of posture for the structuring of psychotherapeutic encounters. Until the 1970s, however, these analyses were performed on the basis of film, which was a difficult medium for analysis. Things changed slowly with the introduction, miniaturisation and technical sophistication of video we have witnessed since then. It was particularly among conversation analysts that this medium gained relevance. This might be surprising since, for a long time (and, to some, until now), "hard core" conversation analysis prohibited the use of data of any other sort than audio recordings. On the other hand, the development of conversation analysis was supported by the use of the audio recorder, and the introduction of the camcorder seemed to extend the kind of data collection conversation analysts had been used to. Charles Goodwin was one of the first to use video in the way. He analysed spoken interaction in such a way as to show how visual aspects (particularly gaze) help to bestow order (Goodwin 1986, Goodwin 1981). Erickson and Shultz (1982) used video in their studies of four school counsellors in their interview interaction with pupils. Also in the early 1980s, Christian Heath undertook video studies, targeting whole social situations such as medical encounters (Heath 1986). By the late 1970s, Thomas Luckmann and Peter Gross (1977) started a project which used video in order to develop an annotation system for interactions which was compared to a musical score. In a way, this project analyzed what has become to be called multimodality, even if most studies in this volume tackle this issue in a rather holistic way. Whereas this gave rise to a hermeneutic (Bergmann, Luckmann & Soeffner 1993, Raab 2001, 2002) and genre-analytic approach to video (Schnettler 2001, Knoblauch 2004), it was the more ethnomethodological approach of video analysis which became increasingly employed in workplace studies, a field of research preoccupied with interaction at work in high technology settings (cf. Heath, Knoblauch & Luff 2000). It was again Christian Heath and his team who has contributed substantially to this field, as well as Lucy Suchman, Charles Goodwin, and Brigitte Jordan, etc. As far as we can see, it is only within this area that serious reflections on an interpretive methodology of video analysis have been undertaken. Thus, Christian Heath and others have sketched the methodological background of video analysis in several essays (1997) and Suchman & Trigg (1991) have explained the ways in which video contributes to workplace studies. Brigitte Jordan and Austin Henderson (1995) have tried to situate video analysis within the larger framework of interaction analysis. In a similar field of research, the French sociology of work, we even find a whole journal issue devoted to the issues of video analysis and visual sociology (see for example Lacoste 1997).

V

The *papers in this volume* build on this type of video analysis; they are, as we have said, all social scientific, interpretive and naturalistic. As we shall see, their subject is human action and interaction. Despite the similarities, the focuses of the papers varies to some degree, so we have decided to put them in an order that reflects this variation.

The first series of papers focuses on *methodological issues* and address the question how video data may be analysed in a scientific manner. This question is addressed by other papers, too, since it is the common topic of the whole book. The papers in this section directly address this topic and propose analytical methodologies. These papers delineate approaches oriented to conversation analysis, ethnography or hermeneutics and, like THOMAS LUCKMANN in his short paper "Some Remarks on Scores in Multimodal Sequential Analysis", interpretive sociology in general. As he indicates, video provides a very helpful instrument for the analysis of interaction since it, despite all technical transformations, preserves the temporal and sequential structure which is so characteristic of interaction. Nevertheless, video analysis faces some serious problems which may be the reason for what he considers the "backwardness" of this method. It is the integration of the many modes of interaction, particularly the integration of the spoken and the visual, which must be addressed by a successful methodology.

CHRISTIAN HEATH and PAUL LUFF ("Video-Analysis and Organisational Practice") address the methodology of video analysis from a quite unusual and enlightening angle. Instead of sketching the ways in which analysis that meets scholarly standards should be conducted, the authors demonstrate very lucidly how video is analysed by lay persons in our societies. In treating actors whose professions require that they watch and on this basis interpret the behaviour of other actors as represented on video, they show how operators in undergrounds, personnel in surveillance centres and members of similar professions act as (sometimes quite sophisticated) "lay sociologists" who must make sense of conduct and interactions. This sense-making is not only accomplished by watching but by also with reference to background knowledge and inferences that build on these professionals' understanding of human conduct.

LORENZA MONDADA ("Video Recording as the Reflexive Preservation and Configuration of Phenomenal Features for Analysis") recommends what she calls a "praxeological approach" to video practices. On the basis of an ethnomethodologically inspired video analytic framework, she strives to take into account not only the question of how data are analysed, but also how they are produced. She addresses exactly what we referred to above as data sorts, i.e. the practices by which data are constructed. One kind of practice she refers to is the "praxeology of seeing", i.e. the setting up of the video camera before the action, the kinds of camera movements and the filmer's interaction with the camera. Moreover, she also hints at the fact that various professions work skilfully with video data, developing their own "professional vision". In conclusion, she draws attention to the practices of editing video records.

HUBERT KNOBLAUCH points to the problems of analysing video data, proposing an approach he calls "videography". His article explores the potential of combining 'focussed' ethnography with a microscopic analysis of video data. The programmatic title expresses the central importance of ethnographic field research for interpretive video-analysis. In combination with the attentive scrutiny of video sequences, ethnography is indispensable in order to make sense of and reconstruct the meaning of relevant details included in the recordings of social situations. Although video is an especially apt instrument for analyzing the details of action and interaction, a systematic collection of additional background knowledge is also of crucial importance. It is necessary to elucidate the visual aspects of the recordings, as the sequences are both situated and situative, that is both depending on and reflecting the larger social context.

In the final paper of the methodological first section, JÜRGEN RAAB and DIRK TÄNZLER suggest an approach they call "Video Hermeneutics". This approach, based on Soeffner's "structural hermeneutics", has at its core a form of sequential analysis that attempts to reconstruct the range of readings, i.e. meanings, possible for single frames. By comparing different readings of key scenes, readings are excluded in order to arrive at a final, "objective" meaning. The interpretation is based on a "score" and proceeds by setting the context in parenthesis. They illustrate this approach in an analysis of two scenes of a television show.

Although they share the interest in methodology, the papers in the volume's second section highlight the contribution of video analysis to specific *research fields*. Thus, DIRK VOM LEHN and CHRISTIAN HEATH ("Discovering Exhibits: Video-Based Studies of Interaction in Museums and Science Centres") demonstrate how fruitfully video-analysis can be used for museum studies. The particular advantage of this method is that it allows us to study the conduct of visitors of museums arising with, at and around exhibits, in this way addressing the practice of aesthetics which has been so often the subject of abstract theoretical debate. In order to do so, they analyse an example from a science museum. Moreover, their article also explains the reasons for conducting video analysis in general and some of the fundamental methodological issues relevant to such an analysis. Thus, they touch on the work of data collection as well as of transcription. They formulate three basic principles for data analysis: it is concerned with the indexical character of practical action, it considers social action as emergent and contingently accomplished, and it explicates the organisation through which participants produce particular actions.

CORNELIUS SCHUBERT ("Video-Analysis of Practice and the Practice of Video-Analysis") also conceives of video analysis as addressing social practice. In particular, he turns to practices in medicine, that is to say in operating theatres in which actors are confronted with technology to such a degree that it seems plausible to him to frame technology as agents in order to clarify the practice observed. In his reconstruction of the practice of video-analysis, he stresses the role of Grounded Theory. Content logs resembling coding procedures may help the researcher to collect and compare data. Video also may be used as a medium for reflection since it allows for feedback and elicitation. Because video data are thus complemented by interview, observation and narratives, he proposes to call this method videographic video analysis.

ANSSI PERÄKYLÄ and JOHANNA RUUSUVUORI ("Facial Expression in an Assessment") address a topic that had been prominent in psychology for a long time: non-verbal behaviour, or, in this case, facial expression. As opposed to the current attempts to analyse facial expression, they take an approach informed by conversation analysis. With respect to their data, which stems from "quasi-natural" conversations, they focus particularly on conversational assessments, i.e. the evaluations of persons and events that are described in conversational speech. In order to account for facial expressions found in the data, they develop a new transcription code which is added to the transcription of spoken utterances. Thus they demonstrate that the interpretation of facial expressions contribute significantly to assessments made within conversational contexts. Not only are facial displays coordinated interactively, but facial activities also incorporate the affective involvements of speakers with what is being assessed.

MONIKA WAGNER-WILLI bases her analysis of interaction in classrooms on the method of documentary interpretation suggested by Ralf Bohnsack ("On the Multidimensional Analysis of Video-Data. Documentary Interpretation if Interaction in Schools"). This method seeks to account for both the sequential aspects of video data as well as the simultaneity of visual information by distinguishing two dimensions of meaning: the explicit communicative dimension is at work when actors relate to the social role or the institutional order, whereas the conjunctive experiential space refers to the more implicit background commonalities of actors. She studies the threshold phase between breaks and lessons. This phase reveals itself as a transitional, liminal phase inbetween the conjunctive experiential space of the peer group and the communicative sociality of the school class.

BERNT SCHNETTLER ("Orchestrating Bullet Lists and Commentaries. A Video Performance Analysis of Computer Supported Presentations") focuses on a relatively new option in face-to-face communication, which in many formally organized social situations quickly became something of an obligation, and that the author therefore claims to be a specific modern ritual: computer-supported presentations. Computer programs such as Microsoft's PowerPoint offer speakers the opportunity to support their presentations with prefabricated and often animated visual impressions, i.e. diagrams and bullet lists, as well as more complex visual forms such as photos and video clips. Schnettler's video performance analysis inquires into the specific new skills a speaker needs to coordinate different kinds of actions during his or her talk in order to gain social acceptance, and to prove him- or herself to be a competent performer. The case study of a computer-supported presentation arrives at the conclusion that 'translating' and 'conducting attention' are two core elements of a unique type of social action the author calls 'orchestration'.

The contributions to the third part of the book share this interest in methodology, while at the same time drawing as well on a particular empirical field. In addition, they are characterised by their interest in the use of video for research (and the role of video for non-scientific practice). In studying classroom interaction, ELISABETH MOHN ("Permanent Work on Gazes. Video Ethnography as an Alternative Methodology") calls for a manner of using video recordings which differs markedly from the "natural situation documentation" used by many. She draws on data collected while doing research in classrooms. Her argument is that the gaze, that is subjectivity of the video ethnographer as well as the visual character of these ethnographies, should be accounted for in the manner in which the data is collected and analysed. She proposes using video recordings as a form of field notes that follow the interests and the observational focus of the ethnographer. Thus, the camera moves according to what seems of importance to the ethnographer. As a result, the analysis, too, will be based on visual data, representing a departure from the word-centred report in favour of a visual display of the result.

In a similar vein, ERIC LAURIER and CHRIS PHILO ("Natural Problems of Naturalistic Video Data") examine the question of the practical use of video in research settings. Although studying "a day in the life of the café", they come to address what one used to call reactivity. Through their video recordings of people in cafés, they came to realise that the presence of the camera (and the absence of the ethnographer) is a constitutive feature of the setting recorded. Instead of getting rid of "reactivity" and thereby creating naturalness as the (artificial) absence of the recording device, they therefore turn to the ways in which subjects "react" to the presence of a video camera. The video, then, creates in their view a "videoactive context", as Shrum, Duque and Brown (2005) would say. In fact, the subjects do not only react, the video triggers action on their part and thus contributes to the interaction.

Practice in a somewhat different vein is the topic of the paper by SIGRID SCHMID ("Video Analysis in Qualitative Market Research – from Viscous Reality to Catchy Footage"). She discusses the importance video has gained within the qualitative market research. In this applied field, video analysis is employed in two ways: as a presentation tool and as an instrument of data collection. It is especially the ability to visualize consumers' habits or a certain lifestyle within an everyday context that accounts for the advantage of video footage compared to more conventional research methods such as surveys, interviews or focus group studies. For the purpose of presentation, video footage can, she argues, first convey a holistic picture of the complex life worlds of individuals or groups of people. Hence, the production of these video images relies on typologies and findings generated in previous investigations. Secondly, and in a stricter sense, video is used in consumer studies as an instrument for data collection, but it also serves to identify new ideas for product innovation, the testing of prototypes or the further development of existing products.

The final paper returns to general issues of visual analysis. Restricting himself to photography, in his article on "Visual Sociology on the Basis of 'Visual Concentration'", HANS-GEORG SOEFFNER addresses an issue that is of major importance of any future video analysis. For, at this point in the field's development, analysis is conducted by going out of one's way via the use of written texts. Opposing this detour, SOEFFNER suggests that we could represent society through visual means themselves. Such an approach has been taken e.g. by Walker Evans and James Agee, by August Sanders in his famous portraits and also by Pierre Bourdieu. It is possible to use photography to the extent that one is successful in making explicit photography's implicit catalogue of rules and its 'interpretation of the world' and thereby to methodologically control the visual displays. Even if SOEFFNER restricts his argument to photography, one could expect that it will become one of the touchstones in the field of video analysis due to its recommendations for finding ways of presenting findings in visual form and, probably, forms of "visual analysis", as well.

Acknowledgments

We would like to express our gratitude to the *Deutsche Forschungsgemeinschaft* for the kind support of the Conference on Video Analysis as well as of our current research project. We also thank Eric Laurier and Polly Kienle for their help with the revision of some of the manuscripts.

References

Aufschnaiter, S. v. & M. Welzel (ed.) 2001: *Nutzung von Videodaten zur Untersuchung von Lehr- und Lernprozessen.* Münster: Waxmann
Banks, M. & H. Murphy, 1997: *Rethinking Visual Anthropology.* New Haven: Yale
Bateson, G. 1958: Language and Psychotherapy: Frieda Fromm-Reichmann's last project. *Psychiatry 21*, 21, 96-100

Bateson, G. & M. Mead, 1942: *Balinese Character. A Photographic Analysis.* New York: New York Academy of Sciences

Bergmann, J., T. Luckmann & H.-G. Soeffner, 1993: Erscheinungsformen von Charisma – Zwei Päpste. In: W. Gebhardt, A. Zingerle and M. N. Ebertz (ed.) *Charisma – Theorie, Religion, Politik.* Berlin/New York: 121-155

Birdwhistell, R. L., 1952: *Introduction to Kinesics. An Annotation System for the Analysis of Body Motion and Gesture.* Louisville, Kentucky: University of Louisville

Birdwhistell, R. L., 1970: *Kinesics and Context: Essay in Body-Motion Research.* Philadelphia: University of Pennsylvania Press

Breckindrige, S. P. & E. Aboth 1910: Chicagoe's Housing Problems. Families in Furnished Rooms. *American Journal of Sociology*, XVI, 3: 289-308

Büscher, M. 2005: Social life under the microscope? *Sociological Research Online*, 10, 1: http://www.socresonline.org/10/1/buscher.html

Collier, J., 1967: *Visual Anthropology. Photography as a Research Method.* New York: Sage

Collier, J., 1979: Visual Anthropology. In: J. C. Wagner (ed.) *Images of Information. Still Photography in the Social Sciences.* London: Sage, 271-282

Collier, J. & M. Collier, 1986: *Visual Anthropology. Photography as a Research Method.* Albuquerque: University of New Mexico Press

Curry, T. J. 1984: A Rational for Visual Sociology. *International Journal of Visual Sociology*, 1, 13-24

Curry, T. J. & A. C. Clarke, 1978: *Introducing Visual Sociology.* Dubuque: Kendall/ Hunt

Davies, C. A., 1999: Using visual media. In: C. A. Davies (ed.) *Reflexive Anthropology.* London, New York: Routledge, 117-135

Denzin, N. K., 2000: Reading Film – Filme und Videos als sozialwissenschaftliches Erfahrungsmaterial. In: U. Flick, E. v. Kardoff and I. Steinke (ed.) *Qualitative Forschung. Ein Handbuch.* Reinbek bei Hamburg: Rowohlt, 416-428

Dittmar, N., 2002: *Transkription. Ein Leitfaden mit Aufgaben für Studenten, Forscher und Laien.* Opladen: Leske + Budrich

Ekman, P. & W. Friesen 1969: A Tool for the Analysis of Motion Picture Film or Videotapes. *American Psychologist*, 24, 3: 240-43

Emmison, M. & P. Smith, 2000: *Researching the Visual.* London: Sage

Erickson, F. & J. Schultz, 1982: The counsellor as gatekeeper. Social interaction in interviews. In: E. Hammel (ed.) *Language, Thought and Culture: Advances in the Study of Cognition.* New York: Academic Press, 237-260

Finn, K. E., A. J. Sellen & S. B. Wilbur (ed.) 1997: *Video-Mediated Communication.* Mahwah: Erlbaum

Fiske, J. 1998: Surveilling the City. Whiteness, the Black Man and Democratic Totalitarianism. *Theory, Culture and Society*, 15, 2: 67-88

Fyfe, N. R. (ed.) 1999: *Images of the Street. Planning, Identity and Control in Public Space.* London, New York: Routledge

Goffman, E., 1961: *Encounters (dt.: 1973).* Indianapolis: Bobbs-Merrill

Goffman, E., 1967: *Interaction Ritual. Essays on Face-to-Face Behavior.* New York

Goffman, E., 1971: *Relations in Public.* New York: Basic Books

Goodwin, C., 1981: *Conversational Organization: Interaction Between Speakers and Hearers.* New York: Academic Press

Goodwin, C. 1986: Gestures as a Resource for the Organization of Mutual Orientation. *Semiotica*, 62, 1/2: 29-49

Gottdiener, M. 1979: Field research and video tape. *Sociological Inquiry*, 49, 4: 59-66

Grimshaw, A. 1982: Sound-image data records for research on social interaction: some questions answered. *Sociological Methods and Research*, 11, 2: 121-144
Heath, C., 1986: *Body Movement and Medical Interaction*. Cambridge: Cambridge University Press
Heath, C., 1997: The Analysis of Activities in Face to Face Interaction Using Video. In: D. Silverman (ed.) *Qualitative Research. Theory, Method, and Practice*. London: Sage, 183-200
Heath, C. & J. Hindmarsh, 2002: Analysing Interaction: Video, Ethnography and Situated Conduct. In: M. Tim (ed.) *Qualitative Research in Action*. London: Sage, 99-121
Heath, C., H. Knoblauch & P. Luff 2000: Technology and social interaction: the emergence of ›workplace studies‹. *British Journal of Sociology*, 51, 2: 299-320
Heider, K., 1976: *Ethnographic Film*. Austin: University of Texas Press
Henney, L. M., 1986: *Theory and Practice of Visual Sociology (Current Sociology 34, 3)*. Lonon
Holliday, R. 2000: We've been framed: visualizing methodology. *Sociological Review*, 503-521
Jordan, B. & A. Henderson 1995: Interaction analysis: Foundations and Practice. *Journal of the Learning Sciences*, 4, 1: 39-103
Knoblauch, H., 2003: *Qualitative Religionsforschung. Religionsethnographie in der eigenen Gesellschaft*. Paderborn, München, Wien, Zürich: Schöningh/UTB
Knoblauch, H. 2004: Die Video-Interaktions-Analyse. *sozialer sinn*, 1, 123-128
Koch, S. C. & J. Zumbach 2002: The Use of Video Analysis Software in Behavior Observation Research: Interaction Patterns of Task-oriented Small Groups. *FQS*, 3, 2
Lacoste, M. 1997: Filmer pour analyser. L'importance de voir dans les micro-analysis du travail. *Champs Visuels*, 6, 10-17
Lomax, H. & N. Casey 1998: Recording social life: reflexivity and video methodology. *Sociological Research Online*, 3, 2:
Luckmann, T. & P. Gross, 1977: Analyse unmittelbarer Kommunikation und Interaktion als Zugang zum Problem der Entstehung sozialwissenschaftlicher Daten. In: H. U. e. a. Bielefeld (ed.) *Soziolinguistik und Empirie. Beiträge zu Problemen der Corpusgewinnung und -auswertung*. Wiesbaden: Athenaum, 198-207
MacLean, A. M. 1903: The Sweat-Shop in Summer. *American Journal of Sociology*, IX, 3: 289-309
Marks, D. 1995: Ethnographic Film: From Flaherty to Asch and after. *American Anthropologist*, 97, 2: 337-347
Mead, M., 1975: Visual Anthropology in a Discipline of Words. In: P. Hockings (ed.) *Principles of Visual Anthropology*. The Hague, Paris: Mouton, 3-10
Mittenecker, E., 1987: *Video in der Psychologie. Methoden und Anwendungsbeispiele in Forschung und Praxis*. Bern: Huber
Pink, S. 2001: More visualising, more methodologies: on video, reflexivity and qualitative research. *Sociological Review*, 49, 1: 586-599
Raab, J., 2001: Medialisierung, Bildästhetik, Vergemeinschaftung. Ansätze einer visuellen Soziologie am Beispiel von Amateurclubvideos. In: T. Knieper, Müller, Marion G. (ed.) *Kommunikation visuell. Das Bild als Forschungsgegenstand - Grundlagen und Perspektiven*. Köln: Halem, 37-63
Raab, J. 2002: ›Der schönste Tag des Lebens‹ und seine Überhöhung in einem eigenwilligen Medium. Videoanalyse und sozialwissenschaftliche Hermeneutik am Beispiel eines professionellen Hochzeitsvideofilms. *sozialer sinn*, 3, 469-495
Rammert, W. & I. Schulz-Schaeffer, 2002: Technik und Handeln. Wenn soziales Handeln sich auf menschliches Verhalten und technische Abläufe verteilt. In: W. Rammert and I. Schulz-Schaeffer (ed.) *Können Maschinen denken? Soziologische Beiträge zum Verhältnis von Mensch und Technik*. Frankfurt am Main: Campus, 11-64
Ruby, J., 2000: *Picturing Culture: Explorations of Film and Anthropology*. Chicago: UCP

Scheflen, A. E. 1965: The significance of posture in communication systems. *Psychiatry*, 27, 316-331
Schnettler, B. 2001: Vision und Performanz. Zur soziolinguistischen Gattungsanalyse fokussierter ethnographischer Daten. *sozialer sinn. Zeitschrift für hermeneutische Sozialforschung*, 1, 143-163
Shrum, W., R. Duque & T. Brown 2005: Digital video as research practice: Methodologies for the Millenium. *Journal of Research Practice*, 1, 1: Article M4
Silverman, D. 2005: Instances or Sequences? Improving the State of the Art of Qualitative Research. *Forum Qualitative Sozialforschung / Forum: Qualitative Social Research [Online Journal]*, 6, 3: Art. 30, availiable at http://www.qualitative-research.net/fqs-texte/3-05/05-3-30-e.htm
Suchman, L. & R. H. Trigg, 1991: Understanding Practice: Video as a Medium for Reflection and Design. In: J. Greenbaum and M. Kyng (ed.) *Design at Work. Cooperative Design of Computer Systems*. Hillsdale: Lawrence Erlbaum, 65-89
Thiel, T., 2003: Film und Videotechnik in der Psychologie. Eine erkenntnistheoretische Analyse mit Jean Piaget, Anwendungsbeispiele aus der Kleinkindforschung und ein historischer Rückblick auf Kurt Lewin und Arnold Gsell. In: H. Keller (ed.) *Handbuch der Kleinkindforschung*. Bern, Göttingen, Toronto, Seattle: Hans Huber, 649-708
Walker, N. 1915: Chicago Housing Conditions. Greeks and Italians in the Neighbourhood of Hull House. *American Journal of Sociology*, XXI, 3: 285-316
Woodhead, H. 1904: The First German Municipal Exposition. *American Journal of Sociology*, IX, 4: 433-458

Methodologies of Video Analysis

Thomas Luckmann

Some Remarks on Scores in Multimodal Sequential Analysis

Introduction

It is hardly necessary to repeat the old sententious saying that no two witnesses to an event will agree in their testimony. A look at old-fashioned field notes such as those of Malinowski and other ethnologists of times past and present show how difficult it is to record and interpret social interactions adequately, even while they are being observed or reconstruct them shortly after observation. Nonetheless they can be fascinatingly informative. That can be hardly said for the somewhat later, more "scientific" sociological attempts to analyze experimentally arranged or, at best, quasi-natural interaction. Using the Parsons-Bales or some similar scheme (counting, *e.g.*, how often A initiates interaction with B and vice-versa) deformed the data in a way which told us substantially less of what actually went on.

Looking at these circumstances in retrospect, the early twentieth century advance in the technology which permitted the recording of sight and sound would seem to have provided an unparalleled opportunity to broaden the empirical foundation of social theory by new forms of social research. However, the record of the period from the twenties to the fifties and even sixties of the last century demonstrates that the opportunity for an analysis of social life based on audio-recordings was seized only hesitatingly. Video-analysis lagged behind by at least another decade or two.

At first glance, this seems surprising. Audio- and video-recordings of social interaction made possible, in principle, a previously unattainable accuracy in the analysis of social interaction. The recordings preserve an essential, constitutive trait of interaction, its distinct temporal, sequential structure. (One should perhaps speak of interacting rather than interaction in order to stress the step-by-step process rather than the goal at which the process is directed). Of course everybody is aware of the temporality of interaction and various often quite sophisticated narrative strategies are employed in everyday life as well as in literature – long before Proust and Joyce – to represent it. However, in social science the narrative reconstruction of the past in interviews as a datum was used with remarkable theoretical simplicity and methodological naiveté. By preserving a record of the interacting process and making it available for repeated inspection in replays, the new technologies made it possible to take account of and to describe the specific temporal structure of interaction and thus the way in which an interaction was accomplished. Compared to the laborious and unreliable reconstructions of social interaction and of social life in general by interviewing, use of the new recording technologies offered the material basis for a qualitative leap in social research.

Yet the interpretive re-construction of interaction that makes use of recordings has its own theoretical and methodological problems. These were perhaps the main reason for the backwardness of the social sciences in embracing the possibilities of the new technology. In addition, there was probably a technical one, the cumbersomeness of the recording equipment, especially of film and video recording, until well past the middle of the last century. That proved a strain on the "naturalness" of the situations in which recording was being done.

Leaving aside the theoretical reasons, among which the most important was the failure to see the importance of sequential reconstruction of social processes, I should like to discuss what was and is, arguably, the chief methodological problem of such analysis. It pertains to sequential interpretation in general and is shared by audio- and audio/video-analysis, but it is particularly acute in the latter.

Not only is multimodal sequential analysis more unwieldy than analysis limited to a single modality, merely because there are more details of potential relevance to be reconstructed. The particular difficulty lies in the fusion, in shared time, of two structurally disparate modalities. Although movement obviously has a temporal structure, visual perception as a key sensory modality in social interaction does not have a similarly obvious focus as communication by speech. Visual perception is involved both in the original interaction as part of the reciprocal orientation of the actors to one another, as well as in viewing the record of interaction. Video recordings seem to preserve every detail, whether potentially relevant or irrelevant. The early advances in sequential analysis were made in analyses based on tapes of telephone conversations. This made analysis substantially simpler but of course it was still extremely valuable as pioneering work in sequential analysis. Incidentally, because telephone calls are "naturally" restricted to sound, their selection by the first generation of conversational analysts did not violate ethnomethodological principles derived from Garfinkel's reading of Schutz's theory of action and of the relation of common sense to science.

As is well known, in the decades that followed the earlier work in conversational analysis was extended with considerable success to video recordings. However, even when audio- and video-recordings began to be more widely used in social research, their real potential was not realized by everybody. Not only was the richness of concrete detail in such recordings often brutally reduced, the very point of the recording, the possibility to inspect the temporal structure of the interaction step by step, was ignored. Instead, some "hypothesis-directed" interactional coding scheme was applied to the recordings – just as it had been earlier applied to observation of interaction in "experimental" settings – in order to provide the "hypothesis" with quantifiable data. The results of such procedures were uninterestingly abstract, for the simple reason that the "hypothesis" imposed criteria of relevance that arbitrarily disregarded that which was relevant to the actors and in consequence disregarded a constitutive element of the interaction.

Preserving the actors' perspective for the observer

If one wishes to preserve the essence of direct interaction in an analytic transcript, all sorts of problems concerning a less distortively simplifying reduction of complex interactional aspects arise. There does not seem to be a simple way to solve these problems. To be sure, the recording is already a first, inevitable reduction of the sensory perceptions, more accurately, apperceptions, of the participants in the "original interaction". Nonetheless, other things *(i.e.,* the "normality" of the perceptual abilities of the participants) being equal, that reduction may be considered sufficiently irrelevant with regard to what is usually important in everyday interaction to the actors themselves. One has reason to assume that the essence of interaction is preserved in the recording. Human bodies being what they are, seeing and hearing are highly relevant. They are the sensory modalities upon which the orientation of normal people is primarily based and which constitute the material substratum of whatever expressive and significatory systems are used in interaction. Usually, sufficiently adequate traces of what was originally seen and heard the in the interaction are preserved in the recordings to permit a reasonable effort at reconstruction. Reasonable but by no means easy: the combination of auditory and visual dimensions in the recording poses problems of reconstruction and interpretation that far exceed the difficulties in the sequential analysis of unimodal interaction.

A moment ago I used the word essence. In my view the essence of direct interaction is, *first*, that it is a multimodal process in shared time and space, *second*, that it is reciprocal, *i.e.,* that the actions are directed at one another in accordance with the projects of the actors. The projects are based on whatever the actors know about social life, including what they know, or think they know, about typical projects of typical actors. This knowledge is used in assessing the projects of the other actors in the situation at hand who, uniquely individual as they may be, are also perceived as typical in regards relevant to their projects. The actors' individual – yet typical – knowledge of the social world is constitutive of the essence of social interaction.

The participants originally, *i.e.,* in the recorded episodes of social interaction, made sense of one another's actions by seeing and hearing each other. The seeing and hearing available to the original participants is preserved in the audio-video recording in a fashion that makes these dimensions of the original interaction permanently available to the analyst. In a manner of speaking, the analyst "re-experiences" the "original" interaction from the distance of an unseen observer, and is able to re-experience it again and again. In repeated replays, aspects, even structural elements of the interactional episode may be apperceived that went unnoticed in the first impression of the replay. At first the recorded episodes of "natural" social interaction often seem overwhelmingly complex and diffuse. Things slowly begin to take shape in replays. If one talks about one's impressions with other observers, first impressions are revised, or reinforced, expanded or simplified. A rough and ready understanding of the episode usually emerges as a result of not entirely implausible interpretations. But that is not enough.

If one wishes to proceed to systematic analysis, such "re-experiencing" is merely a necessary first step. Something more is required, something that transforms interactional experiences, and the corresponding re-experiencing of interaction into publicly manageable data. When other observers on a research team suggest alternative interpretations, based on their "re-experiences" and the intuitive understandings it produces, they should be able to point to the evidence for the alternative interpretations just as the first interpretation, now questioned, should be based on easily identifiable evidence. Under the circumstances, it seems sensible to treat recordings as a kind of difficult quasi-text. The joint hermeneutic effort that must be made to find a reliable interpretation that resolves the arguments between different suggestions, presupposes that the quasi-text is transformed into a genuine text and that the group of observers becomes a community of textual investigators. This goes a long way beyond intuitive attempts at understanding and re-experiencing the episode that was originally recorded and later replayed. Although the text is not yet the final analysis, it is a necessary condition for systematic interpretation.

Some of us have started to use a particular method of transforming audio/video recordings into a "text" some years ago. It consists of what may be called the preliminary reconstruction of the interaction in the form of a multimodal score. The elements of the interaction which the analyst, based on his knowledge of social life, must assume were relevant to the participants in the original interaction, must be noted in a transcript. In a transcript of a purely verbal interaction, as in the case of a telephone conversation, that is relatively simple. The transcript is unimodal, using the conventional script, with adaptations and additions in order to catch intonational, prosodic, paralinguistic and other auditory features. Such conversational analytic transcripts are of course more economic and more easily read by non-linguists than the international phonetic transliteration and will do for most analytic purposes.

Notation and score

But what method serves the purposes of multimodal transcription? What is seen and heard in the recording and must be assumed to have been seen and heard – selected from the flow of sound and movement by the participants in the original interaction as relevant – to be noted onto a score. Evidently, the first decision concerns the notation to be used.

Seeing and hearing are functionally related but structurally dissimilar modalities. For normal people, *i.e.,* those who can see and hear, the sensory modalities of hearing and seeing are heterogeneous vehicles of meaning and signification. (Incidentally, for the deaf-blind, another modality, touch, serves as the material, sensory vehicle of signification. Video-analysis of recordings of deaf-blind interaction obviously poses particularly difficult problems.) Notations to be used for them must cope with the heterogeneity of temporal/spatial form linked to the two modalities. Signification, *i.e.,* conventionalized meaning, is in our societies transcribed in conventionalized alphabetic scripts, and the conversational-analytic scripts which we normally use to transcribe them are based on them. For what is heard, some variant of conversational analytic transcription serves very well. Typical meanings of facial expression, gesture and posture, however, are either coded in what is for most research purposes hopelessly uneconomic detail, or reduced to simplified mannequin-like sketches, or translated into rough and ready vernacular designations. Scripts, including paralinguistic notations lend themselves fairly well to sequential analysis. But what about codes for body movement and facial expression? And what about vernacular designations for movement and expression? In transposing the visual and auditory components of a video recording to an interactional score, decisions about such notations must be made which should at least recognize the problematic synchronicity of such heterogeneous notations.

Let me add a few remarks about the term *interactional score* that I just mentioned. I use it in analogy to *musical score*. The latter is defined by the Oxford Universal Dictionary as *a written or printed piece of concerted music, in which all the vocal or instrumental parts are noted on a series of staves one under the other.* (In German, the corresponding term, *Partitur,* is defined by Brockhaus as *die schriftliche Fixierung eines vielstimmigen Tonwerkes, bei der die Instrumentenggruppen Takt für Takt untereinander angeordnet stehen.* The Brockhaus definition is more precise inasmuch as the merely implicit sequentiality of the OUD entry is here made explicit: *Takt für Takt.)*

The application of the principle of a musical score to the notation of interaction is not new. Although I did not study its history, I would not be surprised if it went back a long way. The applications were perhaps neither quite as multidimensional nor as strictly sequential as what we like them to be for our purposes today, but they were beginnings. A fairly well known example was the notation of dance developed by Laban. Approximately half a century later, the Ithaca *First Five Minutes* programme was greatly more ambitious (cf. Pittinger, Hockett & Danehy 1960). It was a Cornell University linguist, Charles F. Hockett, who collected specialists for the coding and analysis of various communicative dimensions of, and interpretive procedures for interaction, including mimetics and kinesics; among them Adam Kendon, Paul Ekman, as Erving Goffman. Each was to analyze a short piece of interaction, the famous first five minutes, of an interactional episode. The original purpose was to produce an integrated account from different analytic perspectives, more precisely, from perspectives for different interactive modalities. Interesting as were the contributions, as far as I remember not much by way of integration resulted.

With several colleagues and assistants I incautiously started a similarly ambitious project many years later in 1978. I called it "Data about Data" (Luckmann & Gross 1977). Its intention was to ascertain with some precision what and how much is lost of relevant aspects of interaction when one moves from very detailed representations and coding of audio/video recordings to more economic transcripts and vernacular reconstructions. I am sorry to say that this project, after much effort by many people, was also doomed, just as had been the Ithaca project. Ours did not even see publication. One reason was that the detailed coding of facial expression and gestures could not be easily mapped on a common temporal scale with the phonetic representations and these with the more ordinary transcripts. There were other reasons. I never could entirely get rid of a feeling of guilt toward the foundation which gave financial support for this venture.

However, later work by some of the participants in the project profited at least indirectly from the experiences gathered in those days. It was then, for example, that the notion of an interactional score acquired some shape. Jörg Bergmann, who had been an assistant in that project, Hans-Georg Soeffner, and I later applied the notion in an investigation of the presentation (and representation) of papal charisma on film and television (Bergmann, Luckmann & Soeffner 1993). Still later, Soeffner used the method with his assistants in further projects.

In my own later work, I tried, to apply with my assistants, the notion of an interactional score to the study of the aesthetic dimensions of everyday interaction. I had hoped that we would perfect the method beyond its somewhat crude beginnings, but for various reasons the project came to a formal end before the method was extensively applied. At that time, our interpretations were still mainly based on verbal conversational-analytic transcripts. We of course also interpreted gestures and facial expressions, but these interpretations had an auxiliary function and were somewhat anecdotal. We had barely started to use a multidimensional score consistently as a basis for interpretations that systematically integrated the different modalities of communicative interaction. Nevertheless, it seems to me that such an integration will be the crucial task of any analysis of interaction by video.

References

Bergmann, J., T. Luckmann & H.-G. Soeffner, 1993: Erscheinungsformen von Charisma - Zwei Päpste. In: W. Gebhardt, A. Zingerle & M. N. Ebertz (ed.) *Charisma - Theorie, Religion, Politik*. Berlin/New York: 121-155

Luckmann, T. & P. Gross, 1977: Analyse unmittelbarer Kommunikation und Interaktion als Zugang zum Problem der Entstehung sozialwissenschaftlicher Daten. In: H. U. e. a. Bielefeld (ed.) *Soziolinguistik und Empirie. Beiträge zu Problemen der Corpusgewinnung und -auswertung*. Wiesbaden: Athenaum, 198-207

Pittinger, R. E., Hockett, C. F. & Danehy, J. J., 1960: *The First Five Minutes. A Sample of Microscopic Interview Analysis*. Ithaca, NY: Paul Martineau

Christian Heath & Paul Luff

Video Analysis and Organisational Practice

> "5 September 1898: Tried to take cinematograph photo of fire making by Pasi, Sergeant and Mana [?] in morning. 6 September 1898: Tried to take cinematograph photos of Murray I.Kap in Australia corrobora (beche de mer men on board the lugger Coral Sea belonging Fred Lankester [...] Bomai-Malu cinematographed [?] at Kiam [...]"
>
> Haddon, A.C. Diary 10 March 1898-25 March 1899
> (in Long & Laughren 1993)

Introduction

There has been a long-standing interest in the social sciences and in particular social anthropology in using visual media to represent and analyse human conduct and activity. A.C. Haddon (1898), during the project on the communities of the Torres Straight Islands', is frequently cited as one of the first examples of the use of the cinematograph to cultural practice and soon after Baldwin Spencer used film in his studies of Australian aborigines. There are however numerous instances of visual media being used to portray and analyse human activity that foreshadow Haddon and others and yet they are not conventionally seen as part of a professional, anthropological tradition. In this regard, it is interesting to note, that despite a number of convergent theoretical and methodological developments in sociology and social anthropology over the least century, the use of film, video and even photography in sociology remains relatively neglected. Indeed, even the inclusion of photographs with an article causes some consternation among many leading journals in sociology and there is little acknowledgement that visual media have much to offer even qualitative, ethnographic research. There are however important exceptions, not least of which is the growing corpus of studies, primarily informed by ethnomethodology and conversation analysis, concerned with social interaction and in particular the ways in which practical accomplishment of everyday activities, including highly specialised organisational activities, arises in and through the interplay of talk, bodily conduct and the use of tools and technologies. In this regard, video has proved invaluable as an analytic resource enabling research to address and reveal the fine details of socially organised human activities as it arises within everyday, naturally occurring environments.

Video, like other visual media, however, is not simply a technology used by the occasional social scientist to analyse human conduct and events. Increasingly, video is becoming a pervasive resource, used by a whole host of agencies, both public and private sector organisations, with which to scrutinise behaviour and where necessary intervene. For example, over the past decade or so, we have seen the wide spread deployment of video surveillance equipment throughout most major cities in Europe. Perhaps most remarkable, are the ways in which closed circuit television (CCTV) has become a pervasive resource for the management of behaviour in public places in the urban environments (Lyon 1994, Norris & Armstrong 1999, Norris, et al. 1998). It is said for example that in UK there are more than two and a half million CCTV cameras operating in public domains, and that in taking a short walk along Oxford Street in Central London a pedestrian is likely to recorded by more than one hundred cameras. The wide-spread deployment of video technology has led to the rise and further development of a particular form of workplace, namely the surveillance or operations centre which for some is a disturbing realisation of Bentham's Panopticon. It is also led to a growing consideration within many occupations with surveillance and in particular the skilful, situated analysis and assessment of human behaviour and activities as they arise within everyday environments. For sociologists this may be of some relevance, since aside from our own use of video, there is a growing number of professions and occupations that have as a key responsibility the analysis of human behaviour using video technology.

In this paper, we wish to draw on our own video-based studies of work, interaction and technology, to explore the indigenous, organisational use of video for analysing human conduct and events. The case in question, are the station operation centres on London Underground. In these settings, organisational personnel have developed, and rely upon, a body of practice and reasoning through which they use video to examine the conduct of people in public environments, identify problems and events, and develop a coordinated solution. The paper addresses the ways in which station operators use video to make sense of the conduct and interaction of passengers and how they transform the ways in which both passengers and staff see, and respond to, each other's conduct. We wish to suggest that the personnel in question are sophisticated, lay sociologists, whose ways of working and indigenous practices, raise some relevant lessons for ethnographers interested in using video for social research.

In this regard, it is worthwhile raising two further issues that of methodological relevance to those interested in using video for social science research. In one of his early lectures Sacks (1963, 1992) makes a methodological recommendation that resonates with one or two of the concerns of this paper and recent sociological studies of surveillance. He suggests that in addressing a particular analytic issue or substantive problem, it can be of some interest to identify an occupation or group that deals with the issue or problem as part of their everyday practice or organisational responsibilities. We have a long-standing interest in using video to investigate behaviour and social interaction in public places, but for various reasons it has proved a highly intractable and difficult analytic domain. In this light, when the opportunity arose to undertake studies of control centres on London Underground we were interested in developing the research in order to explore resources and reasoning on which personnel who have a occupational responsibility for managing public space analyse and assess behaviour and interaction. In various ways therefore, this paper is concerned with examining how people in practical situations and organisational environments undertake a form of sociological analysis of behaviour in public and whether their analysis is relevant to professional sociological investigations.

Social science, and in particular social anthropology and sociology, are not the only fields with an academic interest in video and video analysis of human behaviour. The wide-spread deployment of video for surveillance has led to a growing interest in engineering and computer science, in particular amongst scholars concerned with image processing technology, in developing systems that can scrutinise data from cameras and automatically identify events (Velastin, et al. 1994). In a sense therefore, these systems are concerned with a form of behavioural, or even sociological, analysis; an analysis that can identify events by virtue of discriminating patterns in images. Such systems presuppose the possibility, that there may be a correspondence between behavioural parameters, in particular the visual elements of movement and types of action and interaction. The project of which this paper forms part, known as PRISMATICA, involved the development of a system known as MIPSA (Modular Integrated Passenger Surveillance Architecture) that is designed to link into a control room environment, scrutinise real time data from CCTV and inform operators of particular problems and events. In this paper we would like to reflect on the ambitions of such systems and their sociological significance.

Organisational geography and the temporality of events

Each major station on London Underground houses an area which is known as the operations room or 'ops room' for short. It is normally staffed by one of the station supervisors who are responsible for overseeing the day-to-day operation of the station and with developing a coordinated response to problems and emergencies. At any one time there will be up to thirty additional staff out and about on the station, mostly station staff who are responsible for platforms, the barriers and even the main entrance gates to the station. The operations rooms are normally located in the main entrance foyer to the station and include a large window which overlooks passengers entering and leaving the station, the barriers, the top of the escalators, the ticket machines, and ticket office.

This panorama is enhanced by a series, normally eight monitors, embedded within a console which provide views of various locations around the station. The supervisors or operator selects his views from the numerous cameras, up to about one hundred and fifty at Piccadilly Circus. The supervisors also have access to omni-scan' cameras in a few locations which allow one to zoom in and out where necessary. An additional monitor provides information concerning the running times and location of particular trains on specific lines. Communications equipment includes conventional telephones and direct lines to line control rooms, a fully duplex radio which allows all staff in the station to speak to each other and hear both sides of all conversations, and a public address systems which allows the supervisor or operation to make announcements to an area within the station. Additional equipment includes alarms, switches to automatically open or close the barriers, for example in the case of an evacuation, and in some cases switches to illuminate 'no entry' signs at the entrances to station. It should be added that station control rooms are part of a broader network of control centres through which they receive information and to which they provide information. These include the Line Control Rooms, the London Underground Network Control Centre and the British Transport Police Operations' Centre.

Figure 1: Operations rooms in stations on the London Underground, from left to right, Victoria, Piccadilly Circus and Leicester Square.

Stations on London Underground, like those on other networks, suffer characteristic or routine problems and difficulties. Though these vary from place to place, if one considers major interconnecting stations such as Victoria, Piccadilly, Oxford Circus, Liverpool Street and the like, then it is not unusual to find similar events arising. These include for example overcrowding in the morning and evening rush hours, security threats including the discovery of suspect packages, begging and unregistered busking, pick-pocketing and minor robberies, unruly behaviour, fare avoidance, and the like. More unusual but nonetheless 'normal' problems also include vehicle breakdowns, passenger accidents and, what is known euphemistically by station staff as, 'one unders'.

In contrast to the conventional view of surveillance and monitoring, supervisors are highly selective in what they look at and when. There is an organisational geography to the station; routine problems and difficulties typically arise in particular locations at certain times of the day, week year and so on. Supervisors configure the CCTV views of the station to enable them to see, determine and manage the sorts of difficulties that will typically arise in particular locations at certain times. For example, at Victoria overcrowding occurs during the morning rush hour on the Victoria north bound platform, and this in turn affects certain escalators and queuing at particular ticket barriers. The supervisor will select and maintain those views for the morning peak and switch to them to the southbound Victoria platform by the mid afternoon in expectation of the afternoon rush. Later in the evening ticket touts attempt to trade in the main foyer and it is not unusual to select a couple of views of the stairwells. Buskers ordinarily use particular locations, such as the bottom of an escalator, on long interconnecting passageway, so once again we find supervisors selecting and keeping an eye those particular images. And, so forth and so on; identifying next trains, keeping an eye for pick pockets, watching out for drug trafficking, and in general knowing where this and that occur, where those are things we should deal with, provide supervisors with highly motivated and organised ways of viewing the 'space' or better the conduct of people and passengers. Moreover, in many cases, it is not simply selecting a single view, but configuring a number of potentially related views that is critical, to that you can track the progress of passengers and in some cases the movement of a problem.

The supervisors' geography of events therefore provides an important resource in overseeing the station and in selecting a relevant and useful set of views at some particular moment. This is not to suggest that as problems and contingencies arise that the view of the world is not reconstituted to enable a particular problem to be seen, identified and managed, but rather that staff are not in continued state of 'cognitive overload' where they are attempting to monitor a disparate collection of continually updated images. It is worth mentioning in this regard, that the supervisors ability to configure a relevant set of views and to see and manage events, using CCTV, is thoroughly dependent upon his practical knowledge and familiarity with the station; its passageways, tunnels, escalators, equipment, facilities and the like. The images, and in particular the conduct which arises within the myriad of domains, is intelligible by virtue of the supervisor's understanding of the ecology both within and beyond the image(s). Without even a relatively simple understanding of which passageways connect to which platform, or why people tend to gather at particular locations on a platform, the CCTV images, for doing the work that the operators do, would be of little use. We will return to this issue later in the paper.

Recognising events: deploying organisation

In a number of major stations on London Underground overcrowding is a severe problem in particular during the weekday morning and evening 'peaks' or rush hours (roughly 8.00 to 9.30 am and 5 to 6.30 pm). Overcrowding is a particular problem for stations which interconnect with major overland stations such as Victoria, Liverpool Street, and King's Cross which serve the major dormitory towns in the South East. Overcrowding not only causes discomfort and irritation to passengers and reduces the free flow of traffic through the station but also leads to particular dangers. For example escalators can become severely congested and unless passengers can exit quickly from the foot of the moving stairs then the pressure of people above can lead to individuals tripping. More serious still, overcrowding on platforms can place passengers standing near the edge in some danger as the pressure from behind pushes them forward. Indeed, overcrowding has led some new lines, for example the Jubilee Line extension, to include housing on the platform edge so that there is no danger of passengers inadvertently being pushed on to the line. At Victoria for example, the entrance to the northbound platform on the Victoria Line is at one end, and passengers disperse rather slowly which causes severe overcrowding during the morning such hour, when this particular platform is one of the busiest on the network.

Station staff and in particular the supervisor in the operations room has to continually monitor overcrowding throughout the morning and evening rush hours. Aside from encouraging passengers to disperse the full length of the platform and removing obstacles, his or her main strategy is at times to reduce the number of passengers at particular areas of the station. In particular he can ask the station assistants to 'close the barriers' that is to have passengers queue behind the barriers until passengers have cleared from the platform(s) below. Or, 'close the entrance gates' so that passengers have to queue outside the station (actually within the mainline station) until numbers are reduced down below.

Identifying and managing overcrowding is not as straightforward, however, as one might imagine. In particular, 'overcrowding' is not simply defined or constituted, for organisationally relevant purposes, in terms of the density or numbers of people in a specific area.

Consider the following fragment. We join the action as the supervisor is looking out through the glass window at the entrance foyer whilst chatting to the field worker.

Fragment 1

    Station Supervisor (SS) looks through window and then glances at platform monitor. Sets public address system).

®   SS: Station Control Vic Way In please. Station Control Vic Way In, please

    (0.4)

  SS: Ladies and gentlemen we are asking you please to remain behind the barrier(s). Remain behind the barriers: please. Remain behind the barriers.

The supervisor momentarily turns from the foyer and glances at the Victoria Line northbound platform monitor. He immediately sets the PA system to the foyer and asks the station staff to implement station control; that is, stop incoming passengers passing through the barriers. A few moments he follows the request with a public announcement asking passengers to remain behind the barriers. The passengers begin to queue and are released some moments later when the platform clears.

The supervisor makes a practical assessment of overcrowding and implements a course of action to reduce the number of passengers arriving on the platform. The assessment, and the course of actions it entails, involves a number of critical considerations. The assessment is not based simply on seeing that the platform is crowded, it is crowded most of the time during the morning rush hour, – but rather with regard to interweaving distinct domains within the station; – the foyer and the platform. The supervisor sees what is happening within the foyer with regard to the number of passengers waiting on the platform; just as seeing people crowded on the platform recasts the significance of the number of people within the foyer. The supervisor configures an ecology, then and there, with which to examine and assess people and conduct within the station, and in particular to make a determination, then and there, concerning the density and crowding of passengers.

The 'relevant' ecology is temporarily linked and constituted with respect to the routine patterns of navigation by passengers through the station. The people within and entering the foyer, given the normal pace and path of human traffic, will arrive on the platform in a few minutes time. The foyer and platform, including on their way the escalators and short passageway are constituted as an interdependent ecology, where conduct and events in one affect, within a short period of time, another. For example, even though the platform may not be particularly overcrowded at this moment, given how people progress through the station, it is likely that there will be problems in a few minutes time.

Critically therefore, overcrowding is not just constituted with regard to the interdependence of different spaces within the station, here and now, but prospectively, with respect to what is likely to happen and where. For the supervisor, identifying and managing overcrowding cannot ordinarily wait until passengers are about to spill on to the track or back up on the down escalators. Rather they have to envisage, anticipate, when overcrowding is likely to arise and set in course practical action to avoid problems arising. To envisage overcrowding it is not enough, to simply inspect a single scene, but rather to compare and contrast different domains and thereby assess and see conduct and events. In the case at hand we can see how the build of passengers in the foyer provides a vehicle for constituting the state of play on the platform; just as seeing the platform here and now, is relevant to 'now' seeing so many people in the foyer.

The assessment and perception of conduct and passengers in a particular location therefore derives from interweaving scenes of conduct and passengers from a variety of domains. The perception of a densely 'overcrowded' platform, derives not simply from seeing a substantial number of people waiting for a train, but juxtaposing that view with other scenes, and in particular envisaging how conduct elsewhere will affect the particular scene in question. Indeed, whilst cameras provide successive views of a particular platform, it is relatively difficult for the supervisor to judge the actual density of waiting passengers, once it is quite busy. The juxtaposed scenes of what is happening elsewhere, provide ways of inferring and envisaging what is/may happening. This current and prospective orientation, also takes into account, what it will take to clear passengers, and juxtaposes, the arrival of more passengers with the timing of vehicles to remove them. The 'reading' or 'interpretation' of a particular image therefore, an image of an 'overcrowded' platform which may to us seem obvious, is dependent upon the supervisors ability to invoke a complex configuration of scenes actions and events, and envisage, just what it might take, to becoming dangerous. To belabour the point; a single scene, or image without knowing what is happening elsewhere or about to happen, does not provide the resources to enable supervisors to produce organisationally relevant and accountable solutions.

Detecting Incongruities

The smooth, unproblematic operation of a complex station relies on the good conduct of passengers. They are expected to use stations for particular purposes, know how to navigate through the space, and to do this in appropriate ways so that others can go about their daily business. The operation of a rapid urban transport system such as London Underground relies upon, for want of a better term, the 'well-behaved passenger'. The routine ways in which well-behaved passengers conduct themselves within the station, provide a sense of ordinariness, routine and typicality. Drawing on Sacks (1972) we might characterise this ordinary, daily and routine operation of people passing through the station as providing a framework of 'normal appearances' and 'background expectations'. In turn this framework of normal appearances provides supervisors and other staff with ways of noticing the unusual, the problematic, the different; actions, people, and even objects that stand in contrast with the routine operation and ways of the station. A diverse range of actions, objects and people can become noticeable by virtue of their incongruity with regard to the ways in which things ordinarily happen.

Consider a 'doubler'; an individual who attempts to pass through the ticket barrier without paying. Doublers achieve this by walking so close to the person in front that they manage to squeeze through the gates with them. In trying to identify someone to follow, doublers circle around the foyer looking for a 'mark'. This action is distinct from the ordinary flow of passengers, who typically walk directly to the gates. Or, consider the individuals attempt to throw themselves under a train. Their conduct is noticeable by the ways in which it contrasts with ordinary ways of waiting on platforms and catching trains; they stand in particular locations and routinely allow a number of trains to pass through the station before trying to jump. Or, consider how, at certain stations, a supervisor may watch where people look when people ascending an escalator. Seeing someone looking down at the rear of the person standing directly in front of them, rather than upwards or to one side, can enable the supervisor to spot a potential pick-pocket. In various ways therefore, the typical conduct of passengers, in particular locations, provides resources to enable supervisors and staff to notice the unusual and the incongruent.

It is not only forms of behaviour that can draw the supervisors' notice by virtue of the ways in which they contrast with normal appearances but other sorts of matters and objects. For example consider the following fragment. The supervisor is using the Omniscan camera to look around the foyer at Leicester Square station. As he pans across the foyer he notices what appears to be a waft of smoke above the crowd. With the camera he slowly tracks the smoke to discover its origins, one of a group of young men standing near the cash machines. He then begins to make a passenger announcement just to those in the main foyer.

Fragment 2

    ((beep - ding dong))
SS: ( ) this is for the young man waiting at the cash machine with a blue denim (er) (.) jacket on (0.5) with a striped shirt (0.2) would you put your cigarette out now please
(1.2)

Whilst making this announcement the station supervisor continues to look at the man in the main CCTV monitor. As the supervisor's description of him emerges the man continues to talk to his friends. The station supervisor then repeats his request.

    (1.2)
SS: would you put your cigarette out now please<this is for the gentleman with the blue denim jacket
(3.2)

As the second announcement emerges the young man and his friends start to look around, and the man in question can be seen to duck down. He then reappears, raising his empty hand to the air. The supervisor responds with:

SS: thank you very much- (0.8) very kind of you, you are going redder and redder by the moment

Although accomplished in a light-hearted way, smoking is an important matter for staff working throughout London Underground. Smoking has been considered a significant safety risk since the King's Cross Disaster in 1987, an incident where 31 people died in a fire probably caused by a discarded cigarette (Fennell 1988). It is not unusual for supervisors, if such behaviour is noticed and they are not otherwise engaged, to use the PA to make either general announcements or, as in this case, a quite specific one. In this example, from a general scan of the scene the supervisor notices something incongruous – a waft of smoke – a matter that suggests a passenger is being less than well-behaved, and one which is organisationally consequential.

The supervisors draw upon the background expectancies of the ordinary and the mundane to recognise and analyse incongruent conduct from passengers and other individuals. If appropriate, such behaviour can lead them to undertake some action. In this case the supervisor makes a series of very particular passenger announcements and monitors carefully the response of the recalcitrant passenger. The CCTV system is the means therefore not only to identify and recognise where and when a relevant action or response should be undertaken, but also a way for managing that response, seeing how it is being understood by passengers (and staff) and assessing their conduct in the light of it. The video systems allows them to assess the sequential unfolding of an action and activities.

The World Beyond

The very complexity of many urban stations, both in London and in other European cities, generates severe difficulties for CCTV coverage. Despite the large number of CCTV cameras there are inevitably blind spots due to obstructions, corners or poor lighting which make particular places out of the scope of the cameras or barely visible. These areas are characterised by staff as being 'off the world', the world beyond the scope the CCTV system. An important aspect of the operator's skills is to know the shortcomings and the limitations of the system, to be familiar with what lies beyond the cameras and the images, and to be able to interweave the geography of the station with the images provided on the monitors. In a sense therefore, the images are intelligible, sensible, by virtue of the operator's ability to know how the camera views stand with regard to the actual physical layout of the stations and its routine behavioural characteristics. Many problems and difficulties arise 'off the world' and it is critical that there are ways in which these events can be detected and managed.

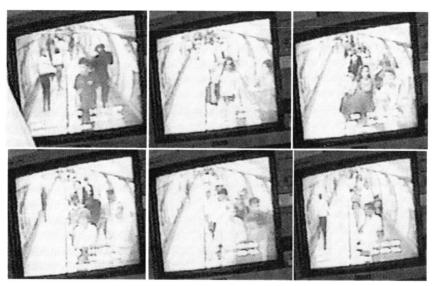

Fragment 3: Passengers on the right of the corridor successively glancing to a busker out of view to the left.

Those who use the stations for activities other than travel also have an interest in the limitations of the CCTV system. Buskers, beggars, pick-pockets, drug dealers, touts and the like, are familiar with the location of cameras in particular stations and will sometimes select areas to undertake their activities that are out of view from the operation centre. So for example, a sharp bend in a passageway, the bottom of a stairwell, even one side of a corridor rather than another, will be known for their inaccessibility to the CCTV system and then become routine locations for particular types of improper activity.

Operators are well aware that these parties are familiar with the location and scope of cameras and draw upon various resources to detect problems and difficulties that may arise. Operators use what they are able to see and their knowledge of routine patterns of conduct to infer what is happening in the actual world beyond.

Consider the example in fragment 3. The images are taken from the CCTV monitors in Leicester Square over a short period of time, and to the untrained eye appear to simply show passengers walking along an interconnecting passageway. The supervisor notices that successive passengers, as they come towards the camera on the right of the passageway, glance to their right. A moment later he calls one of the station staff to go and remove a busker from the interconnecting passageway. The busker has been positioned under the camera in an area away to the left of the image.

As well as noticing the direction of passenger's gaze, supervisors may look at other aspects of passenger conduct to infer what is happening off the world. For example, if they see an arm being extended to the edge of the image or passengers making minor body swerves as they pass a particular point, these may suggest a payment being made or a person standing, sitting or lying out of view (see fragment 4)

Fragment 4. The swerve of the passengers coming down a staircase suggesting the location of a beggar. The person can just be seen towards the bottom right of the image.

The world available on video therefore is not restricted to the domain circumscribed by the images. Personnel can use what they see as a way of determining activities and events beyond the image. Such inferences rely upon their abilities to recognise particular patterns of conduct and the ways in which they are embedded in particular activities; activities which may not themselves be fully visible on the screen. The staff re-configure the elements of an activity from particular actions that themselves may be a small part of the event itself. It should be added that in re-connecting the world in this way, in seeing beyond the image, personnel do not only rely on their understanding of the routine patterns of behaviour, but also knowledge of the spatial and temporal organisation of the local environment – its organisational geography.

Individuals who use surveillance equipment therefore are themselves sensitive to the views on the world beyond the image, and orient to the relationship between their view and the domain itself. They know the views, the limitations and possibilities, by virtue of their familiarity with the 'actual' world beyond. In such ways they configure the context to undertake their everyday work. Their sensitivity to the constraints of their views of the world feature in how they perceive and handle events. They draw on these resources to deploy organisational solutions to problems that arise, and through talk and collaboration with others, co-ordinate the conduct of staff and manage public behaviour.

Conclusion

The video resources, made available through the CCTV system, are critical for the supervisors in London Underground Control Rooms to manage smoothly the operation of the stations. They support the ways in which they can deal with everyday occurrences such as managing overcrowding, people smoking and buskers and beggars within the station, as well as less frequent occurrences such as bomb scares, evacuations and suicides. The video makes locations, objects and the conduct of passengers in remote areas of the station accessible to supervisors in a central control room. However, identifying problematic occurrences and behaviours from these resources is not straightforward. Supervisors and operators do not merely have to be aware of critical changes in the images on the monitors in front of them, but have to make sense of them for their own organisation purposes. In order to do this they have developed practices of seeing and analysing the conduct of others.

These practices depend on understanding the details of everyday conduct made available through video. They rely on seeing particular features of gestures and bodily conduct; an outstretched arm, a step towards a train, a body swerve or a glance across a corridor. But these elements of conduct are not seen in isolation, they are seen with respect to the conduct of others who are either visible in the scene or out of the image or 'off the world'; they are seen in regard to the local context and happenings in the local environment, the time of day, the natural history of typical events, where they happen and how these relate to their temporal organisation – an organisational geography – and, most critically perhaps, they are identified as parts of courses of action; as conduct that is appropriate given particular prior actions and with particular typical actions occurring next. Supervisors have developed a set of background expectations for understanding everyday conduct in a public setting. These inform how they understand appropriate and relevant conduct, but also what is deviant, irrelevant and inappropriate. In some ways supervisors are lay sociologists, and quite sophisticated lay sociologists, developing principles and procedures, a methodology for analysing human conduct. Following Sacks' suggestions, it may be worth glossing some of these principles:

- in making sense of action, you need to consider action with regard to its immediate environment or ecology and how features of that environment bear upon the character of that action;
- particular actions can only be properly understood with regard to a course of action or trajectory of which they form a part;
- in making relevant sense of an action you have to read that action with regard to the 'perspective of the actor'; just as the action can give you a sense of the person's perspective;
- actions have to be read, analysed with regard to the resources that the actor has at hand, in their environment, what they can see and cannot see,
- in many cases, the sense of an action can only be made by reading the action with regard to the actions of others, both those that arise, before and immediately following the action in question; it is important to attempt to discover the sequences of inter-action of which an action forms a part.

These principles may be relevant for those social scientists concerned with developing understandings of human conduct from visual materials. Indeed, a number of researchers do take such matters seriously when analysing video-recordings of everyday settings. In a wide variety of domains analysts have sought to understand the *in situ* practices, concerns and understandings of the participants, from the perspective of those actors, whether those individuals are responsible for controlling trains or aircraft, undertaking scientific experiments, dealing with service enquiries on the telephone or drawing plans on a computer, or whether they are surgeons, doctors or patients (Goodwin 1995, Goodwin & Goodwin 1996, Greatbatch, et al. 1993, Heath & Luff 2000, Heath, et al. 2000, Heath 2001, Mondada 2003, Streeck 1996, Whalen & Vinkhuyzen 2000). These analyses reveal how the talk and visual conduct in these various settings are made sense of with respect to features of the local environment. For example, how in control rooms commands, requests and comments about trains or aircraft, are understood by other controllers with respect to features such as the details of public displays, computer screens or paper documents, or how a gesture by a doctor accompanying a diagnosis can only be made sense of by the patient with regard to locations or features of their body. Or, how colleagues co-ordinate their conduct with a surgeon through monitoring the articulation of the ongoing talk, gestures and manipulation of tools and instruments. In each of these cases these activities are read by colleagues with respect to their places within trajectories of action, whether this is within a particular surgical procedure, a routine handling of a service problem or the ways diagnoses are typically delivered. Moreover, these studies have revealed how conduct is shaped by the immediate local interactional context, how an utterance, a look or a movement is understood by a colleague in the light of an immediately prior action.

It also happens that these methodological and analytic sensitivities inform the analysis undertaken in this paper. As Sacks' suggests when faced with complex methodological problems, an investigation of practitioners who have similar concerns and problems in their occupational or professional life, might suggest ways of overcoming these problems. When tackling contemporary problems in the analysis of video materials we should not overlook the skills of and practices of those who, in the course of their everyday work, collect video data, analyse these materials and present and discuss them with others.

Acknowledgements

We would like to thank personnel on London Underground who generously provided us with access for field work and video-recording and suffer our endless queries and questions. An earlier version of this paper was presented at the International Conference: on 'Video Analysis: Methodological Aspects of the Analysis of Audiovisual Data in Qualitative Sociology' at the Technical University of Berlin in December 2004. We are very grateful for the comments and suggestions from participants at the conference and to Hubert Knoblauch, Bernt Schnettler, Marcus Sanchez Svensson, Jon Hindmarsh, Dirk vom Lehn, David Silverman and Sergio Velastin for their support with the issues and materials discussed here. The project of which this paper is part was funded under the CEC IST 5th Framework Programme. Details of the project, PRISMATICA, can be found on the website: http://www.prismatica.com.

References

Long, C. and Laughren 1993: Australia's first films. *Cinema Papers*, 96, 32-37; 59-61
Lyon, D., 1994: *The Electronic Eye. The Rise of Surveillance Society*. Cambridge: Polity
Norris, C. and G. Armstrong, 1999: *The Maximum Surveillance Society*. Berg
Norris, C., J. Moran and G. Armstrong (ed.) 1998: *Surveillance, Closed Circuit Television and Social Control*. Aldershot: Ashgate
Sacks, H. 1963: Sociological Description. *Berkeley Journal of Sociology*, 8, 61-91
Sacks, H., 1992: *Lectures in Conversation: Volumes I and II*. Oxford: Blackwell
Velastin, S. A., J. H. Yin, M. A. Vincencio-Silva, A. C. Davies, R. E. Allsop and A. Penn, 1994: *Automated Measurement of Crowd Density and Motion using Image Processing*. 7th IEE International Conference on Road Traffic Monitoring and Control, 26-28 April 1994, London, UK, 127-132
Sacks, H., 1972: Notes on Police Assessment of Moral Character. In: D. Sudnow (ed.) *Studies in Social Interaction*. New York: Free Press, 280-293
Fennell, D., 1988: *Investigation into the King's Cross Underground Fire*. Department of Transport, HMSO
Goodwin, C. 1995: Seeing in Depth. *Social Studies of Science*, 25, 2 (May 1995): 237-274

Goodwin, C. and M. H. Goodwin, 1996: Seeing as a Situated Activity: Formulating Planes. In: Y. Engeström and D. Middleton (ed.) *Cognition and Communication at Work*. Cambridge: Cambridge University Press, 61-95

Greatbatch, D., P. Luff, C. C. Heath and P. Campion 1993: Interpersonal Communication and Human-Computer Interaction: an examination of the use of computers in medical consultations. *Interacting With Computers*, 5, 2: 193-216

Heath, C. C. and P. K. Luff, 2000: *Technology in Action*. Cambridge: Cambridge University Press

Heath, C. C., H. Knoblauch and P. Luff 2000: Technology and social interaction: the emergence of 'workplace studies'. *British Journal of Sociology*, 51, 2: 299-320

Heath, C. 2001: Demonstrative suffering: the gestural (re)embodiment of symptoms. *Journal of Communication*, 52:597-616

Mondada, L. 2003: Working with video: how surgeons produce video records of their actions. *Visual Studies*, 18, 58 - 73

Streeck, J. 1996: How to do things with things: objects trouve and symbolization. *Human Studies*, 19, 365-384

Whalen, J. and E. Vinkhuyzen, 2000: Expert Systems in (Inter)Action: Diagnosing Document Machine Problems Over the Telephone. In: P. Luff, J. Hindmarsh and C. Heath (ed.) *Workplace Studies: Recovering Work Practice and Informing System Design*. Cambridge: Cambridge University Press, 92-140

Lorenza Mondada

Video Recording as the Reflexive Preservation and Configuration of Phenomenal Features for Analysis

Introduction

The use of video is becoming a widespread practice within the social sciences interested in the real-time production of social life – and not only within specialized research areas dealing with the visual, such as visual sociology or anthropology and the studies of gesture and multimodality. Video constitutes a fundamental technique for constituting the corpora of data for analysis, as well as an important mean of rendering research results, such as in documentary films or multimedia presentations.

These uses have generated a number of *methodological* texts and handbooks giving advice on fieldwork, on technical equipment and on further analytic exploitation of video records; however, *analytical* studies focussing on video as a timed accomplishment and as a social practice are still very few. Contrary to numerous analyses of visualization practices in the exercise of science (Lynch 1985, 1991; Latour 1986), showing how the organization of images such as diagrams, photographs or maps actively constitute objects of knowledge, working as an "externalized retina" (Lynch 1988), video has not yet been investigated in this respect.

In this paper, we propose a *praxeological approach to video practices*, focussing on the way in which videos are locally and contingently produced by social scientists, as well as in other professional domains. This perspective allows us to describe some basic practices through which scholars studying social interaction actively constitute their primary data and corpora and through which they establish a first preanalytic online interpretation of the very events they document. This perspective operates a conceptual switch: it doesn't deal with video as a mere *resource*, for example in a methodological discussion, but treats video practices as a *topic* per se, within an analytic stance. It allows one to go beyond discussions of video as a methodological tool, as a source of technical bias or as a way of producing records made transparent for the description of the events they document – inviting us to consider that we see "with" the camera and not "through" it (Büscher 2004), and thus to dissipate the fallacy of an independent and pre-existing world transparently offered from "out there" to our observation.

This project thus takes seriously the invitation to develop, as Macbeth puts it, a "praxeology of seeing with a camera" (1999: 151) considering shooting as an embodied exercise of inquiry and analysis, as the "work of assembling visible social fields" (1999: 152). Camera movements, technical choices, and perspective making are an integral part of the social activities of interest here, embedded in talk-in-interaction and synchronized with it, therefore mutually elaborating each other, and further articulated with other bodily conduct, gestures, object manipulations, and material environments. These activities are constitutive of the production of the visibility, recognizability, intelligibility of the phenomena at hand and of the arrangements of phenomenal field properties which are the target of the researcher's analysis. Thus, this perspective focuses on researcher's visual perception as a social and situated action. Seeing as a situated activity (Goodwin & Goodwin 1996), professional vision (Goodwin 1994a, 1995) and the ordered production of visibility as a social accomplishment (Mondada 2005) are therefore a central object of this praxeology.

Turning video practices into a topic of analysis offers a range of possible objects of study: not only the practices and methods by which video records are *produced*, but also the practices by which they are then *edited* – going through multiple transformations thanks to digitalization, compression, cutting, reassembling, clips editing, etc. – as well as the practices by which they are *viewed*, either as films, as in the case of the ethnographic documentaries, or as data, as in the case of interactional studies: in this case, they also undergo temporal manipulations, as they are viewed frame-by-frame, in slow motion, or fast forward. Here we will focus on video as it is produced – but the same approach could/should deal with video as it is exploited and made exploitable: how its details are retrieved, how vision is enhanced by digital media, how it depends on software and their constraints, on compression modes, on types of alignment of the image with its transcripts, etc.

So, we will situate video practices within an ethnomethodologically inspired conversation analytic framework, and deal with video both as an indispensable medium for collecting data and *preserving* their relevant features in a naturalistic perspective and as a *configuring* device – taking into account the professional practices that produce it. In this sense, we focus on the detailed ways in which video recordings are reflexively produced, how they structure and arrange the very data of the analysis, shape them, give them a particular orderliness and meaning. It is therefore of fundamental importance to integrate into the analysis the practical ways in which recordings are produced, with their local contingencies and for all practical purposes. These aspects are neither marginal (so that we may ignore them) nor problematic (so that they might "distort" the phenomena at hand) with regard to the use of the resulting materials for analytic purposes. On the contrary, the very ways of producing images give us central insights into the organizational features of the recorded practices themselves, revealing their local order and intelligibility as reflexively produced by their display to and for the camera.

Documenting naturally occurring interactions

From its very beginnings, Conversation Analysis has been a pioneering movement that has explicitly recognized the use of recorded data, and even claimed that such data are embedded in its specific analytic "mentality". In the early 60s, Harvey Sacks articulated his topics of inquiry with the necessity of working on recordings: aiming at describing the (ethno)methods by which members organize their ordinary social life, he insisted from the start that these methods and the detailed resources they exploited could not be *imagined* but only *discovered* by a close looking at actual recordings of everyday activities.

> "I started to work with tape-recorded conversations. Such materials had a single virtue, that I could replay them. I could transcribe them somewhat and study them extendedly – however long it might take. The tape-recorded materials constituted a 'good enough' record of what happened. Other things, to be sure, happened, but at least what was on the tape has happened. It was not from any large interest in language or from some theoretical formulation of what should be studied that I started with tape-recorded conversations, but simply because I could get my hands on it and I could study it again and again, and also, consequentially, because others could look at what I had studied and make of it what they could, if, for example, they wanted to be able to disagree with me" (Sacks 1984: 26; Sacks 1992, I: 622).

Sacks' arguments concern both fundamental features of human interaction and praxeological features of its analytic practice: first of all, the way in which the tape makes it possible to organize what Garfinkel appropriately calls "another next first time" (2002: 98), but also the ways in which analysis as a social activity can be made possible, through the sharing, the reference to, the discussion and the collaborative analysis of available records. Even if Sacks worked mainly on audio, as early as the start of the 70s, Chuck and Candy Goodwin made an impressive number of videos (used also for Goodwin's dissertation, 1981), much of which got lost, but some of which eventually became "cult" fragments, such as the Auto Discussion – an excerpt of 30 minutes from tape 84, the only surviving fragment of a corpus of 3 days of continuous shots (Goodwin & Goodwin, personal communication). From the beginnings of the 70s, first in Philadelphia, then at the Summer Institute of Linguistics and in California, the Goodwins animated a number of seminars on video data. In parallel, in the UK, in about the same period, Christian Heath began to video tape medical consultations (see his dissertation, published in 1986).

Data production respects the naturalistic orientation of this framework, requiring that participants' activities be observed in their ordinary social contexts, in naturally occurring interactions, i.e. in interactions which have not been orchestrated by the researcher, which would have taken place even if she would be absent – but which represent people's ordinary business. This fundamental demand is related to a specific vision of social activities and of language developed within an ethnomethodologically inspired conversation analytic framework, which insists upon the following aspects:

– a *praxeological view of language and action*: social practices (*versus* representations, cultural beliefs, mental models, norms, etc.) are central to the constitution of the social and the grammatical order. Language is not an autonomous system, but a set of practices and resources. The natural habitat for grammatical resources is the sequential organization of social interaction (Schegloff 1996). Therefore language is

an interactive and emergent phenomenon (Hopper 1988) for which time is an essential feature to be studied (Auer et alii 1999).
- an *endogeneous view of resources* as details oriented to and indexically exploited by participants: details of action constitute the relevant accountably phenomenal field properties which are constantly exhibited and interpreted by participants in order to coordinate their conducts. These details are often "seen but unnoticed" (Garfinkel 1967), or seen "at a glance" (Sudnow 1972) and constitute the "scenic intelligibility" (Jayyusi 1988) of conduct and participants' arrangements (Goodwin 2000). Thus, visual features, and more generally multimodal resources, are fundamental and allow a switch from a logocentric perspective on language and action to an embodied view.
- a *situated view of social conduct*: interactions are *reflexively* structured, i.e. conduct adapt to its context and at the same time, by interpreting it in a certain way, configures it by the very fact that it adjusts to this particular feature and not another – being thus both context-shaped and context-renewing. This makes it impossible to transpose behaviour elsewhere so as to recording it more conveniently, with more sophisticated equipment or in absence of certain noise or lighting problems (e.g. by asking people to "informally chat" in a acoustic room in a academic lab).

Video as preserving relevant details of situated action

These fundamental demands concerning the empirical objects to be studied are integrated and embodied into specific practices and techniques of videotaping (cf. Goodwin 1994b, Jordan & Henderson 1995; Heath 1997; Meier 1998). Recording constitutes less a "registrierende Konservierung" than a "rekonstruierende Konservierung" as Bergmann (1985: 305) puts it. It is a paradoxical action: a dynamic fixation, a "Fixierung", which attempts to preserve the "Flüchtigkeit" of social events and their temporality. What these recordings try to reconstruct are the details to which participants orient when they produce and interpret their own and the others' conducts. If the aim is to develop an endogenous analysis of the members perspectives embedded in their practices, then the very details attended to and exploited by them have to be recorded, as well as their orientation to them (in form of gaze, of body positions, of demonstrable orientations in talk, etc.). This sets the task for a specific way of producing videotapes, consistent with a specific "analytic mentality".

This specific way adheres to an "*availability principle*" (Mondada 2003b): the analytical task of recording (and, in the same way, of digitising, anonymizing transcribing, annotating, etc.) is to provide for the availability of relevant details – which indeed makes the analysis possible. Not recording some of these details (and a part of them are not predictable) would mean not providing for the very possibility of analyzing them and therefore the action they organize methodically. Thus, the ethnomethodological conversational inquiry adopts specific ways of shooting video which preserve key dimensions such as:

– *time*. Openings as well as closings of an activity, its particular length and rhythm are respected: one continuous shot documenting the whole activity is the specific video response to this feature. This poses a series of *analytical* problems, such as the recognizable character of an opening and of pre-opening activities, or the documentation of the active relevant arrangement of bodies, objects and spaces as a precondition for the activity to begin; and also a corresponding series of *practical* problems, such as the renewal of batteries or cassettes – which can alter the very temporal organization of the activity (such as its length, but also its articulation in phases) by imposing an exogeneous temporality: these problems can prompt researchers either to limit themselves to record shorter interactions or to search for technical solutions allowing a maximum of autonomy (e.g. by video recording directly onto more commodious hard disks).

– *participation framework and interactional space*. All relevant participants are considered: this produces video shots avoiding focussing too narrowly on only one participant (for example the established speaker) and, on the contrary, taking into consideration not only the recipient designed character of talk and action – which might be problematic for multiparty interactions but also the artefacts and tools manipulated by participants and their dynamic movements. This requirement implies a way of monitoring not only the ongoing action but all possible participants attending to it and produces a strong sense of the complexity of the *interactional space* – documented either with a static camera (allowing the cameraman to be absent, but then having to anticipate all possible movements done by the participants) or with a mobile camera (imposing the presence of the cameraman, who locally accompanies and projects the next possible action). Possible problems arising from the requirement to document relevant details of space and objects oriented to by participants concern the granularity of the available details (e.g. if participants read a map or look at a screen, the visual details they refer to are often barely visible on the video shot). Devices for preserving the continuity of space or participation framework as well as the complexity of objects do not only concern camera movements and focus, but also further transformations of the video records: in this sense, multiscope videos (using split screen or PIP, picture-in-picture) constitute a technical solution (adopted either during production or post-production), especially for complex spaces of action (workplace studies for example, but also ordinary conversations taking place in different rooms – cf. Zouinar, Relieu et alii, 2004, Balthasar & Mondada, in press; Mondada in press).

– *multimodal details*. Video shooting aims at documenting multimodal resources (language, gaze, gesture, body displays, facial expressions, etc.) as they are locally mobilized and attended to by participants. This means that the relevance of details is endogenously produced within courses of collective action as they are interactively and reflexively constructed moment-by-moment within the contingent unfolding of practices. Video records aim not at the production of descriptive glosses by the analyst, but at making available the ways in which participants themselves deal with these details, by methodically orienting to them and by exploiting them for the subsequent organization of action.

Video as configuring and assembling relevant details

This aim to preserve fundamental features of the events and activities is accomplished through video practices and through the cameraman's embodied analysis of the recorded events, which all contribute to the reflexive configuration of these very features – before and during the shot. In the latter case, participants can take the camera movements into account.

Setting up the video camera before the action

Choices of perspectives and spots from which to record action, choices of the beginning and the end of a recorded segment – which depend often on technical constraints (such as the length of the cassettes, the possibility of placing the cameras in difficult angles and locations, etc.) – and other technical choices – concerning the equipment, its miniaturization, angles and lenses, microphones, etc. – results from a reflexive analysis of the situation even *before* the action takes place. In this respect, fieldwork plays an essential role for the identification of expectable patterns of action to which to adjust the video shot.

For example, videorecording a work session between agronomists and computer scientists discussing about how to draw and to read farmland maps, we decided to use two cameras: one was set to point down from the ceiling, taping the working space of the table covered with maps within a vertical perspective (image A); the other was placed sideways on in order to capture all the participant's upper bodies (image B):

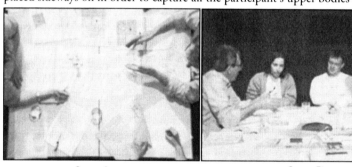

Image A   Image B

These two images offer very different perspectives on what happens: if the first provides a detailed view on the visible features accomplished by pointing and other gestures; the second one documents the bodily postures and gazes A of the participants. In such an activity, the alternation between mutual gazes and a common focus of attention on the artefacts is a key feature that neither one nor the other image alone can capture. Analyzing the way in which turn-taking is projected by finely timed hand movements and not only by talk (Mondada 2004), we discovered that the first and the second image offer different relevant details.

(1a) (e9/agro1-47.00) (transcript based on the vertical view - image A)

```
 1  PAL    et puis à un autre moment:,
            and then at another moment
 2         ben on va échouer, (.) en pâturage, .h
            well we'll wind up (.) with pasture .h
 3         sur l'assemblage +sans parcours. .h +je pense que+
            in an assemblage without any path . h i think that
    viv                    +.........................+moves paper+
 4         +dans le cas du gaec du pr+adou, .h c'est tout l'un,
            in the case of ((name of place)) .h it's either one
    viv    +moves wrist and comes in+
 5         tout l'autre.
            or the other
 6  VIV    +.hh oui. parce que: i m'*sem+ble: eh i*- ici
            .hh yes because it seems to me (that) ehm he- here
           +.........................................+points-->>
    lau                                 *opens booklet*
 7         c'était s::- ce qui: ce que ça voulait représenter.
            it was wh::- what what it was meant to represent.
```

Vivian's turn begins with a pointing gesture (line 6) which is progressively stretched along the table on the document held by Laurence – even prompting her to open the booklet in which the map pointed to by Vivian is located. A systematic feature discovered in our analysis is that pointing gestures are mobilized as multimodal resources for accomplish turn-taking, often projecting turn's begin. Here, this projection is visible in other kinds of detailed body movements, such as hand movements and displacements of objects (lines 3, 4). This movements are done methodically in a specific sequential position: they project the end of Pierre-Alain turn-constructional unit (TCU, finishing with "sans parcours/" 3) at a transition relevance point. However, at that very moment, Pierre-Alain expands his turn by an inbreath (".h" 3) and a new TCU; Viviane projects its end by coming forward with her hand. The pointing gesture line 6 is thus anticipated by other movements timely inserted within the unfolding turn organization.

Now, if we look at the other perspective, we can enrich the transcript with participant's glances:

(1b) (e9/agro1-47.00) (transcript based on the sideways view – image B)

```
 1  PAL    et puis à un autre moment:
 2         ben on va échouer, . en pâturage, .h
 3         sur l'assembla:‡ge +sans parcours, .h +je pen‡se que+
           >>looks LAU->‡looks at VIV----------------------‡looks down->
    viv                      +.........................+moves paper+
 4         +dans le cas du gaec du pr+‡adou, .h c'est‡ tout l'un,
                                     --->‡looks at LAU--‡looks at VIV-->
    viv    +moves wrist and comes in+
```

5   tout l'autre.
6 VIV   +.hh oui. par‡ce que: i'm'*sem+ble: eh i-* ici c'était
        +..+points-->>
  pal   --->‡looks at the pointed document-->>
  lau   *opens booklet*

During his description of an area of farmland, Pierre-Alain visually addresses Laurence, the computer scientist. However, even before Viviane moves her hand, Pierre-Alain moves his gaze from Laurence to her (line 3): in this way he projects the end of his explicating turn and accountably selects Viviane as the next speaker; Viviane's hand movement is responsive to this gesture, aligning with Pierre-Alain's projection. In other cases (Mondada 2004), pointing gestures allow the co-participant to self-select as possible next speaker. The difference between both methods is a matter of timed movements, whose sequential position is fundamental for deciding who is initiating and projecting the next step. The availability of these movements for the participants as well as for the camera/analyst is central too: the camera setting as well as the possibility of consulting two views during the analysis are central for the very results it can produce. In our case, the perspective view was recorded as a PIP, favouring the vertical view: however for this analysis the PIP was not precise enough, and the perspective view had to be resorted to.

Camera movements seeing and anticipating courses of action

Other kinds of reflexive online analysis take place *during* the action: camera movements display the ongoing interpretive practice of the cameraman. Videotaping is a practical accomplishment adjusted to the local contingencies of action and embodying the online interpretation the researcher makes of what happens. The continuous video record is produced within a contingent course of inquiry, where the researcher looks at social life with his camera and his look is made accountable by its record (cf. Macbeth 1999: 140). The camera sees and indeed anticipates the unfolding production of action as it is locally accomplished: the video task consists thus in the work of discovering the local interactional order, as the shot unfolds and as action unfolds.

The cameraman finds and frames the event in a embodied way, the camera being both a resource and a constraint, allowing to see in a particular way, making available a field of view narrower (or a wider, if fish-eye lenses are used) than the eye's. In this sense, as Macbeth puts it (1999) cameras can't glance but can only look or stare at social action.

Again, methods for managing turn-taking are interesting to observe as a practical problem for the participants but also for the cameraman. The classroom setting is a notoriously difficult workplace to videotape (cf. Zungler, Ford & Fassnacht 1998), providing a perspicuous setting for the analysis of the movements of a mobile camera on the selected pupils during a grammatical exercise.

(2) (Brig1-30: 5.23-5.50)
```
 1 AHM   *la terminaison, (.) °de l'im- (.) par- (.) # fait.°
          the ending (.) °of the im- (.) per- fect°
          >>looks at ENS--->
    cam   >>focussed on AHM--->
    im                                             # im.A
 2 CHA   de l'imparfait
          of the imperfect
 3 ENS   de l'imparfait, sophie.Δ (.) der*nière fois Δ hein ?
          of the imperfect sophie (.) last opportunity okay ?
    ahm                   --->Δlooks away---------Δ
    cam                          --->*zoom back------>
 4        après gare à vous* si vous ne connaissez pas tous. (.)
          after that beware  if you don't know (it) all
    cam                --->*general view--->
 5        Δallez *vas-y,
          okay let's go
    ahm   Δlooks at the front right--->
    cam    ---->*moves toward the front, maintaining large view-->
 6 SOP   °alors,° pour former le conditionnel du présentΔ
          °so° in order to create the conditional of the present
    ahm                                              ---->Δ
 7 ?      (   )
 8 ENS   on pren:d,
          one takes
 9 ?     °on prend°
         °one takes°
10 CHA   on prend l'imp- (.) le:=
          one takes the imp- (.) the=
11 VIO   =sch::: tais-toi, sch:::
          =sch::: shut up sch:::
12 ENS   allez,
          let's go
13 SOP   xxxx
14 ENS   mais tu n'écoutes pas,
          but you don't listen
15 NAD   maîtresse, j'peux?
          teacher, can I?
16 ENS   euh:: saΔrina#
          ehm:: sarina
    ahm           Δturns quickly behind--->
    im                 # im B
17        (0.2)*(0.3)+(0.2)+ #
    cam    ->*switches to the left, moving to the last row--->
    im                      # im C
    sar              +adjust on her chair and advances her body+
```

18 SAR   pour ( ) le conditi[onnel
            for ( ) the conditional
19 ENS   [pour <u>for</u>mer, il faut un p'tit
                      in order to create, you need a little bit
            peu de vocabulaire quand même °scientifique°
            of °scientific° vocabulary newertheless
20 SA   °pour former le conditionnel présent°
            in order to create the conditional present

At the excerpt's beginning, the camera is focussed on the pupil being interrogated, Ahmed (line 1-3, image A). In the subsequent moments, camera movements will exploit Ahmed's own orientation to the ongoing action's organization for relevantly framing the interactional space of the classroom: as soon as the sequence between the teacher and Ahmed is closed and another pupil is selected (3), Ahmed looks away from the teacher. Slightly after, the camera operator zooms back, encompassing a more general view of the classroom, waiting for the identification of the next speaker. Again when Ahmed looks to his front right, the camera moves in that same direction, locating Sophie whose answer is being delayed: so, when she begins her turn, the camera is focussed in her direction (6). Interestingly, as Sophie encounters problems in continuing the exercise, another pupil is selected, Sarina (16): on the last syllable of her name uttered by the teacher, Ahmed turns visibly his head behind (image B) and this displays for the cameraman the place where Sarina sits, on the last row of the classroom (image C). During the following brief pause, the camera moves toward her and is thus able to document not only her answer but also her bodily rearrangement and adjustment to her emerging speaker position.

This excerpt shows how member's displays of the relevant interpretation and adjustment to the unfolding interactional order are exploited as resources by the cameraman following and projecting their next actions. In this sense, camera movements as visible on the tape and as transcribable as one detail among other interactional details, provide not only for the documentation of the action but for its temporally emergent accomplishment.

image A
camera focussed on AHM

image B
AHM orienting to the selected next speaker

image C
camera moving to the last row, focussing on the selected speaker

Interacting with the camera

We are concerned, in this paper, with the fact that video shooting actively co-produces the peculiar orderliness of the events, gestures, actions, and talk it displays and documents. Moreover, the cameraman orients to this orderliness in the very production of the visual record, contributing to its accomplishment in accordance with his practical purposes and in a recipient-designed manner, related to the co-participants, audiences, and co-workers he is engaged with:

– participants *inspect* and interpret the movements and focus of the camera, presuming possible topics of research interest; this produces an online analysis of the ongoing situation, comprising the camera, from their side too (this public availability of the camera gaze is even more explicit with a mobile camera than with a static one).
– participants also *adjust* to the camera in the organization of the course of their affairs and for their practical categorization as being filmable or not (orientation to the camera can reveal "embarrassing", "delicate" actions or words, which are categorized as such by the very fact that at that moment the participants make a comment on/to the camera. This can work as a very useful advice for taking into account ethical issues, and for data anonymization, to be related to the local relevance of delicate matters and their emergent categorization – cf. also Speer & Hutchby 2003).
– participants can *exploit* the camera as a resource for their own activities: either for accomplishing the ongoing action (for example by using the video perspective in order to organize a queue or other arrangements of bodies) or for accomplishing another action related to the camera as inaugurating a stage or a scene. In this sense, dealing with the effects of the camera on the ongoing action as a "bias" or considering them in terms of an "observer's paradox" (Labov 1972) misses the very entanglement of the camera and of the action and the very fact that the camera can indeed reinforce and reveal structural elements of the situation and activity (and thus can be enrolled as a resource for the production of its order and accountability).

This shows how these phenomena as well as video taping itself are embedded within the organization of the ongoing action, and have to be integrated within its analysis and not kept separated – In a methodological appendix or in the "backstage" areas of science. In these moments, what happens is a "recorded conversation" and not just a "conversation" – as a phenomenon which itself says something about the local relevancies, the participants, the organization of the ongoing activity (and not only about the way in which data are constituted). However, the relevance of the video device for the local action's organization has not to be supposed a priori and in general, but has to be demonstrated moment-by-moment through the accountable orientations of the participants: orientation to the camera is a phenomenon that can be analyzed as a topic (cf. Heath 1986: 11-13, Lomax & Casey 1998 for good examples). Skilled ways of obtaining an informed consent by the participants and of managing the discretedness/sophistication of the recording contribute to the form these orientations might take: in this sense, the way in which the recording is organized remains fundamental, as it enhances or diminishes the salience of the device for the participants.

Video as a professional practice

As we have seen, videos are not just data made available for research: videos are produced within specific, situated, contingent practices. However, these practices concern various kinds of social members and groups:
- not only the researchers, on which we have focussed our paper, but also
- the amateurs using video for private purposes such as videorecording a friend's wedding, snow holidays, a son's birthday, etc.;
- other professionals skilfully producing and configuring video images for all practical purpose. In this latter respect, video practices and devices are more and more deeply embedded in contemporary workplaces and institutional settings: surgeons use endoscopic cameras explore the anatomy within the course of a laparoscopic operation in order to provide for the relevant visual environment for the next surgical step (Mondada 2003c), TV cameraman and directors produce images appropriate for broadcast (Relieu 1999; Broth, 2003; Mondada, in press b), video are shot by CCTV and surveillance cameras in public spaces (Ball 2000), airport control rooms (Goodwin & Goodwin 1996; Suchman 1996), underground station operation rooms (Luff, Heath & Jirotka 2000). These settings can be studied for the way in which they produce videos as well as for the online interpreting practices by which they exploit them. In the latter case, studies focus on seeing as a professional practice that can also be documented in other settings – dealing with fixed images, computer screens or other objects (Goodwin 1994a, 2000; Heath et al 2002; Lynch 1988).

Video practices as they are organized and promoted by social actors for other than academic purposes produce video records that can be used by researchers themselves, who in this case delegate the production of data to the members they observe. In this case, the objects made available for researchers are either the products of these practices, allowing for the reconstruction of the video movements (as they are witnessable in the image) or the activity of production itself, videotaped by the researcher (for example, Schmitt, in preparation, videotapes a film team shooting a movie). This latter case is a reminder for not reducing the production to its product – this being particularly striking for media analysis (cf. the work of Relieu 1999, Broth 2003).

Working with videos produced by members within their professional activities allows to take into consideration their practical purposes and to analyze how they are materialized and embodied in particular ways of shooting. For example, surgeons operating laparoscopically are firstly interested in the endoscopic image they look at on monitors in the operating room during the procedure (im. A); however, when they broadcast the operation in an amphitheatre for teaching purposes, they add to this endoscopic image another external view of the relevant area of the body, showing where the instruments are inserted - switching between one image and the other or using PIP in order to make both of them available (im. B) (Mondada, in press a). The researcher interested in team collaborative work can shoot her own videos within the operating room, which will produce a very different view, for other practical purposes (im. C). Although these various views can be edited in a composite image (a split screen), they are shot in order to produce very different accountabilities and intelligibilities of action (Mondada 2003a), which can well be incommensurable.

image A	image B	image C
interior endoscopic view used by surgeons during the operation	exterior view used for teaching purposes, often inserted within the interior view	view of the operating room videotaped by the researcher

Thus, video practices embedded within specific professional practices produce specific accountabilities of action. In a project aiming at documenting the experiencies of persons who escaped the Holocaust, historians have recorded a series of testimonies in the form of video taped interviews of witnesses. Their video shootings are focussed on the witness, framing the upper part of his body against a curtain – accomplishing in this way the "officiality" of the settings (image A). Alternative video shootings we produced within an interactional linguistic project consist in views of the witness and the two historians interviewing him, thus constituting a wider view on the setting – which is visible as a video studio – encompassing the whole participation framework

image A	image B
historians' view on the testimony as a monological narrative	alternative view on the testimony as a collective enterprise

and the recording devices such as microphones and some cameras (image B). Whereas the historians' view makes the activity accountable as a testimony's narrative, focussing on the speaker alone, the alternative view produces the accountability of the activity as the collective elaboration of a storytelling within an interview.

Video production as a social practice – to be studied by considering symmetrically both researchers engaged in conversation analysis and other professionals or amateurs involved in the local production of videos for all practical purposes – constitutes a perspicuous setting for the study of embodied seeing practices, namely for a praxeology of seeing with a camera. Their study can show how the accountability of action is variously produced by the cameraman's embedded online choices and analyses, reflexively adjusting to the contingencies of the recorded action.

Concluding remarks

In this paper we dealt with video practices as a topic of inquiry, focussing on video production within the framework of ethnomethodology and conversation analysis. We highlighted the very fact that these videos are practical accomplishments within specific contexts and contingent courses of action, adjusting, anticipating, following the dynamics of sequential unfolding of interaction and of changing participation frameworks. Videos produced within the naturalistic requirements of ethnomethodology and conversation analysis both aim at preserving relevant details and phenomenal field features and reflexively contribute to the configuration of the very interactional order they document. This reflexive dimension of video practices can be studied in depth by also considering other skilled professional video activities, engaged in producing video documentation of events, actions or talk for various practical purposes. Thus video shooting – either by researchers, by professionals or by amateurs – can be a perspicuous setting for the observation and analysis of the way in which members develop endogenous online situated contingent analysis of social life.

Transcript conventions

Data have been transcribed according to conventions developed by Gail Jefferson. Multimodal details have been transcribed according to the following conventions (according to Mondada 2004):

* *	gestures and actions descriptions are delimited between
+ +	two identical symbols (generally one symbol per participant)
Δ Δ	and are synchronized with correspondent stretches of talk
>>	gesture or action described begin before the excerpt's beginning
--->>	gesture or action described continue after excerpt's end
*--->	gesture or action described continue across subsequent lines

```
---->*    until the same symbol is reached
....      gesture's preparation
----      gesture's apex is reached and maintained
,,,,,,    gesture's retraction
lau       participant doing gesture is identifyied when (s)he is not the speaker
cam       camera movements are described
im        the exact point where screen shot (image) has been taken is indicated
#         with a specific sign showing its position within turn at talk.
```

References

Auer, P., Couper-Kuhlen, E., & Müller, F. (1999). *Language in Time. The Rhythm and Tempo of Spoken Interaction*. Oxford: Oxford University Press

Ball, M. (2000). The visual availability and local organization of public surveillance systems: the promotion of social order in public space. *Sociological Research Online (www.socresonline.org.uk), 5*(1)

Balthasar, L., Mondada, L. (in press). Multiscope videos. *Interacting Bodies. Proceedings of the 2d ISGS Conference, Lyon, June 2005*

Bergmann, J. R. (1985). Flüchtigkeit und methodische Fixierung sozialer Wirklichkeit: Aufzeichnungen als Daten der interpretativen Soziologie. In W. Bonss & H. Hartmann (Eds.), *Entzauberte Wissenschaft (Sonderband 3 der Sozialen Welt)*. Göttingen: Otto Schwarz

Broth, M. (2003). Analyse de l'interaction à la télévision. *Moderna Sprak, 2*(2), 193-202

Büscher, M. (2005). Social life under the microscope? *Sociological Research Online ‹http://www.socresonline.org.uk/10/1/buscher.html›, 10*(1)

Garfinkel, H. (1967). *Studies in Ethnomethodology*. Englewood Cliffs, N.J.: Prentice-Hall

Garfinkel, H. (2002). *Ethnomethodology's Program. Working out Durkheim's Aphorism*. Lanham: Rowman and Littlefield

Goodwin, C. (1981). *Conversational Organization: Interaction Between Speakers and Hearers*. New York: Academic Press

Goodwin, C. (1994a). Professional Vision. *American Anthropologist, 96*(3), 606-633

Goodwin, C. (1994b). Recording human interaction in natural settings. *Pragmatics, 3*, 181-209

Goodwin, C. (1995). Seeing in depth. *Social Studies of Science, 25*(2), 237-274

Goodwin, C. (2000). Practices of Seeing, Visual Analysis: An Ethnomethodological Approach. In T. v. Leeuwen & C. Jewitt (Eds.), *Handbook of Visual Analysis* (pp. 157-182). London: Sage

Goodwin, C., & Goodwin, M. H. (1996). Seeing as a situated activity: Formulating planes. In D. Middleton & Y. Engestrom (Eds.), *Cognition and Communication at Work*. Cambridge: Cambridge University Press

Heath, C. (1986). *Body Movement and Speech in Medical Interaction*. Cambridge: Cambridge University Press

Heath, C. (1997). Analysing work activities in face to face interaction using video. In D. Silverman (Ed.), *Qualitative Research. Theory, Method and Practice*. London: Sage.

Heath, C., Svensson, M. S., Hindmarsh, J., Luff, P., & vom Lehn, D. (2002). Configuring awareness. *CSCW, 11*(3-4), 317-347

Hopper, P. (1988). Emergent grammar and the a priori grammar postulate. In D. Tannen (Ed.), *Linguistics in Context: Connecting Observation and Understanding* (pp. 103-120). Norwood: Ablex

Jayyusi, L. (1988). Toward a socio-logic of the film text. *Semiotica, 68*(3/4), 271-296
Jordan, B., & Henderson, A. (1995). Interaction analysis: Foundations and practice. *The Journal of the Learning Sciences, 4*(1), 39-103
Labov, W. (1972). *Sociolinguistic Patterns.* Philadelphia: University of Pennsylvania Press.
Latour, B. (1986). Visualisation and cognition: Thinking with eyes and hands. *Knowledge and Society: Studies in the Sociology of Culture Past and Present, 6,* 1-40
Lomax, H., & Casey, N. (1998). Recording social life: Reflexivity and video methodology. *Sociological Research Online, 3*(2)
Luff, P., Heath, C., & Jirotka, M. (2000). Surveying the scene: Technologies for everyday awareness and monitoring in control rooms. *Interacting with Computers, 13,* 193-228
Lynch, M. (1985). Discipline and the material form of images: An analysis of scientific visibility. *Social Studies of Science, 15,* 37-66
Lynch, M. (1988). The externalized retina: Selection and mathematization in the visual documentation of objects in the life sciences. *Human Studies, 11,* 201-234
Lynch, M. (1991). Pictures of Nothing: Visual Construals in Sociological Theory. *Sociological Theory, 9-1*(1-21)
Macbeth, D. (1999). Glances, trances, and their relevance for a visual sociology. In P. L. Jalbert (Ed.), *Media Studies: Ethnomethodological Approaches* (pp. 135-170). Lanham: University Press of America & Int. Inst. for Ethnomethodology and Conversation Analysis
Meier, C. (1998). Zur Untersuchung von Arbeits- und Interaktionsprozessen anhand von Videoaufzeichnungen. *Arbeit. Zeitschrift für Arbeitsforschung, Arbeitsgestaltung und Arbeitspolitik, 7*(3), 257-275
Mondada, L. (2003a). Describing surgical gestures: the view from researcher's and surgeon's video recordings. *Proceedings of the First International Gesture Conference, Austin, July 2002* (http://www.utexas.edu/coc/cms/International_House_of_Gestures/Conferences/Proceedings/Contents/List_of_Papers.html)
Mondada, L. (2003b). Observer les activités de la classe dans leur diversité: choix méthodologiques et enjeux théoriques. In: Perera, J., Nussbaum, L., Milian, M. (eds.). *L'educacio linguistica en situacions multiculturals i multilingues,* Barcelona : ICE Universitat de Barcelona, 49-70
Mondada, L. (2003c). Working with video: how surgeons produce video records of their actions. *Visual Studies,* 18, 1, 58-72
Mondada, L. (2004). Temporalité, séquentialité et multimodalité au fondement de l'organisation de l'interaction: Le pointage comme pratique de prise du tour. *Cahiers de Linguistique Française,* 26, 169-192
Mondada, L. (2005). Visions controversées de la carte: construire le visible par les gestes et la parole en interaction. In: C. d'Alessandro et alii (eds.). *Espaces, savoirs et incertitudes.* Paris : Belin, 15-31.
Mondada, L. (in press a). Operating together through videoconference: members' procedures accomplishing a common space of action. In: Francis, D. (ed.). *Orders of Ordinary Action.* Washington: University Press of America & Int. Institute for Ethnomethodology and Conversation Analysis
Mondada, L. (in press b). Videorecording and the reflexive constitution of the interactional order: uses of split screen in video practices
Relieu, M. (1999). La réalisation et la réception du produit télévisuel comme accomplissements. In J.-P. Desgoutte (Ed.), *De l'image au verbe. Le jeu interactif dans le discours audiovisuel.* Paris: L'Harmattan
Sacks, H. (1984). Notes on methodology. In J. M. Atkinson & J. Heritage (Eds.), *Structures of*

Social Action (pp. 21-27). Cambridge: Cambridge University Press. (Edited by Gail Jefferson from various lectures)

Sacks, H. (1992). *Lectures on Conversation [1964-72] (2 Vols.)*. Oxford: Basil Blackwell.

Schegloff, E. A. (1996). Turn organization: One intersection of grammar and interaction. In E. Ochs, E. A. Schegloff & S. A. Thompson (Eds.), *Grammar and Interaction* (pp. 52-133). Cambridge: Cambridge University Press

Schmitt, R. (in preparation). Das Filmset als Arbeitsplatz: Einblicke in die Struktur einer komplexen Kooperationsform

Speer, S., Hutchby, I. (2003). From ethics to analytics: Aspects of participants' orientations to the presence relevance of recording devices. *Sociology*. 37, 2, 315-337

Suchman, L. (1996). Constituting shared workspaces. In D. Middleton & Y. Engestrom (Eds.), *Cognition and Communication at Work*. Cambridge: Cambridge University Press.

Sudnow, D. (1972). Temporal parameters of interpersonal observation. In D. Sudnow (Ed.), *Studies in Social Interaction* (pp. 259-279). New York: Free Press

Zouinar, M., Relieu, M., Salembier, P., Calvet, G. (2004). Observation et capture de données sur l'interaction multimodale en mobilité. *Mobilité & Ubiquité* '04, Nice 1-3 June 2004. Nice: ACM

Zungler, J., Ford, C., Fassnacht, C. (1998). *Analyst eyes and camera eyes: Theoretical and technological considerations in "seeing" the details of classroom interaction*. Albany: The National Research Center on English Learning and Achievement. Report Series 2.40

Hubert Knoblauch

Videography
Focused Ethnography and Video Analysis

Introduction

Within the last two decades, video recording has become a more and more accepted instrument of data collection and analysis in the social sciences. However, while the collection of data using video appears largely unproblematic, the analysis of video data is more divided. This analytic variability can be initially simplified by distinguishing two types of analysis: the standardised (including automatised) and the interpretative. The standardised (and automatised) analytic approach begins with a number of pre-defined codes, constructed according to a given categorical frame that are "applied" to audiovisual recordings. After producing some kind of "intercoder reliability" or automatising the codes, audiovisually recorded interactions between pupils, for example, may then be coded as "supportive" or "non-supportive", aggressive" or "non-aggressive" (cf. Mittenecker 1987). In fields such as Computer Supported Collaborative Work or Human Computer Interaction, there are currently more than 40 software programs for standardised analysis available, most of them based on predefined categories (cf. Koch & Zumbach 2002). As useful as these studies may be for certain purposes, they differ from the requirements of the second approach, that of interpretive video analyses which is in the focus of this article (cf. Knoblauch, Schnettler and Raab, this volume). This is an analytic approach that starts from the assumption that actions are oriented to by meanings. Yet, while there are an impressive number of studies which have proven the necessity, importance and relevance of such interpretive video analysis, there have been a few attempts to delineate the methods of these studies, i.e. how to handle video for the purpose of social scientific research. Consequently, the field of interpretive, qualitative and naturalistic social scientific research still lacks any unified methodologies.

My aim in this paper is to build upon the disparate interpretative studies and propose a unified method. This will involve elucidating the methodological assumptions, and methodical steps, applied by a number of researchers in the field of interpretative video studies.[1] Video analysis in the social sciences, I will argue, can be considered as a

---

[1] I am fortunate to have had the chance to work with Thomas Luckmann in a series of projects involving video data, first as a junior researcher, later as a senior researcher. I am also indebted to John Gumperz whose research techniques I became familiar with at Berkeley. Most importantly, however, my gratitude goes to Christian Heath and his WIT group (especially Jon Hindmarsh, Paul Luff and Dirk vom Lehn) at King's College London whose dedication

kind of ethnography using video, to be more exact: a *videography*. As *video*graphy, the focus of video analysis is typically on what may be called visual conduct. Under the current heading of multi-modality, some researchers attempt to cut the forms of such visual conduct into slices, e.g. as gestures (Kendon 2004), kinesics (Birdwhistell 1970) or facial expressions (Ekman & Friesen 1969b). Whereas the attempts to re-synthesise the various slices or modes into a holistic picture, for example in analogy to the musical score, have proved to be utterly complex and so far, not really successful (cf. Luckmann this volume), approaches that take visual conduct as part of a social context seem to be able to cope much better with visual data. Based on Goffman's analysis of social situations and on conversational analysis, one of the central foci of interpretive, qualitative, social scientific video analysis has become interaction. By interaction, I refer to the fact that actors (e.g. those recorded) orientate their action at one another creating what Goffman (1981) has defined as a social situation. Interaction, however, is not restricted to people in co-presence. In fact, quite a number studies using video analysis (e.g. within the area of the Workplace Studies, cf. Heath, Knoblauch & Luff 2000) address forms of interactions in which technologies and visual representations of co-actors (such as documents, telephones, screens etc.) figure as "agents" (simulating co-presence). The focus on interaction, thus, also includes "interactivity" (Rammert & Schulz-Schaeffer 2002), i.e. forms of mediated interaction by means of technology, as well as the situative context. For this reason, it seems adequate to talk of video*graphy*.

In this paper, I will try to clarify in more detail what is meant by videography. Obviously, videography is only one of a number of methods applied when analysing video data. However, as I will argue in part 2, videography is probably the method that best exploits the potential of video for the social sciences since it combines (focused) ethnography with the "microscope of the social sciences". In a next part (3) I shall outline some methodological assumptions and methodical steps in order to make use of this microscope, particularly those addressing its sequential and visual features. And finally (4) I shall come back to the requirements on comparison and sampling that are, again, embedded in the ethnographic frame of videography.

Focused ethnography and video analysis

Studies in the social sciences that employ video data collection and its analysis frequently stress that they augment or complement their video recordings by field studies, participant observation or, more generally, ethnography. Indeed, if one looks more closely at video studies, and reflects upon ones own methodological practice, it becomes evident that the recording of video data is rarely developed in isolation. Most

---

to detailed video analysis has been so influential. I am also most grateful to Neil Jenkings for numerous valuable comments on the paper.

studies, in addition to video data, employ ethnographies which may include: participant observation, information from documents, comments from interviews and discussions, together with elicitations using the visual data recorded. Ethnography is of particular importance in those cases in which technological settings are studied; but also other areas in which the implicit and tacit knowledge of actors needs eliciting in order to understand the action at hand. For this reason, by the early 1980s Corsaro (1981) was proposing that there should be no video recording and analysis without undertaking prior ethnography – a procedure similar to what Albrecht (1985: 328f) already called "scouting". Indeed Erickson (1988) and Cicourel (1992) have stressed that this focusing process presupposes prior knowledge of and prior familiarity with the field and, therefore, prior ethnography. As Heath and Hindmarsh (Heath & Hindmarsh 2002: 107) emphasize, for the analysis of video recordings of naturally occurring activities "it is critical that the researcher undertakes more conventional fieldwork".

The bond between video analysis (in its social scientific, interpretive and naturalistic version) and ethnography has not occurred by chance, instead there is an intimate relation between video and ethnography (cf. also Shrum, Duque & Brown 2005). On the one hand, ethnography and video are both observational in a basic sense: audiovisual observation lies at the core of the activities of ethnography, and it is also audiovisual observation that is automatised or, to use Latour's (1986) terminology, "inscribed" into video-technology. There is, of course, a debate as to what degree this observation by means of video is "participatory", proactive, and contributes to the actions (Suchman & Trigg 1991, Jirotka & Goguen 1994) or "reactive", in affecting and manipulating the situation taped. However, while video equipment can be obtrusive and even obstructive to the local action, there are situations in which video recording may be less distorting than the presence of an (overt of covert) observer (see for example vom Lehn & Heath this volume).[2] Second, the inscription of the audiovisual allows one to address "natural situations" (see Knoblauch, Schnettler & Raab this volume) – the kind of situation that is also subject to ethnography. And finally, ethnography and video converge since they are both oriented to the conduct (or, as it was once more prosaically termed: the manners and folkways) of people in their ("natural") environment. As result of this convergence between video analysis and ethnography, I would argue, it is not misleading, but instead instructive, to talk of *videography* as the method to analyse people acting in social settings by video.

Videography admittedly differs to some extent from ethnography in a classical sense. For example, despite attempts to do multi-sited ethnographies of different organisational units by means of video, videographies typically do not aim at encompassing

---

2 As opposed to doing observations, the technologies of recording also relieve the researcher from other tasks and allow for ethnographical observations, questions and reflections while making the video records. Since the data collection is supported technically, researchers dispose of more time to observe specific features or to inquire into certain aspects of the already focused field.

large, locally distributed social structures, such as tribes, villages or cities. In fact, in contrast to such encompassing "conventional" ethnographies (as I will call them for the sake of brevity), videographies may be said to be *focused* in several ways.³

First, conventional ethnographies may be time intensive requiring a long, continual periods of fieldwork (as a rule for most students about a year). Whereas in contrast to this kind of experience-based ethnography, videographies tend to have shorter periods of data collection. Although even if fieldwork and data collection is over a shorter time period, the projects as a whole require similar amounts of time for completion.

Secondly, it has been suggested that the short periods of fieldwork for videographies can render them "superficial" or "quick and dirty" (Hughes, et al. 1994). This view, however, ignores the fact that, the short time periods covered are compensated for by another type of intensity: videography is enormously data intensive. This type of intensity refers not only to the huge amount of data collected in relatively short time, but to the fact that videography requires intensive and detailed data analysis to a degree unprecedented by conventional ethnographies based on field notes with written records.

Before clarifying the nature of video data analysis below, we should note that videography differs from most conventional ethnographies in a third sense; that of its scope or, to be more exact, focus. It lays a "focus on the particular", i.e. the "particulars of situated performance as it occurs naturally in everyday social interaction" (cf. Erickson 1988: 1083). Videography, therefore, typically analyses structures and patterns of interaction, such as the coordination of work activities, the course of family arguments or professional meetings. Rather than studying, for example the police as a field, videography may turn to the question of how police officers do their patrols; or instead of studying youth clubs, it may focus on the question how young people perform at a certain event; or instead of studying the management of a company, it may focus on the meetings of managers. So whereas classical ethnography has turned towards social groups and social institutions, videographies are more concerned with specific actions, interactions and social situations.

It is this focus on actions, interactions and the social situation that motivates videographers to set their analyses within the framework of interpretive, qualitative and 'naturalistic' approaches in the social sciences. Based on the seminal work of scholars such as Mead and Goffman, particularly conversation analysis has influenced the analysis of video data (cf. Sacks 1992[1964ff]). However, due to the on-going restriction of "hard core" Conversation Analysis to audio data and its opposition to video data and background knowledge, the influence of conversation analysis on video analysis is less than it is with purely audio data (cf. ten Have 1999). However, as noted above, video analysis is not a unified approach and there are alternative ways to do video analysis (cf. the contributions to this volume by Mohn, Raab & Tänzler, Schnettler and Schubert

---

3 At this point I draw on my paper on focused ethnography, first published in German (Knoblauch 2001b) and in English (Knoblauch 2005).

etc.); yet we can say that videographies rely on ethnographic data to a varying degree – and that they account for the effect of ethnographic knowledge to varying degrees.

Video analysis: Sequentiality and Visuality

While ethnography may frame videography, its core lies in video-analysis. Video analysis builds on a number of features of the medium of video filming in general. On the one hand, the desire to record the "natural situation" is founded on the "mimesis" assumption that video recordings do indeed represent to some degree what is going on in situations that could be observed without a technological device. Despite the jeremiads on the "crisis of representation" and opposed to written documents of the situation, even the convinced post-modernist cannot deny that video recordings are accessible to other observers in ways that allow them to make new observations and interpretations and to give evidence for (and possibly against) other analyses. Compared to 'plain' observation, video recordings therefore appear more detailed, more complete and more accurate. Moreover, in a technical sense, they are a much more *reliable* kind of data than written fieldnotes since they allow analytic access for researchers who have not participated the data collection, i.e. independently of the person who collected the data (Peräklyä 1997).

Epistemologically, videography is not characterised by a suspension of belief in the existence of the things seen; on the contrary videography may be said to share a kind of "scientific realism" in that it assumes that people are existent and, that they have been conducting (acting) in ways that are open for reconstruction (capture) by video data.[4] In this way, the video recording allows us to establish what Schutz (1962) has called subjective adequacy, i.e. a kind of correspondence between the statements of the researchers and those that are being researched and represented on video.

The advantage analysing video recordings is, that video is much more easily reproduced, manipulated and analysed than other visual data formats, e.g., film. The technical options of repeated viewings, dissection through slow motion and frame-by frame analysis, comparison through fast forward and data banks allow one to observe details that are not even visible to participants in such detail: often they cannot explain or even remember the bits and pieces of the visible behaviour that is accessible to the video analyst. One may anticipate that advances in digitalisation will enhance these options by enabling researchers to compare a number of different sequences simultaneously on one screen. Additionally, frames and sequences will able to be linked and coded in a nonlinear ways and analysis will potentially become more and more visual (instead of verbal).

Finally, video analysis exploits another feature of this medium: its temporality. Like film, video is also defined by the temporal sequence of pictures (it is the fact that this

---

4 As to "scientific realism" and the distinction between these two levels cf. Luckmann (1978).

temporality is no longer built into the new digital storage medium that may cause the changes just mentioned above.) As a result of their temporality, pictures are watched in a consecutive *sequentiality*. It is this feature of sequentiality which has influenced the particular focus of much video analysis, i.e., actions and interactions, as the medium preserves the time structure of these temporal processes in a fashion unprecedented by earlier media (except of film). As video recordings mimic audiovisual conduct in time, they serve as a perfect medium to analyse the sequencing of action and the coordination of interaction through time. It is for this reason that video analysis can be regarded as akin to forms of analysis which are based on sequentiality, such as conversation analysis, objective or structural hermeneutics (cf. Soeffner this volume, Raab & Tänzler this volume). In other words, they consider sequentiality as the very structure by which social action, and thus social order is accomplished. Hence, video analysis starts with sequences of actions and interactions as its subject matter.

So we can briefly sketch how sequentiality can be considered the basis of interpretation and analysis. Firstly, interpretations of video recordings focus on audiovisual conduct. They assume that what is happening (and what is understood as happening) can be only understood if one looks closely at the actions, action sequences and interactions that are expressed in audiovisual conduct. Actions (as we call this basic category for the sake of convenience – without defining their boundaries) are assumed to be produced *methodically* in certain ways, and it is only by being performed in certain ways that certain things are brought about. Thus, a PowerPoint presentation (to take an example from our current research) would not be regarded as some background activity to what may be considered the core activity (e.g. "knowledge transfer"). Rather, the series of actions involved in doing the presentation will be considered as the very essence of this activity. The focus of analysis then lies in *how* those actions are being performed.

This is linked to an additional assumption which again lays stress on the audiovisual: Whatever is observable and understandable should not be considered as being due to external factors beyond the video recorded scene itself, such as "drives", "subconscious desires", attitudes or interests, but as motivated by the local sequence of action recorded. As Goodwin (1986) has shown, even alleged "adaptors" (as Ekman & Friesen 1969a call gestures such as scratching or coughing) turn out to be not just "outbreaks of nature". Rather, they appear to be sensitively built into the sequential order of actions, and thus proving to be actions themselves. As opposed to conventional sociological lore, actions here are not seen as relating to other factors outside the specific situation in which they occur. This is at the heart of what we mean by sequential analysis where one considers any action (note: action not actors) as motivated by prior actions and motivating future actions. This assumption is often equated to the "situative" character of social action (Suchman 1987). However, I would consider situativeness a methodological principle by the analyst long as possible, and avoid treating it as a substantial feature of social actions. In fact, talking about the situative character precludes the observation of actions which cannot be interpreted by situative, local resources only — and in which institutional regulations, social asymmetries and power may figure.

Reflexivity is another highly important methodological concept. By reflexivity we do not mean that actions are reflected consciously. On the contrary, most studies do address what may be called routinised, implicit knowledge or social practice. Reflexivity means that actors do not only act but also "indicate", "frame" or "contextualise" how their action is to be understood and how they have interpreted a prior action to which they are responding.[5] Thus we do not simply ask a question, we demonstrate that it is a question which we are formulating. It is because of this reflexivity that co-actors can understand what is meant by an action. By "investigating the methodological resources used by participants themselves in the production of social actions and activities" (Heath 1997: 184), it is also the reflexivity of the action that allows analytic interpretation.[6]

The possibility of interpreters and analysts making use of reflexivity does not only demand that they know the culture they are studying. It also demands that they understand situated action, rather than an apriori theory of communicative action. Such an understanding also means that analysts who have not participated in the phenomenon that was recorded are able to make sense of what is going on in the actions and interactions. This understanding has very practical aspects, for words and sentences have to be understood in order to be transcribed: one has to "see" the directions of gazes on the recordings or know what actors are referencing so that all essential parts (sentence, word, movement) of a sequence make sense for the participants. It is at this basic level of everyday understanding that ethnographic knowledge figures principally.

The necessity of interpretation proves that video analysis is basically a hermeneutic activity: the task set is not to only describe and explain "nonverbal" behaviour, but to (a) determine the knowledge which one needs in order to understand what is going on in a situation and (b) to identify the visible conduct that constitutes the situation.

Interpretation may be regarded therefore as the very first step of approaching the data, i.e. the tapes and transcripts. As interpretation that is related to the everyday understanding of what is seen and heard, it may be distinguished from analysis. By analysis we do not mean necessarily the distinction of different modes of audiovisual conduct (visual, verbal, paralinguistic etc.) — although it is necessary at certain points to focus on certain aspects, e.g. pointing gestures during PowerPoint presentations. Analysis, means identifying units of action and their interrelationships with one another in the sequence of their production. Whatever may appear to be a unit is to be interpreted in relation to what has been prior to it, and whatever the interpretation

---

5 This notion of reflexivity differs from notions of reflexivity that address the presentation of research (cf. Ruby 2000). Of course, reflexivity applies here, too, but this is not a feature of research only. What is meant by reflexivity is explained in more detail in Knoblauch (2001a).
6 In conversation analysis, it was assumed that reflexivity of spoken communication is framed in spoken communication only — an assumption that is not adopted by video analysis.

will be, it will be tested for its significance in the next unit (or turn). Hence interpretation is never only done retrospectively.

In conversation analysis, the basic unit of the sequence has been the "turn". In fact, since video analysis still draws on transcripts of texts, turns at talk remain a starting point of the analysis. However, turns are not fixed action units but must be analyzed by looking at exactly how the utterances and the ways transitions and boundaries are produced. In order to understand the utterances, one may first try to look for acoustic cues, such as phrase intonations, pauses and rhythms.

Take as an example the following transcript[7]:

1   (3.3)
2   M: ähm das is jetzt so die klassische Ausrüstung die einem zur Verfügung
    ehm this is now the classical equipment which is available when
3   steht=wenn man eben Reis untersuchen möchte. Sie sehen hier auf
    one wants to investigate rice. You may see here on
4   der rechten Seite eben so ne ähm Lupe.
    the right hand side just such ehm a magnifying lens

The transcript shows a segment of text where M is speaking. By looking at the talk one realises that the description M provides is of some "equipment" he is referring to (2). By his address term (3) one can tell that he is addressing someone else and hints at the magnifying glass as part of the equipment with which to investigate rice. The sequence is structured so that he first gives a general title ("classical equipment") to the topic ("investigate rice"); then he moves to singular item.

Scrutinising the transcript does not only allow us to become more familiar with the transcript and the spoken words (leading often to a continuous refinement and correction of the transcript). It is also the basis for analytical observations on the structure of the sequences studied. Moreover, the reading of the transcript serves a secondary function when watching the video and the visual conduct in more detail. The familiarity with the words spoken makes it easier to identify the sequence of events and "relate" the visual events with respect to the text. The video sequence can be repeatedly watched so as to discover the order of acoustic and visual events (what is happening when) and to identify when things are done or said.

It could be argued that this analysis could be accomplished without the transcript, but experience has shown that the availability of a written transcript functions as a kind of location device orientating the analyst in the video. The analysis of the consequent sequences thus moves from the (transcribed) written to the seen. However, the

---

7   An important requirement and resource of analysis consists in detailed transcriptions of data. Transcriptions (which typically involve a lot of work and confront the researcher in a very intensive way with the data) include paralinguistic and prosodic features (Cook 1990) which, however, do not figure prominently in the example given. As the transcription of data is as time-extensive as is data analysis, it seems decisive to develop strategies of sampling and selecting relevant data.

visual is not treated merely as an addendum to the spoken. Rather, in watching the video recordings, one frequently discovers additional sequences which allow one to make sense of prior interpretations or sequences.

Without the video data and without ethnographic knowledge it would be difficult to tell that M is not just talking; but that in addition he uses a PowerPoint presentation on which what he is talking about is represented.[8] Moreover, that he is pointing at the screen by means of a laser pointer. Thus, the deictic noun "das ist" ("that is") is part of introducing the new slide whereas with the deictic noun "Sie sehen hier" ("you may see here"), M points at the items he is going to talk about.

Image 1: PowerPoint presentation with pointer

In looking at both, the spoken and the visual conduct, one can then discern that the visual conduct is constructed in such a way as to support the text the speaker is producing, and vice versa. The PowerPoint slide shown on the screen (Image 1.) is, in fact, quite complex, but the ways of highlighting the text as well as pointing to the screen create an object which has not been there before and which then may serve as a point of reference in the next turn – the turn itself being constructed by visual (body movement, new slide) and verbal (pause) features. Analyses of this kind aim at the sequential structure of events, the construction of meaningful units, participation structures, the spatial organisation of activities, and the role of artefacts for performing activities etc. (Jordan & Henderson 1995).

Thus, the validation procedure for backing-up the analysis draws on what we may call an immanent criterion of sequentiality. Analysis depends on what occurs audiovisually: every utterance, every gaze, every move of the body or the head is being taken

---

8 The data pertains to a research project supported by the Deutsche Forschungsgemeinschaft (DFG) called "Die Performanz visuell unterstützter mündlicher Präsentationen. Gattungsanalytische Untersuchung einer paradigmatischen Kommunikationsform in der 'Wissensgesellschaft'" ("The Performance of visually supported oral presentations: Genre analytical investigation of a paradigmatic form of communication in the 'knowledge society'").

into consideration if, and how, it forms part of a sequence. Sequences are not identified independently of the sequences prior to, or subsequent to themselves, but by their immediate local context. One needs not to consider everything on the screen, but only that which stands in a recognisable relation to what came before and what comes after. Thus, turns at talk may not be the relevant units of sequences at all. But whatever may be considered as unit must be shown to be bounded by audiovisual conduct itself.

This criterion of sequentiality is complemented by a second criterion: what is of importance in the visual must not be speculated about but be indicated by the actors themselves. Do actors look at the screen before they push a button? Does it ring before A walks away? Does A look at B before A moves towards C? Schegloff (1992) called this the criterion of relevance, i.e. what is of relevance for the analyst must be shown to be of relevance for the actors. Or, as Goodwin (2000: 1508f) formulates: "Rather than wandering onto field-sites as disinterested observers, attempting the impossible task of trying to catalogue everything in the setting, we can use the visible orientation of the participants as a spotlight to show us just those features of context that we have to come to terms with if we are to adequately describe the organization of their action". This task can be accomplished by an analyst who knows both the field and the video data well. In addition, it is beneficial to regularly hold data sessions in which the analytical observations of sequential orders are subjected to the critical gazes of other observers who can gradually become familiar with the data. Finally, data workshops with other researchers and students who are less familiar with the data can be organized which may provide additional perspectives and/or help in testing more encompassing observations.

Up to this point, the analysis has focused only on the sequence of actions (including technical devices, such as the screen on which the items are represented). This focus must not be considered a problem since the example refers to a focused kind of interaction in which participants themselves establish a common focus. Things change however if the events recorded are not focused interactions, if spoken words are only of minor importance and if, therefore, the visual gains in importance. For the spoken may be represented in a sequential and linear order corresponding to time, that is a diachronic order. Yet the visual denotes an additional synchronous dimension of simultaneity, i.e. the visually represented courses and resources of action, features of actors and thus the contexts may not be organised on a turn-by-turn basis.

One way to approach this problem in video analysis has been suggested by Goodwin (2000). He suggests that semiotics may be able to grasp these visual features. Thus, talk is embedded in multiple sign systems (such as graphic codes, gestures and other features of the environment). To Goodwin, actors orient to what he calls "semiotic fields" that include different kinds of sign phenomena instantiated in diverse media. In accordance with the principle of relevance, these semiotic fields may be of local relevance in that the actors demonstrably orient towards them (Goodwin calls this "contextual configuration").

There is no doubt that the concept of semiotic field works in cases of well developed sign systems (such as graphic systems of professional experts or the sign elements of children playing hopscotch). One must, however, question if semiotics will help to remedy the problem of visuality in general, since semiotics presupposes that the signs visible are organised in a more or less systematic way. Even if one may admit that words form part of a system, one may doubt that gestures can be considered as forming a real system, let alone other visual elements (such as expressions, clothing, furniture, the order of things in space etc., cf. Hodge & Kress 1988).

Returning to Ethnography

Validation by the criterion of relevance may often turn out to be an intricate task. In order to clarify the meaning and signification of visual elements of the recorded data, therefore, one further possible procedure is elicitation, auto-confrontation or video-based interviewing.[9] This means that the actors involved in the recorded data are presented with the recordings themselves. Thus, Schubert for example (this volume) presented medical personal he had been videoing with recordings of the their operating theatre work and asked them to clarify actions they were involved in. This method does not only potentially allow the reconstruction of actors' perception and orientation in the captured action. It may be seen to also give access to background knowledge relevant to understanding what is going on as actors may able to explicate the functioning and significance of items visible in the scene, but not available to the analyst.

The importance of background knowledge that elucidates visual aspects of the recordings proves again the importance of ethnography for doing video analysis. For it is by way of observation, interviews, expert interviews etc., i.e. ethnography, that we get familiar with, and make sense of, the settings in which we produce the video recordings. We acquire the knowledge necessary to understand the audio-visual action temporally, i.e. the series of actions (which, in many empirical cases, also involves intricate technologies and their activities). Thus videography still addresses the emic perspective of the natives' point of view, yet in a very specific sense: specified with respect to certain situations (situated), activities and actions. This does not mean that one needs to reconstruct the stock of cultural knowledge (i.e., members' knowledge) necessary to act in the domain as a whole. The task of the researcher is to acquire sufficient knowledge, particularly those elements of knowledge, partly embodied, relevant to the activity on which the study focuses. When studying technological activities, for example, especially those elements of knowledge necessary and relevant to understand the practices involved in handling that technology are sought.

---

9   Cf. Bayart, Borzeix & Lacoste (1997). The method goes of course back to Jean Rouch, cf. Jackson (2004).

Typically, it is these types of sequences that are the focus of videographies: Ways of managing technologies, forms of cooperation between personal and their use of technology at certain circumstances (for example in routine actions or crises interventions), kinds of interactions between lay and professional actors etc. The focus may vary strongly depending on the research topic and the structure of the field. Nevertheless, one of the principal goals of the analysis will be to identify common features of what is being studied. In order to do so, the analysis will not only need to interpret and analyse single cases, but will also utilize case comparisons. Such comparison means that similar cases, according to the features that are identified in the analysis, can be located. Comparisons can be associative and look for similarities, or they will be identfying minimal and maximal contrasts. In general, these comparisons will help to determine certain patterns in the sequences studied, be they institutionalized (as e.g. certain organisational "problem solutions") or context dependent and situational.[10] These sequences may consist of series' of individual actions, of interactions between various actors and of actions of technologies. Therefore, analysis tends to demonstrate the kinds of interrelationship of these actions in the situations recorded.

For this reason, single instances may be compared which are stored in the data corpus. In order to retrieve these instances, one draws on a content log.[11] On the basis of such a content log, activities can be analysed across a given corpus of video data, e.g. locating forms of pointing from a corpus of data of video recorded PowerPoint presentations in order to identify the specific features of pointing with this technology, the role of the technology and the effect it has on presentations.

As is often stressed, these situations do have *situative*, contingent properties realized only in the situations which provide a resource for the actors. On the other hand, one should be aware that situations also include *situated* properties, that is, they have properties that are observable across situations and form part of "larger context" (Goffman 1983), be it the kind of rooms and their micro-ecologies; the technologies available, the ranks of persons present and their representations as well as features of the decorum; the situations recorded form part of settings, institutions, organizations and other contexts. There is no doubt that these contexts are subject to the ethnography, be it social welfare agencies, underground stations or management offices. Thus, instead of just comparing interactive sequences, the analysis may then return to the larger context which has been subject to the ethnography (Whereas the first comparison, then, may be regarded as analysis within a data sort, this one resembles to a triangula-

---

10 As far as we look for patterned features, we investigate what we call "communicative patterns", that is forms of interaction that exhibit communal structures beyond the situative actions that relate to extra-situational functions and social structures. Cf. Knoblauch & Guenthner (1995).
11 A content log contains the temporal sequence of events, a rough transcription of activities, gestures and talk, reflections and codings of sequences according to the research topic. Cf. Jordan & Henderson (1995).

tion across data sorts, cf. Flick 2004: 36ff). This context may be kept constant in some studies. Thus, one may concentrate on counseling activities in social welfare agencies, on cooperation between actors in underground control rooms or in ticket-sale interactions between service personal and clients in stations. In these cases, the ethnographic details which enter into the background knowledge of the analysts are to some degree constant. In other cases, however, the contexts in which certain activities that are shown or claimed to be recurrent may vary across various settings, institutions or milieus. To give an example, we may ask if PowerPoint presentations in academic settings differ from the same genre in private companies or in administrative settings. In order to avoid misunderstandings these different settings are not considered as "external factors", but they may prove to denote relevant settings according to which certain interactional sequences may differ or (what could be of even more interest) exhibit strong similarities.[12] Analysis, then, means not only considering interactive situations but also the larger social context (and showing how the former constitute the latter). It is for this reason that analysis can be seen to begin in the data collection process and to guide the sampling of video recordings at every stage. Throughout the research process it is related to, and dependant upon, ethnography. It is due to this close relationship between video analysis and ethnography that I suggest the term videography adequately accounts and describes the unified core of what constitutes the interpretative video analysis methodology.

References

Albrecht, G. L. 1985: Videotape Safaris: Entering the Field with the Camera. *Qualitative Sociology*, 8, 4: 325-344
Bayart, D., A. Borzeix and M. Lacoste 1997: Les traversées de la gare: Filmer des activités itinerantes. *Champs visuels*, 6, 75-90
Birdwhistell, R. L., 1970: *Kinesics and Context: Essay in Body-Motion Research*. Philadelphia: University of Pennsylvania Press
Cicourel, A. V., 1992: The interpretation of communicative contexts: Examples from medical encounters. In: A. Duranti and C. Goodwin (ed.) *Rethinking Context: Language as an Interactive Phenomenon*. Cambridge: Cambridge University Press, 291-310
Corsaro, W. A. 1981: Something old and something new. The importance of prior ethnography in the collection and analysis of audiovisual data. *Sociological Methods and Research*, 11, 2: 145-166
Ekman, P. and W. Friesen 1969a: The Repertoire of Nonverbal Behavior: Categories, Origins, Usage and Coding. *Semiotica*, 1, 63-68

---

12 It is the goal of genre analysis to identify these kinds of similarities and differences and show in which way they contribute to the construction of situations and larger social structures. Cf. Knoblauch & Günthner (1995).

Ekman, P. and W. Friesen 1969b: A Tool for the Analysis of Motion Picture Film or Videotapes. *American Psychologist*, 24, 3: 240-43
Erickson, F., 1988: Ethnographic description. In: U. Ammon (ed.) *Sociolinguistics. An International Handbook of the Science of Language and Society*. Berlin, New York: de Gruyter, 1081-1095
Flick, U., 2004: *Triangulation. Eine Einführung*. Wiesbaden:
Goffman, E., 1981: *Forms of Talk*. Philadelphia: University of Pennsylvania Press
Goffman, E. 1983: The Interaction Order. *American Sociological Review*, 48, 1-17
Goodwin, C. 1986: Gestures as a Resource for the Organization of Mutual Orientation. *Semiotica*, 62, 1/2: 29-49
Goodwin, C. 2000: Action and embodiment within situated human interaction. *Journal of Pragmatics*, 32, 1489-1522
Günthner, S. and H. Knoblauch 1995: Culturally Patterned Speaking Practices - The Analysis of Communicative Genres. *Pragmatics*, 5, 1: 1-32
Heath, C., 1997: The Analysis of Activities in Face to Face Interaction Using Video. In: D. Silverman (ed.) *Qualitative Research. Theory, Method, and Practice*. London: Sage, 183-200
Heath, C. and J. Hindmarsh, 2002: Analysing Interaction: Video, Ethnography and Situated Conduct. In: M. Tim (ed.) *Qualitative Research in Action*. London: Sage, 99-121
Heath, C., H. Knoblauch and P. Luff 2000: Technology and social interaction: the emergence of 'workplace studies'. *British Journal of Sociology*, 51, 2: 299-320
Hodge, R. and G. Kress, 1988: *Social Semiotics*. Ithaca and New York
Hughes, J. A., V. King, T. Rodden and H. Anderson, 1994: Moving out of the Control Room: Ethnography in System Design. In: R. Futura and C. Neuwirth (ed.) *Transcending Boundaries. Proceedings of the Conference on Computer Supported Cooperative Work*. Chapel Hill: 429-439
Jackson, J. 2004: An ethnographic flimflam: Giving gifts, doing research, and videotapiong the native subject/ object. *American Anthropologist*, 106, 1: 32-42
Jirotka, M. and J. Goguen (eds.) 1994: *Requirements Engineering: Social and Technical Issues*. London
Jordan, B. and A. Henderson 1995: Interaction analysis: Foundations and Practice. *Journal of the Learning Sciences*, 4, 1: 39-103
Kendon, A., 2004: *Gesture. Visible Action as Utterance*. Cambridge: Cambridge University Press
Knoblauch, H., 2001a: Communication, contexts and culture. A communicative constructivist approach to intercultural communication. In: A. di Luzio, S. Günthner and F. Orletti (ed.) *Culture in Communication. Analyses of Intercultural Situations*. Amsterdam, Philadelphia: John Benjamins, 3-33
Knoblauch, H. 2001b: Fokussierte Ethnographie. *Sozialer Sinn*, 1: 123-141
Knoblauch, H. 2005: Focused Ethnography. *Forum Qualitative Sozialforschung / Forum: Qualitative Social Research [Online Journal]*, 6, 3: Art 44, Available at: http://www.qualitative-research.net/fqs-texte/3-05/05-3-44-e.htm
Knoblauch, H., B. Schnettler and J. Raab, this volume: Video-Analysis. Methodological Aspects of Interpretive Audiovisual Analysis in Social Research. In: (ed.)
Koch, S. C. and J. Zumbach 2002: The Use of Video Analysis Software in Behavior Observation Research: Interaction Patterns of Task-oriented Small Groups. *FQS*, 3, 2
Latour, B., 1986: Visualization and Cognition. Thinking with eyes and hands. In: H. Kucklikc and E. Long (ed.) *Knowledge and Society. Studies in the Sociology of Cultural Past and Present*. New York: Jai, 1-40
Luckmann, T., 1978: Philosophy, Science and Everyday Life. In: T. Luckmann (ed.) *Phenomenology and Sociology*. Harmondsworth: Penguin, 217-253

Luckmann, T., this volume: Some remarks on scores in multimodal sequential analysis. In: H. Knoblauch, B. Schnettler, H.-G. Soeffner and J. Raab (ed.) *Video-analyis.*
Mittenecker, E., 1987: *Video in der Psychologie. Methoden und Anwendungsbeispiele in Forschung und Praxis.* Bern: Huber
Peräklyä, A., 1997: Reliability and validity in research based on tapes and transcripts. In: D. S. Silverman (ed.) *Qualitative Research.* London: 199-220
Raab, J. and D. Tänzler, this volume: Video-Hermeneutics
Rammert, W. and I. Schulz-Schaeffer, 2002: Technik und Handeln. Wenn soziales Handeln sich auf menschliches Verhalten und technische Abläufe verteilt. In: W. Rammert and I. Schulz-Schaeffer (ed.) *Können Maschinen denken? Soziologische Beiträge zum Verhältnis von Mensch und Technik.* Frankfurt am Main: Campus, 11-64
Ruby, J., 2000: *Picturing Culture: Explorations of Film and Anthropology.* Chicago: UCP
Sacks, H., 1992[1964ff]: *Lectures on Conversation. Edited by Gail Jefferson and Emanuel A. Schegloff.* Oxford: Blackwell
Schegloff, E., 1992: On talk and it institutional occasions. In: P. Drew and J. Heritage (ed.) *Talk at Work. Interaction in Institutional Settings.* Cambridge: 101-136
Schubert, C. this volume: Video-Analysis of Practice and the Practice of Video-Analysis.
Schutz, A., 1962: Common Sense and Scientific Interpretation of Human Action. In: (ed.) *Collected Papers I: The Problem of Social Reality (ed. by Maurice Natanson).* The Hague: Nijhoff, 3-47
Shrum, W., R. Duque and T. Brown 2005: Digital video as research practice: Methodologies for the Millenium. *Journal of Research Practice,* 1, 1: Article M4
Soeffner, H.-G., this volume: Visual Sociology on the Base of 'Visual Concentration'
Suchman, L., 1987: *Plans and Situated Actions. The Problem of Human-Machine Communication.* Cambridge
Suchman, L. and R. H. Trigg, 1991: Understanding Practice: Video as a Medium for Reflection and Design. In: J. Greenbaum and M. Kyng (ed.) *Design at Work. Cooperative Design of Computer Systems.* Hillsdale: Lawrence Erlbaum, 65-89
ten Have, P., 1999: *Doing Conversation Analysis. A Practical Guide.* London
vom Lehn, D. and C. Heath, this volume: Discovering Exhibits: Video-Based Field Studies in Museums and Science Centres

Jürgen Raab & Dirk Tänzler

Video Hermeneutics

Video technology offers new perspectives for sociologists. Above all ethnographic approaches, which have been eager to adapt the new technique as a means of data production, have had a crucial impact on the field of qualitative social research. *Video hermeneutics* have recently been developed as a procedure for the understanding of audiovisual data. Sociological hermeneutics are closely related to the theory of the social construction of reality (Berger & Luckmann 1966). The fundamental idea of this approach is to consider social data as manifestations of the protagonists' perception and recognition of reality as well as of their self-representation and self-interpretation. Consequently, *video hermeneutics* as a reconstruction procedure shows how facts are fabricated by human beings under certain socio-historical conditions. It also obliges the researcher to take on a self-reflexive stance and take into account his or her subjective presuppositions under which he himself or she herself constitutes the reality he or she is observing. Only in this way social scientists do justice to the intention of an ethnographic approach.

In the following, we outline some characteristic features of the methodology (I) and the method (II) of *video hermeneutics*. A few, but significant theoretical elements of the hermeneutical procedure are presented. Problems of the transcription, the description, and the interpretation of audiovisual data are discussed more or less theoretically. Finally, we demonstrate the practice of *video hermeneutics* in a brief case study (III).

Understanding Images as a Way of Understanding Culture

Modern societies are characterised by the increase of medial and visualised forms of communication which have deep impact on social relations. Medial representations of reality tend to overlay the 'natural' perceptions generated by the human senses. In other words, media products not only increasingly surround people in their everyday-life, but photographs, movies, TV-broadcasts, video-productions, and virtual computer-worlds influence their perception of reality fundamentally. Half a century ago Marshall McLuhan formulated his favourite thesis on communication that "the medium is the message" (McLuhan 1964), and he recently contributed the prophetic vision of a "global village" (McLuhan & Powers 1989). But it is still a challenge for sociologists to explore the ramifications of audiovisual media to culture and society.

Researchers must answer questions like: To what extent do technical constructions of reality alter the *forms* of human self-interpretation and self-representation? How do the audiovisual media shift and extend the *potential* for the human construction and attribution of meaning? And not least, which new requirements for the interpretation and which new challenges to the understanding of meaning come into being in everyday-life (e.g. in the reception of mass media), as well as in social-scientific interpretation?

In the humanities and the social sciences, images were overshadowed by a focus on analysis of written language and of texts for many years (Goody 1981, 2000). However, since the 1990's, boundless discussions on the *pictorial turn* (Mitchell 1994), the *imagic turn* (Fellmann 1995), and the *iconic turn* (Boehm 1994) have indicated that the paradigm of the *lingustic turn* (Rorty 1967) and therefore of speech and text are beginning to lose their privileged positions. All these turns suggest a change of paradigm in the humanities and the social sciences and stand for the rediscovery of the relevance of images – especially and above all in view of the new forms and the new dimensions of pictorial communication and audiovisual recording techniques available in modern societies. They are propelled by the attempt to at last do theoretical, methodological, and methodological justice to the historical, cultural, and social function of images.

In his famous definition, Max Weber calls for "a sociology [...] as a science concerning itself with the interpretative understanding of social action and thereby with a causal explanation of its course and consequences" (Weber 1978: 4). *Video hermeneutics* as a new branch of sociological hermeneutics represent perhaps one of the most thorough and probing attempts to realize Max Weber's program of an interpretative sociology (Soeffner 2004). Furthermore, for *video hermeneutics*, human perception and social action, the human constitution of meaning, and the social transmission of knowledge are always conducted through symbolic forms. In brief, social action takes place by means of symbolic exchange (Mead 1967, Schutz & Luckmann 1974, 1989, Berger & Luckmann 1966). However, even hermeneutic approaches in the social sciences fail to consider sufficiently or simply oversee the fact that images are a quite particular medium for the constitution of meaning and for the social construction of reality. Most importantly, images call for entirely different approaches to the process of interpretation than those used for speech and texts.

Developing Ernst Cassirer's idea of symbolic forms, Susanne K. Langer makes the fundamental and therefore useful differentiation between *discursive* and *presentative symbolism* (Langer 1967). In language, only those things can be expressed that fit into a discursive order. A discursive order is a linear sequence of already significant elements. Any idea that cannot be adapted to this form of projection is unutterable and cannot be communicated by means of words and sentences. In contrast, images are characterised as a simultaneous and integral symbolism that Langer calls presentative. All elements that constitute the meaning of an image are simultaneously present.

Applying Langer's differentiation to the phenomenon of video, we can say that audiovisual data represent a *hybrid* of discursive *and* presentative symbolism. In this kind of data simultaneity and succession of symbols are affiliated and constitute a specific mode of signification on three levels. Firstly, these are *events and objects before the camera* – always accompanied by language (spoken or written, dialogues or monologues, narratives or commentaries), sounds, and music. Secondly, *camera actions* are present – the image itself is moving (changing camera positions, pan shots, moving cameras, and zooms). Thirdly, *editing techniques* mold the data– offering an opportunity to separate and to link units of meaning (cutting and montage) as well as to embellish, to pad, and to optimise the material in many ways.

This brief phenomenological description has crucial consequences for the methodology of *video hermeneutics*. The integration and the combination of different levels of action and different symbolic forms make audiovisual recordings the most complex procedure of data-production in the social sciences. However, it is for this reason that audiovisual recordings present the greatest challenge for interpretation. Due to the richness of their content, to their complexity, and to their variability audiovisual data require appropriate procedures for transcription, description, and interpretation both in their discursive succession and in their presentative simultaneity. In the following, we give a rough sketch of the three central methodic principles of *video hermeneutics*: sequentiality, parenthesis of context, and contrasting.

Methodic Principles

Sequentiality

At the core of *video hermeneutics* lies the *sequential analysis*. The meaning of sequentiality here is twofold. On the macro-level it means, that not the whole datum – for example the film or video-record as a totality – but only key scenes are interpreted. On the microlevel it means, that these key scenes are interpreted step-by-step, i.e. picture-by-picture.

The key scenes are selected by an interpretation group – the procedure functions optimal only when a research group conducts the analysis, not so well by a lonesome researcher – after they have watched the recorded data in its entirety. On the macrolevel there are really no guidelines that determine the choice of a particular sequence for detailed analysis. Instead, the researchers themselves decide spontaneously in view of their project goals and thematic focus, which sequence they find most intriguing and prefer to interpret. The idea of the sequential analysis is, to conceive the motives underlying the intuitive selection of a key scene by the interpreters. The understanding of the interpreter's attraction to the key scene coincides with the attempt to reconstruct and explain the structure of the datum. The restriction to an analysis of key scenes is a consequence of the aim of providing a non-reductive and extensive interpretation of the data in all recognisable details and aspects (events and objects before the camera, camera actions, and editing techniques).

Assuming that social reality is a meaningful and regulated order, at the micro-level we follow the temporal sequence of the data in an exact and strict manner. To this end, the researchers 'freeze' the flow of pictures and create motionless stills. At this point, they begin to describe the stills in all details. The descriptions are noted in a formula developed for the transcription of film and video-documents called a *score* (see the score in the appendix, also Bergmann et al. 1993 and Luckmann in this volume).

In general, the *score* is a technical instrument used to translate visual and acoustic data into written language. For hermeneutics, *text* is a fundamental prerequisite to interpretation. The score requires that the interpreters not only verbalize their thoughts in spoken language, but that they also risk a first translation of their observations into written text. The schematic structure of the score supports them in this effort through the analytic subdivisions it requires. In the first steps of the analysis, they do not yet have to represent the complex relationships within the sequence as a whole. Instead, they can limit themselves to selecting single elements of the action and translating them into written text as a first approximation of the meaning of the sequence. In short, the score is the first *locus of translation*, but it accomplishes this purpose in a special manner adequate to the nature of the video-material. Therefore, the construction of the score must be flexible, i.e. it must adapt to historical changes in general and to technical developments especially in the audiovisual media itself, as well as to the research interests and to the formulation of the scientific question.

Due to the fundamental hybrid character of audiovisual data, the score must record all actions in their simultaneous and successive order. To realise this methodic principle all events are distinguished in their audiovisual dimensions, described en detail and noted in different columns in accordance with the research interests (i.e. setting, camera, body, head, speech, and music). In some cases, it seems necessary to distinguish between different kinds of bodily-actions, in other cases not. The linear *succession* of the events in the dimension of time is fixed vertically ('top-down') in the spatial dimension of the columns, which run parallel to each other. In the horizontal dimension, therefore, all events are shown in the *simultaneity* of their appearance. It is possible then to reconstruct, for example, what happens with the body or on the face of an actor while he is speaking. Thus, the interpreters are forced to look more closely at the data then is perhaps usual, and the score represents an instrument with which they can check for redundancies in the recorded data of the event at any point.

Lastly, the score is an elementary means for monitoring one's own interpretation and thus an analytical tool for a methodic approach as stipulated by Grounded Theory (Glaser & Strauss 1967). It is also an instrument for third persons to *check* and to *confirm* the single steps, as well as the entire interpretation, according to general methodological standards.

In principle, *video hermeneutics* perceive the practice of notation and that of interpretation as inextricably linked to one another. A notation is not only a description, but at the same time the beginning of an interpretation of the observed social action.

The score is an intermediate step enabling the interpreters to progress from a highly complex, synaesthetic perception of social action, to finally arrive via a structured analysis at a description and interpretation in the form of a coherent text. It is obvious that the score can replace neither the real object of the analysis nor the interpretation in the form of a text. The last reference for all understanding and interpretation is the datum in its original appearance and not a text of any kind. But, nevertheless for hermeneutics text is a fundamental condition for interpretation.

In contrast to understanding as a spontaneous act, interpretation is an experimental setting in which hypotheses about the observed social reality are constructed on the basis of a text. We can say that the sensual phenomena of the audiovisual datum are translated in the score as an abstract form of text. In the sense of Alfred Schutz (1953) a 'natural' "first order construction" is transformed into a "second order construction". Two aims are realised in this way. The data are interpreted in accordance with the research interest, and the interpretation is set down as an adequate representation of the datum in its 'natural' order. Thus, methodic constructivism is linked with epistemological realism.

Parenthesis of Context

Establishing *parenthesis of context* is perhaps the most important procedure in sociological hermeneutics. However, it is also one that is most likely to be misunderstood. Beginning with an image-by-image interpretation, we do not attempt to secure and install *one* particular interpretation of the social action. On the contrary, we intend to delay the process of attributing meaning to our data, and remain in the role of inquirers as long as possible.

Sociological hermeneutics are not procedures for the empirical testing of theoretical hypotheses. Instead, they serve to generate conjectures on the subject. By *parenthesis of context* we free ourselves from common sense and all standardised explanations in everyday-life and scientific understanding – i.e. from orthodox and dogmatic worldviews – to achieve a fresh perspective offering new and innovative insights into social reality. In short, *parenthesis of context* is the methodological technique that enables us to become conscious of and to account for the social construction of contexts, in which the recorded data gain meaning and relevance. Just as was crucial to Goffman's sociological approach of the understanding of human action (Goffman 1974), we ask ourselves: What is really going on here? Why are the protagonists behaving the way they do, and why not otherwise? And: why have they chosen these options while rejecting others?

In order to find answers to these questions, it is important to design possible contexts in which certain data can occur and fit best. We are obliged to develop a multitude of interpretations that may indeed be mutually contradictory. However, in order to do so, we must take recourse to an artifice that, as Karl Mannheim put it, dissociates us from the principal 'position-boundedness' (*Standortgebundenheit*) of our own knowledge (Mannheim 1960). Through this artificial installation the researcher is alienated from the 'natural' given data as well as from the ordinary worldview he takes for granted. He is thus forced to create a multitude of possible interpretations of the data under changing fictitious contexts as in an experiment 'in vitrio'.

Seen this way, *parenthesis of context* means that, in the first step of the interpretation, we ignore as much of our knowledge about the data that constitute the data we are studying as possible. We thereby achieve distance to what had seemed self-explanatory, above and beyond the image-by-image interpretation already mentioned.

According to Hans-Georg Gadamer, "understanding begins [...] when something addresses us. This is the primary hermeneutical condition. We know now what this requires, namely the fundamental suspension of our own prejudices. But all suspension of judgements, and hence, a fortiori, of prejudices, has logically the structure of a question. The essence of the question is the opening up, and keeping open, of possibilities" (Gadamer 1975: 266). This hermeneutical stance coincides with Max Weber's intention to establish an interpretative sociology as a science of historical possibilities. To realise the objective opportunities in the historical data, we must distance ourselves from the given social reality and allow ourselves for that moment to become alienated from it. Or, as Helmuth Plessner put it, "the art of alienated perception fills therefore a necessary condition for all true understanding. [...] Without alienation there is no understanding" (Plessner 1983: 94).

Contrasting

The interpretation of the first sequence is finished when no new hypotheses on the meaning of the sequence can be formulated by rational means. At this point, this first probe will seem to be valid in relation to the sequence and perhaps to the research goal, but not necessarily in relation to the datum, i.e. the video-record as a whole. Consequently, the video-record as a whole must be examined in search of a second sequence that should contrast maximally to the first sequence and therefore offer a opportunity to falsify the first interpretation. For our case study, we contrasted a computer-animated sequence with a scene of face-to-face-interaction.

To widen the scope for new aspects or features of the case, we might look for other key scenes and repeat the procedure as long as all hypotheses on the meaning of the case can be reduced to a single one. Finally, when all elements of the material will have been reconstructed as moments that fit together and constitute a whole, the interpretation has to be considered as exhausted to the empirical data and valid as a theoretical model of the case in study.

The "GDR-Show" – A Case Study

Generally speaking, we do not treat video as an instrument to generate data, but instead understand it as a fully-fledged social construction of reality. This means that, even if we record data by video for scientific usage, we interpret them as 'natural' in the sense of Alfred Schutz' concept of "first order construction" (Schutz 1953) – whatever the 'real' nature of the data might be. We will demonstrate this on the basis of the interpretation of two sequences from a video-record of a TV-show: a computer generated artefact on the one hand and a 'real' social interaction in front of the camera on the other hand.

From the Ostalgia-shows broadcasted by German television in the summer of 2003, we chose a video-record of the most successful Ostalgia-show on the private RTL network. The "GDR-Show" was seen by six and a half million Germans, or twenty percent of all TV-households in the country. It was the last programme in a series of similar shows in the retro-format presenting retrospectives of West German popular culture from the 1970's and 1980's. The popular culture of Eastern Germany was adapted to this blueprint. More or less prominent persons took the stage. Accompanied by media flashbacks, they reported their personal experiences in former times.

Image 1: Intro to the "GDR-Show"

The TV-format imposed by the presence of a presenter forced the guests of the show to distance themselves from their former lifestyles in an ironic way. The two following sequences from the "GDR-Show" demonstrate the ironical dissociation as a basic principle of the actors' performances.

For a systematic analysis, we have chosen the introductory sequence to the "GDR-Show" as a first key scene. The introductory sequence appears at the beginning, after every commercial break, at the end of the show, and functions like as a bracket that ties up all parts of the process of communication. During the show, the introductory sequence mutates into a shibboleth of the TV-serial and – as the following analysis will demonstrate – represents form and content of 'Ostalgia' in a nutshell. Thus, an interpretation of this short piece as a condensed model of 'Ostalgia's' metaphorical contend will give us insight into the structure of the phenomenon as a whole. This first hypothesis is contrasted by the sequential analysis of a second key scene from the show: a face-to-face interaction, which will be analysed with particular regard for the dialogues and for the body language of the presenter and a guest-star.

When the introductory sequence starts, we see a golden garland of corn emerging from darkness and moving from the right to the middle of the screen. A bundle of rays illuminates the scene, revealing a red background. The circle formed by the garland and its glow call a halo to the viewers mind. The manner in which the garland throws its shadow against the red background, and the rolling rays radiating from the centre behind the garland generate enchantment. Then moving letters appear on the screen which after a moment which arrange themselves to form the writing "Die DDR

Show" at the centre of the garland in a funny style. The use of moving letters as if they were pieces of a puzzle suggests that the previously established aura has been broken. All this lead us to infer a ritual. From this 'in-between' perspective, a state rooted in the interplay between numinocity and profanity is constituted. The modified GDR-emblem symbolises the virtual reality of the show. Right away, we cannot help but notice that the hammer and compasses, the core elements of the former East-German national emblem, are missing. The hammer, symbolising the working class and the compasses, representing the technocratic avant-garde, both elemental to the socialist state, have vanished. Only the garland of corn remains in a slimmed-down form as a reminiscence of the pastoral component of the GDR. Finally, the symbolic character of the emblem is depoliticised and replaced by a consumer good's trademark.

At this point, the three letters break ranks, a spotlight falls on the middle of the letter 'D', and the camera dives into the inner blank space of this letter. At this moment of being 'in-between', the stage appears and the show starts. The symbol that had functioned as 'a bridge to transcendent realities' is transformed into a frame for a virtual sphere of action, thereby making the end of our analysed sequence.

During the sequence, we hear the "Prinzen", a pop-band well-known both in the GDR and now in reunified Germany, singing "All this is Germany. All this is us" ("Das alles ist Deutschland. Das alles sind wir"). Each single phrases alone represents a statement. When the sentences are joined, they become normative imperatives, requiring identification of the viewer. After each sentence has been sung, it is immediately punctuated by the expressive phrase "oh-oh-oh", which serves as a comment. The meaning of the "oh-oh-oh" is ambiguous. It might be an expression of admiration or an indication that these are delicate issues. This song is also heard at the beginning of the second key scene, in stilling it with a sense of ambiguity.

In the analysis of the first sequence, we identified a distinct pattern, constituted by three binary oppositions: (de)politicisation vs. commercialisation, auratisation vs. profanation, admiration vs. reservation. In the following, we attempt to show that these binary oppositions constitute the framework of the "GDR-Show" as an experimental setting in which the actors must

Image 2: World-star and presenter

prove themselves as the avant-garde of a new collective identity construction. This was no easy undertaking, as, even in 2003, Eastern German traditions and mentalities were still regarded as a culturally archaic burden in the politically and economically reunified German Federal Republic. Both, the improvement of the actors and the construction of a collective identity will be realized if all the contradicting elements will fit together in one figure.

The former world champion of ice-skating and Hollyday-on-Ice-Princess Katharina Witt is introduced as an "Eastern-star", a "Western-star", and in the end as a "world-star" by the presenter. When the world-star descends the big steps of the stage wearing the uniform of a "Young Pioneer", i.e. dressed as a member of the former communist youth organization, the audience is surprised. This discrepancy in the appearance of Witt is expressed by the ambiguity of the phrase "oh-oh-oh" in the theme song. The presenter refers to the incoherency in Witt's appearance when he opens the talk with the remark "fesch", which means, (am.) 'fresh' or 'fine', or (engl.) 'bold' or 'keen', but also 'smart', 'elegant' or even 'sexy'.[1] By addressing her as 'smart' he expresses his admiration for Witt's attractiveness, but also for her courage in wearing a costume that is taboo in reunified Germany. The ambiguity of the first comment is stressed by the second statement referring to the uniform ("Eine Jungpioniersuniform"), which manifests the presenter's reservation respect to Witt's outfit and its political correctness.[2]

This contradicting evaluation of Witt's appearance by the presenter defines the limits of the space; the 'in-between' Witt must prove herself as a competent actor and 'world-star'. She is confronted with the task of overcoming the contradiction of her appearance by performing a role in which the contradicting tokens 'admiration' and 'reservation' form one unit.

The audience's reservation arise from the fact that the uniform is a communist symbol originally worn by children. Used as a prop in service of an adult women's self-representation the uniform transforms itself into a fashionable accessory, thereby loosing its political meaning. Witt confirms the presenter's remark with the words: "Yes, I am here today as a Young Pioneer, so to speak" ("Ja. Ich komme sozusagen als Jungpionier heute"). In the German sentence the parenthesis "so to speak" ("sozusagen") and the adverbial phrase "today" ("heute") mark the distance to and the playful character of her role as Young Pioneer. She rejects an interpretation of the uniform as a symbol of uniformity, suggesting that she now lives in a 'multi-optional world'. Nevertheless, her attitude of distance to the socialist past is counteracted by her posture, her gestures, and her facial expression. Sitting up straight, she proudly presents her scarf by pushing up the lappets. Finally, when she enunciates the word "Young Pio-

---

1 For the following analysis see the score in the appendix.
2 The choice of the presenter's term "fesch" (engl. 'smart') as an expression for Witt's attractiveness is motivated by her uniform. In German "fesch" is an idiomatic expression for the appeal of somebody in uniform.

neer" ("Jungpionier") with affection, she closes her eyes and, metaphorically spoken, outgrows beyond herself. In this way, her body-language indicates a regressive identification with her former role as a Young Pioneer and confirms the presenter's comment "fesch" ('smart'). By performing her personal identification with the role of a Young Pioneer, she solves two problems of self-representation: the contradiction between girl and woman and between being smart and appearing in a traditional communist outfit.

However, there is one element in Witt's performance, that still does not fit with the interpretation we have offered so far. Sitting up straight, Witt keeps her hands on her knees which are pressed together. This attitude of reservation is a reaction to the presenter's phrase "fesch" ('smart'), which is much less a comment on the outfit, but rather a compliment to the person wearing this outfit. The gesture is even a rejection of the sexual allusion contained within this compliment. Then, moving her hands to the scarf, she reacts to the presenter's second statement referring to the uniform and diverts his and the audience's attention away from her body to the accessory of the costume that defines it as a uniform. Proudly presenting the lappets of her scarf she brings out the attractiveness of the uniform and at the same time she gives the situation an erotic timbre.

Summarizing this scene we can say, that in a first step Katharina Witt reimbues a depoliticised uniform with infantile innocence, transforming it into a profane commercial commodity. In a second step, she bestows new charm upon this commodity. Marking it as the outfit of an idol of the international entertainment industry, Witt supplies the costume with new attractiveness. All three of the binary oppositions that we identified in the first sequence reoccur in the second sequence: (de)politicisation vs. commercialisation, auratisation vs. profanation, admiration vs. reservation. Here, reservation is still expressed with reservation.

Let's have another look at the scene. Although announcing reservation by putting her hands on her knees in reaction to the compliment and sexual allusion of the presenter, Witt confirms the erotic and sexual undertone in the interaction by her next gesture, that is by lifting the lappets, but – and this seems to be crucial – she defines the eroticism of the situation by *herself*. Generally speaking sexual attractiveness for an actor is a chance to become a media-star, but at the same time represents a high risk of loosing one's face, one's authenticity, one's 'real' identity. The presenter's compliment puts Witt into a risky situation. She solves this problem opting for coquetry. She transforms the seduction of the presenter in his double role as a show-master and a man into an erotic interplay dominated by the woman. Coquetry is the reversal of the classical situation of seduction that follows the cultural definition of passivity as a female and activity as a male characteristic.

The seduction that a man tries to initiate as a representative of the hegemonial culture and in his role of a show-master is transformed into coquetry by the woman. By this redefinition of the situation, Witt's regressive identification becomes recognizable as a mask of her sovereignty and the attempt to prove herself as a self-confident woman *and* as an Eastern German citizen as well. Following Georg Simmel (1996), coquetry is a state of 'in-between' the flirt and the beginning of the sexual intercourse. It is an erotic interplay between two equal antagonists of different gender. From this perspective the play of coquetry between Witt and Geissen is a parable for the newborn collective identity, which stands for an ironical state of 'in-between' Eastern and Western Germany.

Conclusion

Our example might demonstrate that *video hermeneutics* are not the application of a formal method on any object, but rather the representation of the social construction of reality within case studies. Collective identities are social constructions, generated by rituals as a specific kind of social action. In complex societies, it is not possible to fabricate generally binding constructions of collective identities through rituals requiring face-to-face interaction, the presence and participation of community. Today, only medial communication provides near ubiquity, reaching as many people as possible. In this way, the media achieve the condition for construction of collective identities and are bound only by the rules of media reception and not to political participation.

Our analysis has reconstructed the objective meaning of the media-product, not the aesthetic, ideological or economic intentions of the producers of the show. Neither these intentions of the producers nor the reconstructed objective meaning of the media-product has any social relevance. As symbolic orders in the sense of Ernst Cassirer (1965), the media are a reality of their own. Only the viewers, through their perception, give a pragmatic accent of reality to the fictitious medial constructions. Form and content of media-products gain historical relevance if the recipients attach value to them in reference to social action in everyday-life. As a consequence, *video hermeneutics* enable us to reconstruct the conditions under which media-products are designed. Furthermore, we can formulate not only well-founded hypotheses regarding the modes of perception and acceptance of these audio-visual constructions, but also with respect to their impact on social action in everyday-life.

References

Berger, P.L. & T. Luckmann, 1966: *The Social Construction of Reality. A Treatise in the Sociology of Knowledge*, Garden City, New York: Doubleday

Bergmann, J.R., H-G Soeffner, & T. Luckmann, 1993: Erscheinungsformen von Charisma – Zwei Päpste, in: W. Gebhardt, A. Zingerle & M. N. Ebertz (eds.) *Charisma. Theorie-Religion-Politik*, Berlin: de Gruyter, 121-155

Boehm, G. 1994: Die Wiederkehr der Bilder. In: G. Boehm (ed.) *Was ist ein Bild?*, München: Fink, 11-38

Cassirer, E., 1965: *The Philosophy of Symbolic Forms. Volume 1: Language*, New Haven: Yale University Press

Fellmann, F., 1995: Innere Bilder im Licht des imagic turn. In: K. Sachs-Hombach (ed.) *Bilder im Geiste*, Amsterdam: Rodopi, 21-38
Gadamer, H.-G., 1975: *Truth and Method*. New York: Crossroad
Glaser, B.G. & A.L. Strauss, 1967: *The Discovery of Grounded Theory. Strategies for Qualitative Research*, Chicago: Aldine
Goffman, E., 1974: *Frame Analysis. An Essay on the Organization of Experience*, New York, Evanston, San Fransicso, and London: Harper and Row
Goody, J., 1968: *Literacy in Traditional Societies*, Cambridge: University Press
Goody, J., 2000: *The Power of the Written Tradition*, Washington: Smithsonian Institution Press
Langer, S.K., 1967: *Philosophy in a New Key. A Study in the Symbolism of Reason, Rite, and Art*, Cambridge: Harvard University Press
McLuhan, M., 1964: *Understanding Media. The Extension of Man*, London: Routledge
McLuhan, M. & B. R. Powers, 1989: *The Global Village. Transformations in World Life and Media in the 21st Century*, Oxford: Oxford University Press
Mannheim, K., 1960 [1936]: *Ideology and Utopia: An Introductory sequenceduction to the Sociology of Knowledge*, London: Routledge
Mead, G.H., 1967: *Mind, Self, and Society from the Standpoint of a Social Behaviorist*, Chicago: University of Chicago Press
Mitchell, W.J.T., 1994: *Picture Theory. Essays on Verbal and Visual Representation*, Chicago: University of Chicago Press
Plessner, H., 1983: Mit anderen Augen, in: ders.: *Gesammelte Schriften VIII: Conditio humana*, Frankfurt a.M.: Suhrkamp, 88-104
Rorty R. (ed.), 1967: *The Linguistic Turn. Recent Essays in Philosophical Method*, Chicago: University of Chicago Press
Schutz, A., 1953: Common-Sense and Scientific Interpretation. In: *Philosophy and Phenomenological Research*, 14, 1-37
Schutz, A. & T. Luckmann, 1974: *The Structures of the Life-World, Vol. 1,* London: Heinemann
Schutz, A. & T. Luckmann, 1989: *The Structures of the Life-World, Vol. 2,* Evanston: Northwestern University Press
Simmel, G., 1996 [1918]: Die Koketterie, in ders.: *Hauptprobleme der Philosophie - Philosophische Kultur, Gesamtausgabe Band 14*, Frankfurt a.M.: Suhrkamp, 256-277
Soeffner, H.-G., 2004 [1989]: *Auslegung des Alltags - Der Alltag der Auslegung. Zur wissenssoziologischen Konzeption einer sozialwissenschaftlichen Hermeneutik*, Konstanz: UVK
Weber, M., 1978 [1921]: *Economy and Society. An Outline of Interpretative Sociology*, Edited by G. Roth and C. Wittich, Berkeley, Los Angeles, and London: University of California Press

Appendix: Score "DDR – Show"

Cut	Time (sec.)	Visual Data			Audio Data	
		Setting	Camera	Body	Head	Speech	Music
1	1	Witt and Geissen sitting on a modern sofa in front of a background, dominated by red and brown colours.	Knee shot slightly from the left.	Distance between the bodies 1 meter. Geissen's right arm outstretched on the sofa's backrest in direction to Witt. His left arm resting on his thigh.	Geissen stares at Witt's blue scarf, smiling.		
	2	Witt wears a dark blue pleated skirt, which ends at her knees, a formfitting white blouse with epaulettes, and a knotted scarf. Her short braids are held together by rubber bands. Geissen in a dark blue striped suit, orange shirt with opened collar, styled scrubby hair.		Witt sitting upright, both arms outstretched and hands on her closed knees.	Witt turns her head to the right side.		
				Witt turning to the right and sitting up grasps and lifts the lappets of her scarf with both hands	Witt turns her head to the left side. Looking at Geissen.	Geissen: "Eine Jungpioniers-uniform."	
	3				Geissen still staring at the scarf.	Witt: "Ja."	
2	4	Bright background; two bright spots right to Witt's mouth.	Close-up view on Witt, slightly from the right side; Witt slightly right from the center of the picture; her mouth in the golden section.	Witt plays with the lappets of the scarf.	Witt turns her head to the left side, lets her head fall on to the right.	Witt: "Ich komme sozusagen"	
				Witt drops the lappets.	Witt raises head and chin, eye impact, purses her lips.	als Jungpionier	
	5			She lifts her shoulders and stretches her back.			
	6			Witt drops her shoulders and unbends her back.	Witt closes her eyes and smiles at Geissen.	heute." Geissen "Ja."	

Research Fields of Video Analysis

Dirk vom Lehn & Christian Heath

Discovering Exhibits: Video-Based Studies of Interaction in Museums and Science Centres

Introduction

There is a growing recognition that our understanding and appreciation of exhibits in museums and galleries arises within social interaction, both with those we are with and others who happen to be in the same space. Despite the emerging corpus of studies of the behaviour of visitors, and the burgeoning interest within sociology with the object, the conduct and interaction of people in museums and galleries remains surprisingly neglected. Video, augmented by field work, and coupled with relevant methodological resources, provides unprecedented resources with which to address the multi-modal actions and activities of visitors and to begin to explore the ways in which the constitution of objects and artefacts in museums and galleries arises in and through co-participation and collaboration.

In this paper, we briefly present a distinctive approach to the analysis of social interaction in museums and galleries, an approach that places the situated and concerted accomplishment of practical action at the heart of the agenda. The approach draws from methodological developments within sociology and in particular ethnomethodology (Garfinkel 1967) and conversation analysis (Sacks 1992). These general methodological developments are augmented by a growing body of research that has come to be known as 'workplace studies' (Heath & Luff 2000, Luff, et al. 2000, Suchman 1987). These studies have directed analytic attention towards the action and interaction with and around the material environment and in particular the ways in which tools, technologies, objects and artefacts feature in, and gain their occasioned sense and significance through, practical collaborative activity. They include for example studies of control centres, newsrooms and operating theatres. Many of these investigations use video, augmented by field studies, to examine the fine details of interaction and to explore how people, in concert with others accomplish social action and activities. We are interested in drawing on these methods and antic commitments to explore the behaviour and experience of visitors in museums, galleries and science centres.

Background

This paper is part of a programme of research we have been undertaking for a number of years concerned with conduct and interaction in museums and galleries. The research was originally driven by an interest in practical aesthetics and the ways in which people responded to works of art and decorative art. More generally, we were interested in exploring how people encountered objects and artefacts in museums and galleries through their interaction with others, not only those they were with, but those who just happened to be in the same space. These concerns have led to a number of projects, funded by the Wellcome Trust, the UK research councils as well as the European Commission (Disappearing Computer Programme). These projects are exploring, both the character and organisation of people's response to exhibits and exhibitions and how their response emerges in and through social interaction, talk, visual and material conduct. They also address the design of exhibits and exhibitions and the assumptions or presuppositions concerning the response and behaviour of visitors that inform their development and deployment. Underlying these analytic issues, is an interest in the ways in which we can enhance participation and collaboration in museums and galleries and the ways in which new techniques and technologies can create new forms of engagement (Heath & vom Lehn 2004, vom Lehn, et al. 2001).

As part of the projects we have undertaken studies of conduct and interaction in a range of museums, galleries and science centres in the UK and abroad – including the Science Museum, the Tate Britain and Tate Modern, the Victoria and Albert Museum, the Courtauld Institute of Art, the science centres Explore-at-Bristol and Green's Mill, the Glasgow Science Centre, the Musee des Beaux Arts Rouen, Beatrice Royal Arts and Crafts Gallery, Nottingham Castle, the Zentrum für Kunst und Medien (ZKM, Karlsruhe), the Sculpture and Functional Arts Exposition (Chicago) and Shipley Art Gallery.

Data collection

In undertaking this programme of research we have gathered a substantial body of data. The data consists of audio-visual recordings of the conduct and interaction of people, their talk, visual and material conduct, at exhibits in museums and galleries. It also consists of field observations, and interviews and discussions with visitors, museum managers, designers, educationalists, and curators. With our interest in social interaction however, it is the audio-visual recordings that form the principal vehicle for analysis. They offer certain advantages over more conventional qualitative data. They provide the resources through which we can capture (versions of) the conduct and interaction of visitors and subject their actions and activities to detailed, repeated scrutiny, using slow-motion facilities and the like. They expose the fine details of conduct and interaction, details that are unavailable in more conventional forms of data, and yet details that form the very foundation to how people see and experience exhibits in museums and galleries. Unlike other forms of data, audio-visual recordings also provide the researcher with the opportunity to share, present and discuss the raw materials on which observations and analysis are based, a facility that is rare within the social sciences and that places an important constraint on the analysis of data.

The analysis of the audio-visual materials is augmented by field observation and data gathered through interview and discussion. These and related materials, such as exhibit specifications, requirement documents, copies of labels, instructions, gallery guides and the like, provide important resources with which to situate and understand the conduct and interaction of visitors. For example, it is not unusual for people to selectively voice instructions or labels to others as they approach or examine an exhibit. The analysis of the interaction needs to consider how participants occasion, embed, or transform, this information within talk and action. Moreover, video and audio recording inevitably provide a selective view of events, and while this view may encompass a broad range of actions and activities that arise at an exhibit, it can be useful to know what else may be happening more generally within the scene. As part of data collection therefore we systematically interleave field observations, information from materials and comments from interviews and discussions, with recorded data, and where relevant, take these into account in the analysis of the participants' action and interaction.

Undertaking video-based field studies raises a number of ethical issues that are widely discussed within textbooks and monographs in qualitative research. In discussion with museum personnel and visitors we have developed a set of practices that are designed to publicise the research and its aims and objectives to maximise opportunities for participants to withhold or withdraw cooperation if they so wish. We place notices informing visitors of the research at the entrance to the museum and the relevant galleries; notices that invite potential participants to discuss data collection with the researcher, and if they have any reservations, before, during or after the event offering to cease recording or destroy any records. In general visitors have shown great deal of interest in the research and willingness to participate.

Audio-visual recording is preceded by a period of fieldwork in museums and galleries. Fieldwork, including discussions with museum staff, provides useful information concerning exhibits and exhibitions and areas in galleries that might be of particular interest. It also provides an opportunity to consider how it might be best to position the camera(s) and place microphones. An important consideration is how to position equipment so as to minimise the obtrusiveness of the equipment and the recording. In this regard, it is important to position and focus the camera so that it captures the conduct and interaction of the participants within the scene whilst not demanding that the researcher remains behind the camera. Indeed, it is not unusual for potentially interesting data to be undermined by the ambitions of the person filming the scene, who mistakenly believes that through subtle operation of the camera, it is possible to encompass the interaction of the participants. We remain in the gallery to undertake field observation, answer any queries from visitors, whilst having set the camera to record, avoiding being seen to operate the equipment. In this regard, audio-visual recording coupled with background fieldwork can prove far less obtrusive than conventional participant and non-participant observation.

Initial data collection is followed by a review, in which we examine the materials to assess the quality of the images and sound and to identify any issues that might be relevant to further data collection. We also undertake preliminary analysis of a selected number of fragments and begin to reflect upon any particular actions and activities that might inform how we gather further data, be it through video, fieldwork or even interview. The preliminary analysis is followed by further data collection that in turn is subject to more detailed analysis. Data collection and analysis therefore is an iterative and complimentary process designed and refined with regard to the practical issues and analytic insights that emerge through detailed inspection of the data (Goodwin 1994, Heath 2004, Heath & Hindmarsh 2002).

Analyzing audio-visual data

Our approach to the analysis of data draws from methodological developments within sociology and in particular ethnomethodology and conversation analysis. The approach is driven by three principal assumptions that direct analytic attention towards the local, practical accomplishment of social actions and activities. In the first instance, we are concerned with the indexical character of practical action and inextricable relationship between action and 'context'. To put it another way, – the intelligibility of action, its sense and significance, is inseparable from the occasion, moment and circumstances in which it is produced. Secondly, social actions and activities are emergent and contingently accomplished with regard to each other; – to use Heritage's (1984) characterisation, the action is both context sensitive and context renewing. This emergent, ongoing, interactional accomplishment of social action and activity is perhaps most manifest in talk and conversation and the ways in which a next utterance, a turn at talk, is produced with regard to the immediately preceding action(s) and in turn, implicates, provides the framework for (a) subsequent utterance(s). The emergent and socio-temporal character of human action is a critical feature of context and situation; indeed, the real time contributions of others are the most pervasive 'contingency' for social action. The situated character of practical action therefore does not simply point to the circumstances in which an activity arises, but rather to the ways in which social actions and activities emerge, moment by moment. Thirdly, the analysis is concerned with explicating the organisation through which participants produce particular actions and make sense of the actions of others; that is, it is directed towards the practices and reasoning that inform practical accomplishment of everyday, emergent, context embedded activities.

Analysis proceeds on a 'case by case' and involves the highly detailed examination of particular actions with regard to the immediate context and a particular interactional environment in which they arise. The specific location and character of an action, be it vocal, visual or material, and its relationship to, embededness in, the immediately surrounding framework of activity, the preceding and proceeding action(s), is critical, not just to how the participants produce and coordinate their actions, but to the ways in which it is scrutinized. Analysis focuses on the 'work' that particular actions are accomplishing in situ, then and there, and in particular on the ways in which they reveal interactional relations to the immediately prior and proceeding action(s). For example, we might consider how particular action such as an assessment of an exhibit, creates an opportunity for, and engenders, a specific action from a co-participant, that in turn, implicates subsequent action. These sequential relations between actions therefore form an important focus of analytic enquiry and provide a foundation to the ways in which people accomplish activities in interaction, with each other.

The importance of the location and form of an action within the emergent accomplishment of an activity demands a procedure, a system that enables the researcher to capture and represent features of the participants' conduct. There is a long-standing convention in conversation analysis and cognate approaches for the transcription of talk, a convention that is primarily concerned with representing the interactional features of talk (Atkinson & Heritage 1984, Drew & Heritage 1992, Sacks 1974).

The transcription of visual, and material conduct such as handling an object has proved a long-standing problem for students of social interaction and there remains no conventional procedure through which the visual is represented. Our own solution, a solution we believe that is used by others who are interested in multi-modal interaction, is transcribing at least the onset and completion of the visual and material features of the participants' conduct with regard to the talk and/or silence or pauses. To provide a more suitable spatial representation of the participants' conduct and its relationship the transcription is laid out horizontally (Goodwin 1981, Heath 1986).

It is critical however to underscore that the data on which the analysis is based is the audio-visual recording. The transcription provides an important vehicle for becoming familiar with the complexities of a particular fragment and beginning to explicate the relations between actions and activities. It also provides an important resource for documenting observations and recalling insights and analytic observations.

Although data collection and analysis are primarily undertaken by the principal investigator we regularly hold data workshops involving some or all members of our research group. In those workshops we discuss one or two short video-fragments. This discussion aids the refinement of transcripts and helps to further develop the analytic focus of our research. The participation of external researchers and practitioners *is of value* as they often are able to provide a distinct perspective on the data which supports the relevance of our investigations. However, such data workshops should not be confused with the data analysis. In a sense, they only are "aids to sluggish imagination" (Garfinkel).

Discovering functionality

It has long been recognised that the design of exhibits for museums, galleries and science centres poses major challenges. They have to be developed to enable visitors from very different backgrounds and with a variety of interests to access and understand the function and purpose of the exhibit – not infrequently within a few moments. Labels and associated information displays and the like, provide a critical resource in this regard, facilitating engagement with the exhibit and giving a rationale to the presence and purpose of the object or artefact. So called 'interactive' exhibits are particularly interesting, since they demand that, in some cases a quite complex, functionality is immediately accessible to the visitor and that they have a overall purpose that lies beyond simply playing with various aspects of the exhibit. This purpose and the functionality is not infrequently portrayed in the labels and information displays that accompany the exhibit, labels that children and other visitors may not necessarily be eager to read. Moreover, these exhibits rarely enable more than one individual to engage the functionality, or even read the label, at the same time, so that a negotiation arises in and through which participants establish a form of fragmented, but interdependent engagement in the exhibit. In the following fragment we wish to briefly consider aspects of this negotiation and the ways in which the participants, a mother and her son, progressively discover, and align towards particular aspects of the exhibit.

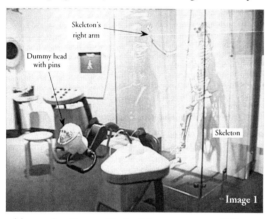

The example is drawn from a science centre in Bristol known as Explore-at-Bristol. The exhibit is known as "Jumping Skeleton" and is part of an exhibition area entitled 'Your Amazing Brain'. The Jumping Skeleton demonstrates how certain parts of the brain are related to bodily movements. It consists of a skeleton, a plastic head with an open skull that reveals a plastic brain and a probe located on a small table nearby (Image 1). A visitor can move different parts of the skeleton, such as the legs, arms, head and jaw, by pointing the probe onto one of six pins implanted within the brain positioned in front of the skeleton. When a visitor points the probe at, for example, the second pin to the right in the brain, the skeleton's right arm moves slowly up and down, or when pointing it to the pin on the far left of the brain the jaw opens and closes.

A text panel is on the wall to the right of the skeleton. It encourages visitors to manipulate the skeleton using the probe, "Can you make him jump?" and to understand the relationship between different parts of the brain and the skeleton's movement, "Which part of the brain makes him move? Do different parts produce different movements?".

We join the action as Jenny suggests to her son, Ben to apply the probe on a particular pin on the dummy's head.

Fragment 1 Transcript 1[1]

    ...
10 J: Try that one (.3) that's about here
11   (1)
12 J: Oh <u>look</u> it makes your legs move
13   ...

With her suggestion, "Try that one" Jenny points to the area in question (Image 2). The utterance and the accompanying gesture encourage Ben to turn towards the pin and apply the probe. As he begins to move the probe to its new position, Jenny touches a spot on Ben's head that corresponds to the location of the pin in the dummy head. She looks up and sees the skeleton's left leg moving up and down (Image 3). A moment later, she points at the moving leg and encourages Ben to look up, "Oh look it makes your legs move" (Image 4).

J: Try that one   J: That's about here   J: Oh it makes your legs move

The child's manipulation of the probe arises in the light of Jenny's suggestion; the utterance and the accompanying gesture occasion a particular action by the child. The response of the child however fails to establish a recognisable connection between the manipulation of the probe and the movement of the skeleton. The mother monitors the conduct of the child in applying the probe and encourages him to see and experience the legs' movement; a movement that has been engendered by virtue of the child's actions. Jenny's suggestion implicates a course of action from the child that would enable him to interconnect his own conduct with the movement of the skeleton and yet, she has to undertake actions to secure the appropriate alignment and response. It is interesting to add, that Jenny attempts to establish for the child the relationship between the skeletal movement and the brain and the child himself; prodding his head in an attempt to establish a correspondence. Certainly, if this is the case, it may well fail, since the child, at least at that moment, fails to connect the skele-

---

1 The transcription of the talk draws on Jefferson's (1984) conventions. A '?' stands for a lowering of the voice, '(spurts)' for an utterance the analyst could not properly hear and is not entirely sure about, and '(.)' for momentary but audible pauses and (3.3) for a pause of three seconds and a third of a second.

ton's movement to the probing brain let alone the operation of his own mind. We can begin therefore to gain a sense as to how the participants' orientation to and experience of the exhibit arises through sequentially organised, multi-modal interaction involving talk, gesture and tactile conduct.

The sequence through which Jenny encourages Ben to create a particular action and appreciate the skeleton's movement evolves within a framework of activity through which the participants discover the exhibit. As they arrive at the exhibit, Ben takes hold of the probe and immediately attempts to prod areas of the skull. Jenny on the other hand turns to and reads the accompanying text panel. The participants progressively interweave and transform their seemingly distinct courses of action and as we have seen establish mutual orientation towards the skeleton's movement and its provenance. As Jenny arrives and looks at the text panel she begins by reading aloud one of the queries it poses for the visitor.

Transcript T2: JS T1-02608
1   J: <u>Uh:</u>, can you make him jump?
2   (3.3)
3   J: Which part of the brain makes him mo::ve?
4   (3.5)
5   J: Uh:, that part of the brain makes your hands move
6   So your head, that's about there
7   (.9)
8   J: That bit makes your head move
9   (2.3)
10   ...

Jenny attempts to pose Ben the puzzle; whether he can make the skeleton jump. The child disregards the utterance and continues to thrust the probe at different areas of the brain without inspecting the effects on the skeleton. The query elicits, or attempt to elicit, a two part action from the child, probing the brain and turning towards the skeleton to see the effects and thereby discovering what might make it jump. It fails, and Jenny makes a second attempt to encourage the child to discover the relationship between the probe and the movement of the skeleton. Once again the child disregards the query and continues to orientate towards and probe different areas of the skull. She then transforms the way in which she attempts to secure an appropriate orientation from the child to enable him to see and appreciate the actions with the probe. As he prods the skull, Jenny moves behind Ben, points at the moving arm of the skeleton and says, "that part of the brain makes your hands move" (Image 5). When Ben still fails to respond, she touches his head and explicates the relationship between his use of the probe and his head, "So your head, that's about there" (Image 6). The boy continues to apply the probe to the dummy head without visibly responding to his mother's actions. When his actions cause the skeleton's head to move back and forth Jenny touches the corresponding spot on Ben's head and again articulates the relationship between the dummy's and the boy's head, "That bit makes your head move" (Image 7).

J: Uh:, that part of the brain makes your hands move

J: So your head, that's about there

J: That bit makes your head move

The fragment illuminates that Jenny progressively displays her discovery of the functionality of the exhibit; she has understood the relationship between the pins in the dummy head and the skeleton's movement and how the hands-on exhibit can be seen with regard to the functioning of the human body. The analysis reveals that her discovery of the exhibit's functionality arises in the light of Ben's interaction with the exhibit and her understanding of the information in the text-panel. Her questions and explanations can be seen as attempts to realign her understanding of the exhibit with the boy's orientation to and interaction with the artefact. Curiously, up to this point in the fragment the boy shows little response to his mother's actions, leaving her in a position where she cannot be sure that he has understood what the exhibit does and what it is about. Her doubt in his understanding of the exhibit stimulates the instruction of his action that follow on her discovery of the exhibit's functionality.

Notwithstanding the design of the exhibit and the associated labels and information resources, the ways in which the son and his mother discover the functionality of the Jumping Skeleton and its purpose is fragmented, yet interdependent, and progressively coalesces around particular features of the artefact. The participants discover the exhibit in different ways, that are independent and yet oriented to the actions and trajectory of actions of the other. The very ways in which they arrive at the exhibit, what comes to hand and is accessible, differentiates their ability to participate and yet within this differentiation, they are sensitive to, and coordinate, their actions with each other. This sensitivity and coordination does not simply arise from some generalised awareness of the other's actions, but rather through successive sequentially oriented attempts to secure particular actions and establish a mutually aligned collaborative activity. Indeed, we find that Jenny uses the discovery of the functionality to progressively become involved in the interaction of the exhibit. Ben aligns towards the instructions of his mother and thereby, through the juxtaposition of utterance and manipulation they develop a concerted focused collaboration with the exhibit. How the exhibit therefore is discovered and used by the participants arises in and through their interaction, an interaction that selectively discriminates and manipulates aspects of the artefact, as the participants contingently negotiate their emerging engagement.

The analysis demonstrates how the detailed analysis of audio-visual data help to reveal how participants socially organise their talk, bodily and tactile actions with each other when examining exhibits. The inspection of the woman's talk alone could not uncover how it is fashioned with regard to the boy's actions. The examination of the audio-visual data provides access to the ways in which the talk arises in the light of Ben's tactile actions. It helps to uncover how the two participants gradually align their orientation to the material environment in and through their verbal, bodily and tactile actions.

Summary

We can begin to see therefore that the conduct of visitors and their experience of particular exhibits contingently arise in and through their interaction with others. The characteristics of an exhibit, the organisation of exhibitions and the various resources with which visitors are provided, offer, at best a framework, in which a range of activities emerge;– activities that have a profound effect on the visitors' experience and conclusions that they may draw. In turn these activities consist of and are accomplished through the spoken, visual and tactile actions of the participants themselves; actions that emerge, sequentially within the developing course of the interaction. The participation and engagement of the visitors is accomplished in and through their interaction with each other; an interaction that in various ways is sensitive to and progressively invokes features of the exhibit. The spoken, the visual and the tactile are thoroughly interdependent and it is through these 'multi-modal' resources that the participants' actions and activities are accomplished. Unlike other forms of data collection in the social sciences, video provides the researcher with access to (versions of) the talk and bodily conduct of visitors, the resources in and through which activities within museum spaces are systematically accomplished. Indeed, they enable researchers to begin to consider conduct and interaction at the exhibit face and the practices and reasoning on which people rely in discovering exhibits in concert and collaboration with others.

The interactional and sequential organisation of the participants' conduct provides both, topic for analysis as well as a resource. As we can see the actions of the participants are produced with regard to the contribution(s) of the co-participant, and in turn, provide resources to which subsequent action(s) is addressed. As we have seen, action does not simply respond to the prior, but in various ways implicates action, even a potential trajectory of an activity. A participants' subsequent action provides resources therefore to consider the ways in which a prior action is being treated and managed, just as examining the next action can enable us to consider how a co-participant is responding to the response to previous action. Interaction therefore, and its moment by moment concerted accomplishment provides resources to enable us to begin to consider action from the standpoint of the participants' themselves; actions that are interdependent and accomplished and made sense of with regard to the immediate conduct of others.

We believe that the approach may also be able to begin to make a small contribution to the growing interest in the social production of people's experience of exhibits and exhibitions (Falk & Dierking 2000, Hein 1998, Leinhardt, et al. 2002). It is widely recognised that the ways in which people examine and make sense of exhibits are highly contingent and circumstantial, arising in and through interaction. As yet however, there are relatively few studies that have examined the talk and bodily conduct that arise with and around exhibits in museums and galleries. In directing analytic attention towards the participants' conduct and interaction at the 'exhibit face' we have the opportunity to begin to identify the actual activities that may contribute to the practices of sense making and understanding and to delineate the forms of interaction, in and through, which they arise. We can also begin to reflect upon the character and organisation of exhibits and the information resources we provide in order to discover how they contribute to the interactional accomplishment of particular activities. In this brief chapter, we have begun to show how visitors may use resources provided by the museum such as questions in labels, to configure their interaction with and around exhibits.

Video-based field studies that explore people's conduct and interaction in museums can provide observations and findings to inform and contribute to the design of resources developed to enhance people's experience and understanding of exhibits and exhibitions. For example, they can help to develop an understanding of how people 'naturally' use labels and other kinds of information resource, such as gallery cards, information kiosks or portable computer systems when exploring and inspecting particular exhibits both alone and in concert with others. They are particularly useful to reveal how the deployment of new technologies not only affect the user's way of looking but also the ways in which s/he organises and coordinates her interaction with others. For example, in a recent study in a contemporary art museum shed light on the difficulties visitors using a Personal Digital Assistant (PDA) face in navigating and exploring the museum together with their companions (Heath & vom Lehn 2004, vom Lehn & Heath 2005). Video-based naturalistic research of the conduct and interaction in museums and galleries can also contribute to the design and development of 'low and high tech' resources for visitors, providing insights and observations that can inform the requirements for systems and set the criteria through which they are assessed. Video-recordings not only enable the detailed analysis of visitor behaviour as it arises in situ, but also provide a record of events that can be shown and discussed with designers, curators and museum managers. It can also provide the resources for examining and assessing related initiatives including for example the ways in which people use guidelines, programmes, worksheets and the like, when actually visiting a museum and navigating exhibitions. In other words, we have only just begun to touch the surface of the ways in which video and a relevant methodological framework can help to examine, assess and inform the conduct and communication of visitors in museums and galleries.

Acknowledgement

This work has been supported by a grant funded by the ESRC Science in Society Programme (Project No. RES-151-25-0047). We would like to thank the staff at Explore-at-Bristol that kindly allowed access to carry out research in their exhibitions and particularly the visitors who participated in the investigation. We would like to thank all those visitors who kindly agreed to participate in the research and the curators, educationalists and managers of various museums and galleries for their help with the research. We would also like to thank Paul Luff, Jon Hindmarsh, James Bradburne, Jonathan Osborne and Ben Gammon for their help with the ideas and materials discussed in this paper.

References

Atkinson, J. M. and J. Heritage (ed.) 1984: *Structures of Social Action. Studies in Conversation Analysis*. Cambridge: Cambridge University Press

Bitgood, S. and D. Patterson 1993: The effects of gallery changes on visitor reading and object viewing time. *Environment and Behavior*, 25, 6: 761-781

Drew, P. and J. Heritage (ed.) 1992: *Talk at work: interaction in institutional settings*. Cambridge: Cambridge University Press

Falk, J. and L. Dierking, 2000: *Learning from Museums. Visitor Experiences and the Making of Meaning*. Walnut Creek, Lanham, New York and Oxford: Alta Mira Press

Garfinkel, H., 1967: *Studies in Ethnomethodology*. Cambridge: Polity

Goodwin, C., 1981: *Conversational Organization: Interaction Between Speakers and Hearers*. New York: Academic Press

Goodwin, C. 1994: Recording human interaction in natural settings. *Pragmatics.*, 3, 181-209.

Heath, C., 1986: *Body Movement and Medical Interaction*. Cambridge: Cambridge University Press

Heath, C., 2004: Analysing face-to-face interaction: video, the visual and material. In: D. Silverman (ed.) *Qualitative Research. Theory, Mehtod and Practice*. London, Thousand Oaks & New Delhi: Sage, 266-282

Heath, C. and J. Hindmarsh, 2002: Analysing Interaction: Video, Ethnography and Situated Conduct. In: T. May (ed.) *Qualitative Research in Action*. London: Sage: 99-121.

Heath, C. and P. Luff, 2000: *Technology in Action*. Cambridge: Cambridge University Press.

Heath, C. and D. vom Lehn 2004: Configuring Reception: (Dis-)Regarding the 'Spectator' in Museums and Galleries. *Theory, Culture & Society*, 21, 6: 43-65

Hein, G., 1998: *Learning in the Museum*. Cambridge/MA: Routledge

Heritage, J., 1984: *Garfinkel and Ethnomethodology*. Cambridge: Polity Press

Jefferson, G., 1984: Transcript notation. In: J. M. Atkinson and J. Heritage (ed.) *Structures of Social Action. Studies in Conversation Analysis*. Cambridge: Cambridge University Press, ix-xvi

Leinhardt, G., K. Crowley and K. Knutson (ed.) 2002: *Learning Conversations in Museums*. Mahwah, NJ: Lawrence Erlbaum Assoc

Leinhardt, G. and K. Knutson, 2004: *Listening in on Museum Conversations*. Walnut Creek: Altamira Press

Litwak, J. M., 1996: *Using Questions As Titles on Museum Exhibit Labels to Direct Visitor Attention and Increase Learning*. Minnesota: University of Minnesota

Luff, P., J. Hindmarsh and C. Heath (ed.) 2000: *Workplace Studies. Recovering Work Practice and Informing System Design.* Cambridge: Cambridge University Press

Sacks, H. 1974: A Simplest Systematics For The Organization Of Turn-taking For Conversation. *Language. Journal Of The Linguistic Society Of America*, 50, 696-735

Sacks, H., 1992: *Lectures on Conversation.* Oxford: Blackwell.

Serrell, B., 1996: *Exhibit Labels. An interpretive approach.* Walnut Creek: Altamira Press.

Suchman, L., 1987: *Plans and Situated Actions. The Problem of Human-Machine Communication.* Cambridge: Cambridge University Press

vom Lehn, D. and C. Heath 2005: Accounting for New Technology in Museums. *International Journal of Arts Management*, 7, 3: 11-21

vom Lehn, D., C. Heath and J. Hindmarsh 2001: Exhibiting Interaction: Conduct and Collaboration in Museums and Galleries. *Symbolic Interaction*, 24, 2: 189-216

Cornelius Schubert

Video Analysis of Practice and the Practice of Video Analysis
Selecting field and focus in videography

When practicing videography, interrelations between the empirical field, the analytic focus and the technical instrument need to be taken into account. This article will address the issue of selecting data in various stages of research by using Grounded Theory's *theoretical sampling* as an exemplar of how to make selections that are both based on data and controlled by theory. The different aspects of selection will be illustrated by examples from a study about the work of anaesthetists in operating theatres.

Videography

Videography as a method is still young and no fixed rules exist as to how to go about filming and analysing real life situations. As a form of observation, videography has its ancestry in the ethnographic research tradition (cf. Mohn this volume), but video recordings are necessarily different in scope and focus from observations made with the naked eye. This article will be especially concerned with how scope and focus are related to theoretical assumptions, i.e. the apparent contradiction between classic ethnographic research, which insists on openness, and videography, which should be considered as a way of focusing. For this purpose, the method of *theoretical sampling* proposed by Glaser and Strauss (1967: 45) for selecting and comparing data in a process of controlled data collection will be illustrated by examples of videographic research conducted during an ethnographic study of work practices in a surgical operating room (OR).
 The main question to be answered in considering the interrelation of video cameras and the sociological perspective is the question of how the researcher's knowledge of the field as well as prior theoretical assumptions are involved in the process of configuring the videographic focus. Glaser and Strauss state that theoretical sampling "is *controlled* by the emerging theory" (1967: 45) and based on general assumptions. Even though they reject the idea of using preconceived theoretical frameworks for making initial decisions of what to study, there is still room for *theoretical sensitivity* in the sense of the sociologist's "theoretical insight into his area of research" (ibid.: 46). Since the sociologist can neither shed all prior knowledge, nor should preconceived theoretical frameworks interfere with data collection, there remains only the solution of commencing research by explicating the theoretical research focus, while at the same time remaining open to the peculiarities of the field. To remain sensitive to both theory and field is a persistent facet of videographic research. In our case, the study was con-

cerned with the interrelation of human and non-human agency in the OR against a background of Science and Technology Studies, especially Actor-Network-Theory. We were especially interested in the distribution of activities between the OR-personnel and the OR-equipment, with respect to the routines and risks that such *distributed actions* (Rammert 2002) might pose.

It follows that because of the intention to highlight the interrelation of theory and data, the arguments in the following chapters will alternate between rather abstract theoretical considerations and very practical empirical explications.

Video-Analysis of Practice

The sociology of work in a wider sense has a long tradition in sociology in general (cf. Hughes 1971) and the work of doctors has drawn specific sociological attention from a number of scholars (eg. Freidson 1970, Strauss, et al. 1997[1985]). The ethnographic research of work sites and work practices has also been widely used in constructivist laboratory studies within Science and Technology Studies (Knorr-Cetina 1981, Latour & Woolgar 1979) and the ethnomethodologically orientated Workplace Studies (cf. Heath, Luff & Knoblauch 2004), the latter already making extensive use of video recordings. In the last two research areas, observations of practices are reconstructed in the light of the research question: laboratory studies set out to deconstruct the 'hard facts' of natural science and the workplace studies aim to reveal the social organisation of cooperation in high-technology work settings. In terms of Grounded Theory (GT), they remained theoretically sensitive with respect to their analytical background while producing naturalistic accounts of real world phenomena. In this way, observations can be conducted that are naïve, yet not so naïve in the way that they reveal the contingency and inconsistency of normal, every day routine action and interaction.

Filming in the operating room is different to 'simple' observation of daily practices. In addition to theoretical considerations, technical and ethical considerations shape the way in which practices can be recorded. First of all, access to the OR is controlled for technical and ethical reasons, making it largely inaccessible to the public. Secondly, because of the privileged access to the OR, there is little common knowledge about how work is done and in which ways people interact. Therefore, before videotaping highly skilled and specialised work practices, the observer has to accumulate a large amount of contextual knowledge in order to be able to understand what is going on. The ability to make sense of the observed procedures is an indispensable prerequisite to analysing work practices and prior participant observation lends itself well to gaining knowledge about the field.

As mentioned above, the study this paper draws on was conducted against the background of Actor-Network-Theory (ANT) proposed by Michel Callon (1986) and Bruno Latour (1988). Without going into the details of ANT, its contribution to study practices in the OR is the so-called *symmetry principle*, which states that human and non-human activities should be considered as equal contributions in the analysis of an actor network. Therefore, both humans and non-humans are considered to be *actants* in an actor network and their relations are the relevant unit of analysis (Akrich & Latour 1992). By using this approach, two assumptions, one lay and one professional, that could obstruct the view of the interrelations between humans and non-humans in high-tech work situations, are replaced by the analytic perspective of ANT. The lay assumption is so-called *anthropomorphisation*, i.e. that users treat machines like human beings. In this case, doctors and nurses talk about the operating equipment in terms of its personality, especially in cases of dysfunction, attributing this to poor motivation or hostile attitudes of the equipment. The professional assumption is the sociological consensus that only human beings can really act, which translates to a (undoubtedly useful) *anthropocentrism* in sociological theory. Either way, the relation of humans and machines cannot be adequately described in terms of anthropomorphisation or in terms of anthropocentrism.

In order to observe, it is necessary to dispose of knowledge taken for granted. This is more troublesome than it sounds, since knowledge taken for granted has the virtue of blending itself into the routines of daily life. To observe humans and non-humans as equal in their contributions to collective work processes certainly distorts the assumptions taken for granted in either lay or professional perspectives, because artefacts are not usually perceived as an active element of cooperation. Thus ANT, in our case, is used not as a theory, but as a methodological instrument for epistemic purposes, putting the researcher in the position of a stranger. It is now possible to qualify the naïve, yet not so naïve, observations further. They are naïve in the sense that they need to be open to the phenomena of the field without a predetermined set of observation criteria, yet they are not so naïve, because a large amount of contextual knowledge needs to be generated first and the relevant analytical perspective needs to be constructed in order to frame the observations.

For the relation of participant observation and videography this means that the latter must follow the former. In addition, one must abandon the hope of being able to 'film it all'. Users will always find unobserved areas to communicate or shield relevant areas from scrutiny with their bodies (cf. Lomax & Casey 1998). The videographic perspective has a scope defined by the research interest, not by a desire for exhaustive documentation. Here, the importance of theoretical sampling for selecting scope and focus becomes clear. The knowledge generated by participant observation guides the scope of the camera and the researcher is able to define relevant areas of interest, both temporal and geographical, with respect to surgical operations.

This led in effect to the use of handheld video camera in this research project, which was mainly used in the beginning of the operation during anaesthetisation. In early stages of the research project we used two tripod mounted cameras in two opposite corners of the OR, but this setup turned out to be inadequate in capturing the rather small scale manipulations of machines and patients by the hands of doctors and nurses. Also, once the operation commences, surgeons gather around the incision, effectively blocking views from the peripheral areas of the room. The anaesthetist's workplace is also framed by the operating table and various machines block the scope of the cameras. A third aspect that led to us renouncing stationary cameras is the limited space available in operating rooms. Tripods are by no means allowed to stand in the way and sometimes it happened that while the mobile technical inventory was moved around in the OR, the tripods were accidentally displaced and the camera's angle shifted. Last but not least, the handheld camera can be quickly moved out of the OR, e.g. in critical situations when the feeling of being under surveillance might only put more stress on the staff. Thus the decision to switch from a stationary to a mobile camera was motivated by technical, ethical and practical considerations. But the use of a handheld camera is more selective than use of a stationary one. The mobile camera follows the researcher's gaze, highlighting certain situations while at the same time blinding out the rest.

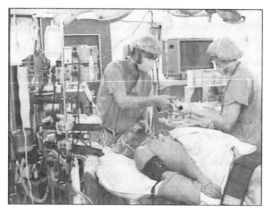

Fig. 1: Intubation by an experienced doctor

The video recordings produced by a handheld camera contain dramaturgic elements with respect to the composition of the recorded scenes. Zooming in and out are ways of scaling the focus from spoken human-human interaction down to the movements of a single hand manipulating instruments. The researcher can also follow the actors into the preparation rooms or to the telephone if sequences of interest are carried on outside the OR. Activities may be centred on the patient's body or may require a certain distance. If the operation becomes complicated, staff tend to move all marginal work away from the surgeons so as not to disturb them. A mobile camera can follow the doctors and nurses in action and in their movements through the OR and adjacent rooms.

Consequently, the video recordings are highly idiosyncratic. To overcome the limits of mere snapshots of interactions, one can follow Glaser and Strauss by *selecting comparison groups*. Since procedures in routine anaesthetisation are rather standardised, it is possible to define different stages and activities that can be compared with one another. In GT the groups are selected according to their *theoretical relevance*: group comparisons "are made by comparing diverse or similar evidence indicating the same conceptual categories and properties" (Glaser & Strauss 1967: 49). In the study of cooperative work sites, this often translates to comparing the interactions in mixed teams (humans and non-humans).

For example, we recorded a number of intubation sequences where either an experienced or a novice anaesthetist performed the procedure. During intubation (specifically transoral endotracheal intubation), a plastic tube is inserted through the patient's mouth into the trachea in order to administer artificial respiration. Depending on the shape of the tube and the patient's body, intubations can be more or less difficult to perform and if the anaesthetist misses the trachea, the food tube can be intubated by mistake. The ability to perform good intubations mainly comes from repeated practice, so novices need to be trained in the practice in order to become competent. For experienced doctors, the procedure is part of daily routine. In the scenes we recorded, the doctor is assisted by a nurse who hands over the instruments and takes them back. In figure 1 we see a nurse handing over the laryngoscope (an instrument for looking down the throat at the larynx) to the anaesthetist. This is an experienced team and the nurse has already turned her head away from instrument and anaesthetist to reach for the tube. An intubation usually takes between 30 to 90 seconds to perform and is supposed to happen quickly, since the patient does not breathe during this time. Such situations are well suited to videographic scrutiny, because they are locally confined and temporally finite, they happen without a lot of talk, and interaction is conducted swiftly. The details of cooperative work on such a small scale are hard to observe with the naked eye.

By the same token, the study of interactivity with machines can be appropriately recorded using video, making high-tech workplaces especially interesting for videographic studies (cf. Suchman 1987). The (mostly) nonverbal conduct when operating machines and the swift routine manipulations of artefacts can be better captured by video than by plain observation (cf. Schubert 2002). In our case, we concentrated on the use of the anaesthetic monitoring equipment and syringe pumps. Syringe pumps are microelectronic devices which assist in regulating the administration of accurate amounts of drugs, such as sleeping or pain medication, over time. The interesting thing about syringe pumps is that they do not have the best reputation for being reliable. This is not to say that they cannot be depended upon at all, but their ability for self diagnosis can lead to false alarms and sometimes the digital readout can be misleading.[1] In figure 2 we see an anaesthetist re-

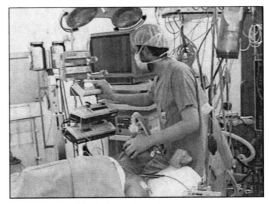

Fig. 2: Operating syringe pump

---

1 A medical doctor concludes her review of a critical paper on syringe pumps thus: "With advances in technology, we tend to put too much faith in machines and their arrogant digital readouts. This paper jogs us back to reality." (http://www.pedsanesthesia.org/newsletter/2002winter/litreview.shtml – 22. June 2005)

programming a syringe pump after several internal alarms. In the daily use of these machines, anaesthetists develop specific routines for normal use and for troublesome situations. The latter can be seen as compensating activities (cf. Hughes 1951) that develop in the interaction with the machines and are connected with the local context. Since these activities are part of the routines taken for granted in everyday work, they are hardly reflected on by the users and the fine-grained documentation available in video recordings is well suited to making these routine practices available for analysis.

Selecting groups of sequences that are relevant to the research question is of course a process which is never absolutely finished, because the research question may shift in the light of new data. As a criterion for adding more sources of data or making an intermediary stop in the selection of other data, Glaser and Strauss propose the term *theoretical saturation*, which will be used for structuring and organising the practice of video analysis.

Practice of video analysis

Once the researcher has returned from the field with written observation protocols and video recordings it is time to analyse the data. One of the first steps in organising the data is to make *content logs* of the video recordings (Jordan & Henderson 1995, Ruhleder & Jordan 1997) in order to discover "easily identifiable behavioural units", or *ethnographic chunks* (Jordan & Henderson 1995: 57). Content logs are not transcripts of a complete tape, but rough descriptions of the filmed situations and may contain references to analytical concepts. The content logs change as the research progresses: they become more detailed when sequences are analysed, which can be seen as a similar process to that of *coding* in GT (Strauss 1987). The role of *theoretical saturation* in the process of identifying ethnographic chunks and creating content logs is that an analysis is always conducted with respect to the progress of the research. Glaser and Strauss define theoretical saturation as "the criterion for judging when to stop sampling the different groups pertinent to a category" (Glaser & Strauss 1967: 61), i.e. the researcher starts coding with theoretical sensitivity, continues to refine the categories by theoretical sampling and the process comes to an (sometimes tentative) end, when theoretical saturation is reached.[2] In the practice of video-analysis, this process resolves into the multiple steps and iterations of analysing videographic data, which are oriented towards the relevance of the material for the research question: a) selecting key sequences: looking at intubations with respect to novice/expert differences, b) repeated

---

2 The different stages of coding (open, axial and selective) will not be elaborated here, because this would require a longer examination of the coding paradigm in relation with predetermined research questions. Suffice to say that it is a process of focusing and organising data guided by theoretical assumptions.

viewing: with slow or fast motion and c) systematically comparing different cases: from large and small hospitals in Germany and abroad for example.

At this point, it is important to note that after the ethnographer comes back from the field, the subsequent analysis is often conducted in groups. After the first step of creating a rough content log and identifying ethnographic chunks, a selection must be made to decide which sequences should be marked for further scrutiny. This can be helped by a collectively generated content log in two ways: firstly, research colleagues can make independent content logs of the same recording in order to broaden perspectives, secondly, they can successively revise an initial content log in an attempt to refine the existing observations, remarks and conclusions. Either way, for the analysis of practices in the OR this means that all the research colleagues must have some knowledge about the context of the situation, i.e. they must be familiar with the peculiarities of the field to some degree. By collectively creating a content log, the problem of individual biases can be countered and the analysis of video recordings can be subsequently conducted in groups.

For our study this was very important, because the research project was part of an interdisciplinary approach to safety in socio-technical systems. Together with colleagues from fields such as psychology, semiotics, ergonomics and computer science, we aimed at producing different accounts of the procedures in the OR according to each individual discipline and then unifying them in an abstract model of OR safety aspects. The video recordings served as a focal point for interdisciplinary research, since the establishment of a common data source (video recordings) made it easier to engage in interdisciplinary discussions of work practices.

Here, a technical benefit of video recordings becomes evident: the capacity to store otherwise volatile interactions, gestures, etc. and the suitability for posterior analysis (cf. Mead 1975). Once a content log is established and the relevant scenes are agreed upon, the detailed scrutiny of selected sequences can commence. Each sequence will be analysed, i.e. repeatedly watched and discussed, until a sufficient level of theoretical saturation is reached. When analysing these sequences, a second technical benefit of video recordings comes into play: the possibility of distorting and altering the temporal composition of perception. By means of playback, a single scene can be endlessly repeated and slow motion and fast motion may reveal phenomena that are hard to perceive in real time.

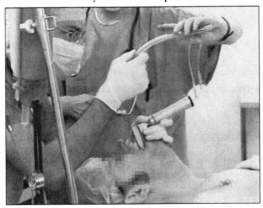

Fig. 3: Intubation by a novice doctor

For instance, the subtle coordination of team interaction (cf. Hindmarsh & Pilnick 2002) during the intubation could only be made visible by slowing the playback speed, sometimes even stopping the film and analysing the interaction frame by frame. In our example, we compared the interaction of experienced nurses with either trained or novice anaesthetists. In the first case, the nurse waited for the signals for coordination from the doctor, which were given in the form of swift gestures. Thus, each sequence in the interaction was initiated by the anaesthetist, which points to two interesting aspects of OR cooperation. First, the nurse recognises the doctor's authority concerning the procedure and takes on the role of an assistant and the traditional hierarchy of doctors and nurses is maintained, secondly, the nurse displays a high degree of competence, since she is able to react appropriately to even the slightest cues, like a quick nod or swift hand movement. The nurse assisting the novice doctor does basically the same, but she does so before the doctor signals her. By presenting the relevant instruments and nodding towards the patient, she is giving cues to the novice as what to do next. She arranges the instruments and tools in a way that makes it easier for the inexperienced doctor to successfully finish the intubation. By manipulating the material environment, she is able to instruct the novice by assisting him without having to use words. In figure 3 she is handing over the tube without letting it go as the novice doctor reaches for it, thus making him aware of the special position the tube needs to be in before insertion. Again, the traditional hierarchy is maintained, but only on a superficial level, with the nurse skilfully coordinating the interaction in a way that is barely visible to the naked eye.

The detailed analysis of such short scenes by means of video is obviously well suited for the task and it is the patterns of interaction and the adjustment of actions in problematic situations that especially render themselves visible through videography. This understanding of videography links it not only to ethnography but also to ethnomethodology (Garfinkel 1967, cf. also *video-interaction-analysis* Knoblauch 2004). The scope of video adds to that of participant observation by focusing on relevant scenes which are selected according to theoretical sampling and analysed until theoretical saturation is reached.

But video has one more advantage that should be noted: video recordings can be returned to the field in order to generate feedback, making video, in essence, a *medium for reflection* (Suchman & Trigg 1991). Feedback strategies are well known to ethnographers and visual techniques, e.g. *photo elicitation* (Harper 1984), are part of the repertoire of visual sociology. In our study we conducted *video-based interviews* with anaesthetists, using short scenes as a stimulus for comments and discussions. For the analysis of practices in the OR, this is relevant especially in validating the sociological interpretations of medical work and generating new perspectives on the data. The anaesthetists can assess whether a situation is typical for their everyday work and give background information about certain procedures or rate the difficulty of the task. Although the video sequence functions as a stimulus, the following discussion between sociologist and anaesthetist makes it different to Merton's *focused interview* (Merton & Kendall 1946). The aim is not to study the reaction to a stimulus, but to use the stimulus as a starting point for a problem-centred talk, in which sociologist and medical doctor engage in the reconstruction of the scene from social, technical and medical perspectives.

In addition to validating sociological accounts of medical procedures and introducing a medical perspective into the analysis, we were interested in the way that these video sequences initiated oral stories of similar situations. The importance of *war stories* has been noted before (Schulman 1996, Rochlin 1999, Orr 1986, Barley & Orr 1997) and during the participant observation it was often the case, that when an experienced doctor instructed a novice, anecdotes of critical situations were used to highlight the central problems and to supply the novice with a memorable story concerning problematic situations. When the doctors were asked to describe the situation seen on video and to assess its potential for complications they very often interwove short episodes of critical incidents that they themselves or other colleagues had witnessed. These might range from patients waking during the operation or the breakdown of electronic instruments when transporting a patient, say, in an elevator. These anecdotes serve to make the novice more alert to practical hazards or undocumented interactions, e.g. between technologies and drugs. This rich corpus of anecdotes, episodes, war stories and practical accounts is what generally makes up the narrative structure of medical knowledge (Atkinson 1995, Hunter 1991). That these narratives are also produced in interaction with sociologists in discussing video sequences, indicates their widespread use in medical settings.

Thus video can be used not only for refined analysis, it can – in the sense of a medium for reflection – be a source of new kinds of data, i.e. the accounts given in the interviews. Videography generates multiple forms of pictures, sound and text, which, according to the principles of GT can be considered as *slices of data* (Glaser & Strauss 1967: 65). Within theoretical sampling, slices of data are "different views or vantage points from which to understand a category and to develop its properties" that help to exceed the limited input of only one method. Although most data may be gathered using one primary method, the process of analysis must contain elements of openness. Glaser and Strauss point out that slices of data should not be considered "as accurate evidence for verifications" (ibid.: 66), since "no data is accurate" (ibid.: 67), but should be seen instead as rich sources of information in the process of establishing categories. This does not contrast with the verifying of sociological accounts of medical procedures by doctors. Rather it is a sort of tentative *triangulation* (Denzin 1989 general see pp. 25, with respect to film see p. 225) which, unlike geometrical triangulation, does not try to identify an 'objective truth' of some kind, but attempts to view the phenomenon of interest from different angles, be they different theories, methods, researchers or slices of data.[3]

The previous remarks indicate that the practice of video analysis within videographic research is not confined to a single method of analysis. By the same token, a

---

3 An instructive example of how real world phenomena can be categorised with respect to analytic categories from several different perspectives is the case of *machine work* on hospital wards by Strauss et al. (1997[1985]: 40).

plurality of methods is not advocated for its own sake, but always with respect to theoretical sampling and saturation. Videography can therefore never be a monolithic method, applicable irrespective of the context of the study, but instead is a tentative approach that displays sensitivity both to the theoretical and to the empirical world. The practice of video analysis is thus a process of constant interrelations of theory and field.

Conclusion

The videographic approach put forward in the previous pages aimed at providing a theoretically orientated strategy for selecting and analysing audiovisual data in the continuous process of research. In this vein, there is no single optimal way to implement videography, it needs to be adapted to the respective study. The quality of videographic research does not lie in following strict methodological rules, but in the ability to arrange different methods, slices of data and theoretical assumptions in order to gain a deeper insight into the interrelations of real world phenomena. This is not, however, an invitation to arbitrariness. The researcher has to account for every move and measure in the research process on the basis of theoretical and empirical rationales. Videographic methods may differ for the analysis of school room interactions for example, in contrast to the methods used to observe operating rooms or auctions, laboratories, control centres, etc. Bearing videography's ethnographic tradition in mind, the general requirement is that it remain sensitive to the peculiarities of the field, whereas Grounded Theory additionally requires us to stay theoretically sensitive as well.

The central mode of operation in videography therefore consists of making distinctions and comparisons, iteratively introducing order into the 'messy' phenomena of the empirical world. The video camera and video playback equipment serve as instruments that render specific properties of observable phenomena visible. In contrast to the naked eye, the more confined scope of the video camera makes us aware of the selections we have to make during observation, but video recordings in return offer a very rich corpus of data for detailed analysis. For this reason, video recording and analysis in videographic research should be considered focusing devices which are embedded within a larger context of multiple methods, ranging from participant observations to interviews and producing very detailed accounts of selected phenomena in the field. Using video equipment as a sociological instrument, one has to keep in mind that it does not produce or reproduce 'reality' but that it consists of an array of artefacts which aid in the sociological reconstruction of practices by distorting our perceptual habits and exempting us from some restrictions of space and time.

The possibilities that videographic research offers have not been exploited to their full extent, and critical issues have not been completely solved. In terms of Grounded Theory, this means proposing videography as a flexible research strategy, rather than as a monolithic method, keeping it open for further refinement and modification. The combination of videography with GT's theoretical sampling provides a lead for structuring qualitative research of work practices and the like.

References

Akrich, M. & B. Latour, 1992: A Summery of a Covenient Vocabulary for the Semiotics of Human and Nonhuman Assemblies. In: W. E. Bijker (ed.) *Shaping Technology/Building Society. Studies in sociotechnical change.* Cambridge, MA: MIT,

Atkinson, P., 1995: *Medical Talk and Medical Work. The Liturgy of the Clinic.* London: Sage

Barley, S. R. & J. E. Orr (ed.) 1997: *Between craft and science. Technical work in U.S. settings.* Ithaca: IRL Press

Callon, M., 1986: Some Elements of a Sociology of Translation: Domestication of the Scallops and the Fishermen of Saint Brieuc Bay. In: J. Law (ed.) *Power, Action and Belief: a new Sociology of Knowledge?* London: Routledge and Kegan Paul, 196-233

Denzin, N. K., 1989: *The Research Act in Sociology.* Chicago: Aldine

Freidson, E., 1970: *Profession of Medicine. A Study of the Sociology of Applied Knowledge.* New York: Harper and Row

Garfinkel, H., 1967: *Studies in Ethnomethodology.* Englewood Cliffs: Prentice-Hall

Glaser, B. G. & A. L. Strauss, 1967: *The Discovery of Grounded Theory.* Chicago: Aldine

Harper, D. 1984: Meaning and Work: A Study in Photo Elicitation. *International Journal of Visual Sociology,* 2, 1: 20-43

Heath, C., P. Luff & H. Knoblauch, 2004: Tools, Technologies and Organizational Interaction. The Emergence of Workplace Studies. In: D. Grant, C. Hardy, C. Oswick & L. L. Putnam (ed.) *The SAGE Handbook of Organizational Discourse.* London: Sage, 337-358

Hindmarsh, J. & A. Pilnick 2002: The Tacit Order of Teamwork. Collaboration and Embodied Conduct in Anesthesia. *The Sociological Quarterly,* 43, 2: 139-164

Hughes, E. C. 1951: Mistakes at Work. *Canadian Journal of Economics and Political Science,* 17, 320-27

Hughes, E. C., 1971: *The Sociological Eye: Selected Papers.* Chicago: Aldine

Hunter, K. M., 1991: *Doctors' Stories: The Narrative Structure of Medical Knowledge.* Princeton: Princeton University Press

Jordan, B. & A. Henderson 1995: Interaction Analysis: Foundations and Practice. *The Journal of the Learning Sciences,* 4, 1: 39-103

Knoblauch, H. 2004: Die Video-Interaktions-Analyse. *Sozialer Sinn,* 1: 123-138

Knorr-Cetina, K., 1981: *The Manufacture of Knowledge: An Essay on the Constructivist and Contextual Nature of Science.* Oxford: Pergamon Press

Latour, B., 1988: *The Pasteurization of France.* Cambridge, Mass.: Harvard University Press

Latour, B. & S. Woolgar, 1979: *Laboratory Life: The Social Construction of Scientific Facts.* London: Sage

Lomax, H. & N. Casey, 1998: *Recording Social Life: Reflexivity and Video Methodology.* Sociological Research Online

Mead, M., 1975: Visual Anthropology in a Discipline of Words. In: P. Hockings (ed.) *Principles of Visual Anthropology.* Paris: Mouton, 3-12

Merton, R. K. & P. L. Kendall 1946: The focused Interview. *American Journal of Sociology,* 51, 6: 541-557

Orr, J. E., 1986: *Narratives at work: story telling as cooperative diagnostic activity.* Austin: ACM Press
Rammert, W., 2002: Technik als verteilte Aktion. Wie technisches Wirken als Agentur in hybriden Aktionszusammenhängen gedeutet werden kann. In: K. Kornwachs (ed.) *Technik - System - Verantwortung.* Münster: LIT Verlag, 219-231
Rochlin, G. I., 1999: The social construction of safety. In: J. Misumi, B. Wilpert & R. Miller (ed.) *Nuclear Safety: A Human Factors Perspective.* London: Taylor & Francis, 5-23
Ruhleder, K. & B. Jordan, 1997: Capturing Complex, Distributed Activities: Video Based Interaction Analysis as a component of Workplace Ethnography. In: A. S. Lee, J. Liebenau & J. I. De Gross (ed.) *Information Systems and Qualitative Research. London, UK: Chapman and Hall.* London: Chapman and Hall, http://alexia.lis.uiuc.edu/-ruhleder/publications/97.IFIPWG82.html
Schubert, C., 2002: *Making interaction and interactivity visible. On the practical and analytical uses of audiovisual recordings in high-tech and high-risk work situations.* Berlin: Technische Universität, Institut für Soziologie
Schulman, P. R. 1996: Heroes, organizations, and high reliability. *Journal of Contingencies and Crisis Management,* 4, 2: 72-82
Strauss, A. L., 1987: *Qualitative Analysis For Social Scientists.* Cambridge: Cambridge University Press
Strauss, A. L., S. Fagerhaugh, B. Suczek & C. Wiener, 1997[1985]: *Social Organization of Medical Work.* New Brunswick: Transaction
Suchman, L. A., 1987: *Plans and Situated Actions. The Problem of human-machine communication.* London: Cambridge University Press
Suchman, L. A. & R. H. Trigg, 1991: Understanding Practice: Video as a Medium for Reflection and Design. In: J. Greenbaum & M. Kyng (ed.) *Design at Work: Cooperative Design of Computer Systems.* Hillsdale, NJ: Lawrence Erlbaum, 65-89

Anssi Peräkylä & Johanna Ruusuvuori

Facial Expression in an Assessment

Facial expression in psychology

More than 130 years ago, Charles Darwin (1872) pointed out that facial expression serves important adaptive function in regulating the interaction between humans (and many animals alike). He demonstrated how the expression of major emotions in face and body "could be analysed in terms of adaptive behaviour patterns, of which they were considered to be the rudiments" (Scherer 1996, 286). For example, the ways in which humans express negative feelings having to do with disgust and contempt through facial movements around the mouth and nose, and through turning away, may originate in specific situations where our ancestors have encountered offensive odours which they have tried to expel or exclude (Darwin 1872: 253-277).

Darwin's work got forgotten for almost a century. In early and mid 20th Century, the study of facial expression was not central in the agenda of human sciences. However, in 1960s and 70s, Darwin's work was found again, most notably, perhaps, by Paul Ekman who was involved in a cross-cultural study on facial expression of emotion (e.g. Ekman et al. 1969). Using photos and films of faces with different expressions, Ekman and his colleagues tried to pin down the connections between emotional states and details of the muscular movement in the face, as well as the ways in which people recognize such movements as expressions of particular emotions (for an accessible overview, see Ekman 2003; see also Izard 1971). Although Ekman discusses the uses of facial expression in social interaction (1979), the main focus of his work lies elsewhere, that is, in the ways in which internal emotional states are expressed and recognized in and through the face.

A rather different take on facial expression can be found in the work of Chovil (1991, 1997) and Bavelas (Bavelas & Chovil 1997; 2000). Rather than focussing on the functions of face as an output of internal emotional processes, they examine facial displays[1] as "visible acts of meaning", by considering the ways in which the facial displays "are part of the integrated message with words" (Bavelas & Chovil 2000: 166; cf. Fridlund 1996). Using video recorded data from two-party conversations in a psychology laboratory setting, Chovil (1991) found two major types of facial displays. *Syntactic* displays involve facial expressions (most often, raising or lowering eyebrows) that serve for example in emphasizing or underlining what is said, or mark a question, or the beginning or the continuation (after a side track) of a story. In *semantic* displays, the facial expression for

---

1 Bavelas and Chovil use the term facial *display* rather than facial *expression*, thereby emphasizing the active uses of face in interaction (cf. Parkinson et al. 2005, 177). In this chapter, we will use the two terms interchangeably.

example conveys the personal reaction of the speaker to what is spoken about (e.g., references to particular "disgusting" foods may be accompanied by wrinkling of nose), or it can involve re-enactment of past experiences, or it can signal thinking or remembering. Semantic displays can be either redundant (i.e., the same semantic content is conveyed also by words) or non-redundant (the semantic content is conveyed by face alone). Yet another type of facial display involves *listener comment*: movements of brows or lips which convey that the listener is attending, or more pronounced facial expressions that convey the listener's personal reaction to what is being said.

Through considering the work of Ekman and his colleagues on one hand, and Chovil and Bavelas on the other, we can outline two ways of approaching facial expression. As Bavelas and Chovil (2000, 166) point out, these two approaches involve methodological choices rather than ultimate claims about the "essence" of facial expression.

Table 1: **Two approaches to facial expression**

	EKMAN ET AL.	CHOVIL & BAVELAS
Key aspect of facial expression	Output of internal psycho-physical state	Communicative resource
Meaning of face	Key expressions have inherent meanings	Meaning arises from linguistic context

In our project, we are predominantly informed by the Chovil & Bavelas-approach. However, we want to develop this approach further towards the analysis of moment-by-moment evolving social interaction. Using conversation analysis (CA; see e.g. Heritage 1984, Peräkylä 2004) as a methodological resource, we will focus on the ways in which participants' facial expressions interact, on momentary basis, with each other, with their words, and with other aspects of their non-lexical expression, such as gaze and prosody. An important resource in this effort are Charles and Marjorie Goodwin's seminal studies on mutual monitoring and organization of participation (e.g. Goodwin MH 1980; Goodwin C 1984). In what follows, we will first describe our method of research and discuss the methodological choices. Second, we will describe with the help of a case-study the moment-by-moment interactional work performed by facial expression in a particular conversational action, assessment. Drawing on the analysis, we will then make some hypotheses concerning the uses of face in the activity of assessment, and finally, we will suggest a third way to conceptualize the meaning of facial expression in social interaction.

Studying facial expression in naturally occurring interaction

For a few years, we have been involved in a pilot research focusing on facial expression in everyday social interaction. In launching our research, we had to consider where to get data with adequate technical quality, but also a possibility to observe interaction as it happens in everyday social life. Despite the many advantages of standardized experimental research settings we wanted to observe interaction as it takes place in ordinary settings, outside the social psychology laboratory. Getting naturalistic data with adequate technical quality that would allow for close observation of the faces of all the participants, however, turned out to be problematic. Our solution was to collect 'quasi-natural' data, where we would provide a setting that would come as close to natural as possible, and the participants would be able to decide themselves the direction that their interaction would take (cf. Chovil 1991; Motley & Camden 1988). We requested dyads of students to come and have a free lunch at a cabinet of a local student cafeteria while their conversation would be recorded. The request was sent in several e-mail lists of local student organizations and resulted in five approximately 30-minute conversations between five dyads of students who knew each other beforehand.

The conversations were recorded with three video-cameras. One of these recorded the facial expressions and gestures of the first participant (A), another one those of the other participant (B), while the third camera recorded both participants interacting. The recordings were channelled through a splitter, to result in a three-part picture where all three shots are shown simultaneously. The view of the third camera is shown in frame 0; the rest of the frames consists of two views showing A and B separately.

In experimental studies, the standardization of the setting is an efficient way to get data that is 'focused' on one particular phenomenon. With naturally occurring data, the contingent quality of social interaction poses a problem. Face-to-face interaction is intervowen of a myriad of strands which are not analytically distinguishable at the outset. Conversation analytical research has provided a set of well documented and cumulative findings that show how everyday conversation is orderly and organized in sequences of actions achieved through adjacent turns of talk by the participants. Thus, instead of standardizing the environment, as in experimental studies, it was possible for us to draw upon previous conversation analytical research to find segments in conversation where a similar action was taking place, where the participants were observably 'doing the same thing' as before.

One recurrent activity on which previous literature was available was *assessment* (e.g. Pomerantz 1984; Goodwin & Goodwin 1992). An assessment involves that the speakers and/or recipients evaluate persons or events that are described in their talk (Goodwin & Goodwin 1987), show their stance towards them. Thus, assessment sequences seemed as good candidate for an environment where the facial expression of the participants could be systematically observable.

Assessments have been the topic of a number of conversation analytical studies. Pomerantz (1984) showed how assessments are often organized as pairs, where the first position assessment by one speaker makes relevant a second position assessment by another speaker. Pomerantz described the ways in which the speakers orient to a preference for an agreement in the second positioned assessment. Recently, Heritage and Raymond (2005) have pursued the analysis of first and second assessments by exploring the ways in which the participants' claims to knowledge regarding the assessed referents are intertwined with the organization of the assessment sequences.

Rather than focussing on relations between first and second assessments, Goodwin & Goodwin (1987, 1992, M.H. Goodwin 1980) have explored the interaction between speakers and hearers *during* the production of an assessment. They show how an assessment can involve only a segment within the stream of talk (for example, an evaluative adjective such as "beautiful" prefacing a descriptive noun) or, alternatively, it can occupy the whole utterance (for example, in the speaker saying "it was so good" about referent which has been made available in earlier talk) (Goodwin & Goodwin 1987 and 1992). In particular, the studies by Goodwins demonstrate the ways in which assessments often involve multi-modal expression, involving not only words, but gesture and gaze alike. They show how the collaborative assessment activity is organized in terms of momentary relations between the participants' expressions employing different modalities. The Goodwins (1987, esp. 37) also show how assessment as an activity has phases, proceeding from the emergence of the assessment, via the heightened participation in it, towards trailing off from it. In a case study to be reported here, we will pursue the line of research initiated by their work in conversation analysis. Our research also draws upon some key concepts originating in the early work of Erving Goffman.

```
Extract 1
01  A:   Mä luulen et mä en pääse sillä hakemuksella ihan (.)
         I think I won't get with that application to quite
                                                         (.)
02       semmossiin (0.4) tosi konservatiivisiin lehtiin.
         such (0.4) very conservative papers.
03       (1.4)
04  B:   Se voi kyl pitää paikkansa. .hff hhhe
         It may indeed be the case. hff hff hf hf
05       (0.5)
06  B:   Mut sun kannattais kysyy noilta
         But it would be useful for you to ask those
07       jotka on päässy sinne Hesariin
         who have got a job from Hesari
08       että kuinka #konservatiivista# siellä o,
         that how #conse:rvative people there are,
09       (3.0)
10  A:   Mut emmä nyt haluu antaa niille mitenkään
         But I don't want to give any false impression
11       valheellista kuvaa #itsestäni ↓parem↑pi vaan laittaa
         of #myself↓ bett↑er just send
12       tollassia [epäasiallisia#.
         such      [incorrect ones.#
13  B:              [.hhh
14       (.)
15  B:   ↑N:o<
         Well<
16       (0.3)
17  A:   @Sitte mä ehkä pääsen sellaseen ↓sopi#vaan
         @Then I'll probably get a job that
18       ↓paikkaan#.@
         ↓suits↓me.@
19  B:   Mmm.
20       (0.3)
```

Method

From the transcript of two of the recorded conversations, all assessments were picked out and re-transcribed. For the spoken turns of talk, conversation analytic conventions of transcription were used (see Heritage & Atkinson 1984). The direction of gaze was transcribed using the method developed by Charles Goodwin (1981), and for the facial expressions, a new method of transcription was developed by the researchers.

In the method, three explicit transformations of the basic 'straightfaced' expressions were coded. These included expressions of positive affect (joy/ amusement), negative affect (sadness/disapproval) and surprise. These expressions involved the lifting of the corners of the mouth and sometimes wrinkling of the corners of the eyes (positive), slight lowering of the corners of the mouth, sometimes together with pursing of the lips and frowning (negative), opening the mouth and raising of the eyebrows (surprise).

Extract 1 (continued)

```
21  B:  Mut ↑oothan sie aika konservatiivinen ittekki.
        But you ↑are quite conservative yourself, aren't you
22      (0.3)
23  A:  Nii:.
        Yeah:.
24      (1.0)
25  A:  Eh//kä<
        Fr1
        May//be<
26      (0.8)//(0.2)//(0.2)//(2.8)
        Fr2   Fr3   Fr4
27  B:  t Savon Sanomissa oli (0.7) ei Savon
        tch in Savon Sanomat they had (0.7) not in Savon
28      Sanomissa ku (1.6) Sata#kunnan Kansassa#.
        Sanomat but in (1.6) Sata#kunnan Kansa#.
29      (0.4)
30  A:  Mm//m,
        Fr5
31      (0.4)
32  B:  Oli kehotettu Samia laittaa #suorat hou°sut°<#. //
                                                         Fr6
        They had asked Sami to wear #proper trou°sers<°.#//
33      (0.4)
34  A:  ↑M//:i//(h)tä//:.
        Fr7 Fr8 Fr9
        ↑W//:(h)ha//:t//:.
35      (0.7)
36  A:  Ei kau//h[eet(h)a(h).]
        Fr10
        No that's ho//rr[ibl(h)e(h).]
37  B:  [Et älä si]nne ainakaan hae //t(h)olla.
                                    Fr11
        [So don't app]ly there in any case with //th(h)at one.
38  A:  .hhh Ohoh.
        .hhh oh no.
39      .hhh Minkä paikan lehti siis Satakunnan
        .hhh at which town is that paper so Satakunnan
40      Sa[nomat.
        Sa[nomat
41  B:  [Pori. //
               Fr12
        [At Pori.//
```

This transcription of facial expression turned out to be very useful as an aid for memory and for the classification of data. In particular, the transcripts helped us to consider the detailed timing, relative to talk, of the changes of the facial expressions. At later stages of the analysis, however, our simple system of transcription was not sensitive enough to the variability and momentary fluctuation of facial expression. Rather than using a more complicated coding system – such as the one developed by Ekman and Friessen (1978) – we have worked directly with the visual images, using natural language to describe the variety of expressions. That is the way in which we describe our data also in this chapter.

The preliminary data analysis resulted in a collection of 104 assessment sequences. With assessment sequence we refer to adjacent turns of talk of which the first one is assessing an object and the following speakers have an opportunity to join in the assessment activity. For example, "Well it has been so great in those days" – "My granny thinks it was great" or "It's so expensive" – "That's right but it's so much fun". In the data, the following turns could be either affiliating or disaffiliating, either assessments or not assessments, either verbal or non-verbal (such as a smile and a nod, for example). Moreover, in some cases the first assessment was done through non-vocal means only.

In analyzing the collection, attention was paid especially on the interplay between what was said and what was displayed by facial expression, and the potential reciprocity of the facial expression of the interactants. The result of the first stage of the analysis was the observation that there are at least two different roles of facial expression in interaction: semiotic and relational. The first one implies that facial expression may emphasize or modify the meaning of what is said in the assessment (cf. Bavelas & Chovil 2000), the second one that facial expression serves to signal and monitor affective cues between the participants.

In the following section, we will illustrate the second phase of the analysis through a case study. The split screen recording technique makes it possible for us to examine in great detail the interplay of the facial expressions of the participants during the production and reception of assessments. By examining the uses of face in an assessment, we hope to complement one further aspect to previous CA analysis on assessments, as well as to outline, in a tentative fashion, a CA-informed approach to the study of facial expression in social interaction.

The case study

In a conversation over lunch, A and B, who are female journalism students, talk about the prospects of A finding a summer job working for a newspaper. A has described her application as a very unconventional one. She thinks that due to its unconventionality, she might not get a job in any conservative newspaper. In Extract 1 above, we are particularly interested in the assessment which is verbally delivered in line 36. But to understand it, we need to explore the talk that precedes it. We will illustrate the facial expression of the participants with captured images from the original video-recording. The location of these framegrabs is marked in the transcript with the abbreviation Fr and the number of the framegrab. (The key to transcription symbols is found in the appendix).

In line 21, as an extension to the topic talk about A's chances to get a summer job, B produces an assessment concerning A. The assessment which characterizes B as "rather conservative" is clearly not in line with the presentational self (Goffman 1955) constructed by B in her earlier talk, and thus constitutes a face threatening act (see also Brown & Levinson 1987). A receives the assessment in classical dispreference format (Pomerantz 1984) involving initial gap (l. 22), a response token that conveys, at most, only partial agreement (l. 23; see Sorjonen 2001; the translation "yeah" is only approximate as "nii" is basically untranslable into English) and eventually backing down by saying "maybe" (l. 25). Towards the end of "maybe", the participants reach mutual gaze (frame 1) which persist for a while into the long silence that follows (l. 26). After a moment of mutual monitoring, B gazes down (frame 2), only to return her gaze back to A for another moment (frame 3). When returning her gaze, she also nods, apparently in response to A's "maybe".

Frame 0 (Line 25. A: Eh//kä<)

After nodding, she once more withdraws her gaze (frame 4). During these shifts in B's gaze, A maintains solid orientation towards her. The facial expression of the participants is rather minimal. However, there is a strong sense of negative affect in the interaction. The return of B's gaze after she had first withdrawn, and its subsequent withdrawal again creates an impression of momentary helplessness; this impression is in line with the somewhat worried expression in her face (see especially frame 3). The simultaneous persistence of A's gaze at B, accompanied by the lack of facial display and prevailing silence, hints towards aggression. Very shortly after this A starts to purse her lips as if biting them (see frame 5) which appears to convey a feeling of discontent. In Goffmanian terms, what happens could be understood as a moment of "embarrassment" (Goffman 1956) arising from the failure of B to recognize and protect A's projected self.

The moment of negative affect is encapsulated in frames 1-4. The exact timing of the frames relative to the transcript is indicated by the symbol // below each frame. In Frame 0, also the overall setting is shown.

After a silence of a few seconds (during with A also withdraws her gaze), B initiates new action in line 27. As this new action unfolds, it turns out to be a story about a newspaper and a mutual acquaintance. The story involves a shift of a topical focus from the character of B back to reality external to both participants. By initiating the story, B creates

Frame 1 (Line 25. B: Eh//kä<)

Frame 2 (Line 25. B: Eh//kä< (0.8)//)

Frame 3 (Line 25. B: Eh//kä< (1.0)//)

a context where A's participation as a story recipient is relevant. Thereby, she steers the interaction away from where the negative affect arose. In Goffmanian terms, what B does can be understood as *corrective action* (Goffman 1955) through which the disruption in the face is mended. A's participation, however, is less than enthusiastic. The following details can be noted.

Much of the beginning part of B's utterance (lines 27-28) is occupied by a repair sequence in which she searches and finally finds the name of a newspaper. B stops the progression of her utterance after having named the paper (line 28). By this, she makes possible recipient action from A. B's gap of 0.4 sec ensues, towards the end of which the participants withdraw from mutual gaze. The silence is ended by A's response token (line 30), whereby she acknowledges of the name of the paper and/or of the completion of the repair. She chooses minimal vocal action ("Mmm" as opposed to "Joo" tai "okei"). She purses her lips while voicing the acknowledgment (the pursing began a few moments before) and she uses a level intonation contour and therefore appears as unenthusiastic. As a whole, it appears that the negative affect prevails in A's action here. See frame 5.

After a new gap (line 31), B produces what can be recognized as the punch line of her little story. At the end of line 32, her utterance (and the story) is hearably complete. Towards the end of the punch line (at word "suorat"/"proper") B moves her gaze towards A. A reciprocates with her gaze almost immediately. At the beginning of the next word ("housut"/ "trousers") B begins to smile in a "slight" way, keeping her mouth shut, and she raises her eyebrows for a moment. The prosody of this last word of her utterance is marked: the end of the word is pronounced in a "cut off" manner, creating an impression of something being withheld. After having completed her utterance, B remains silent, maintaining her smile and her gaze on A. See frame 6.

Frame 4 (Line 25. B: Eh//kä< (1.2)//)

Through her gaze, smile and the movement of her eye-brows, as well as through her prosody, and the discontinuation of her talk, B seems here to be involved in an effort to instigate collaborative *assessment activity* (Goodwin & Goodwin 1987): her comportment suggests that the story just completed involved something remarkable, something to be met

Frame 5 (Line 30. A: Mm//m,)

Frame 6 (Line 32. B: #suorat hou°sut°<#.//)

with positive affect. A, however, remains unforthcoming. She reciprocates gaze, but continues the pursing of her lips through the punch line and the ensuing silence. She does not produce any verbal response to B's story. At this moment, therefore, the participants' affective positions towards what has been described, as expressed by their words and bodies, are quite divergent. To say the least, A remains unresponsive to B's effort to instigate collaborative assessment activity.

However, a rather dramatic change in A's comportment takes place after a silence of 0.4 seconds. She raises her eyebrow, makes her eyes round, starts to smile broadly, and and says "mitä"/ "what".

In frames 7-9, we go through this change step-by-step. The change in A's expression begins in the same time with the first sound of her word "mitä"/"what". During the production of the lengthened "m:", she raises her eyebrows and makes her eyes round. These facial features are typically associated with surprise. Her mouth, however, remains closed which is associated with the production of the "m" sound. See frame 7.

Frame 7 (Line 32. 32. A: "↑M//:i(h)tä:.")

Frame 8 (Line 32. A: "↑M:i//(h)tä:.")

Frame 9 (Line 32. A: "↑M:i(h)tä//:.")

By virtue of the change in A's face during the production of the first sound of her "what", her affective response – or at least one aspect of that, namely the surprise – to B's story is displayed *before* the lexical element is at such stage that it can be understood.

The expression of A's face evolves quickly. By the time the first vowel of her "mitä"/"what" is completed, A's mouth and eyes have taken the shape of a broad smile. Now, in her facial expression, smile and surprise are blended. See Frame 8.

Thus, in terms of her facial expression, A's affective response to the story about "Sami's trousers" is fully developed by the completion of the first syllable of her initial lexical response. The dramatic change in A's face – which takes place while the participants are mutually oriented towards each other – constitutes involvement in assessment activity into which B seemed to invite her, through her face and verbal action, at the end of her story. The expression in which smile and surprise are blended remains in A's face until the end of the word "mitä"/"what" and even after that. The participants faces during the production of the last sound of "mitä"/"what" are shown in Frame 9.

The production of "mitä" ("what") is marked in various ways: pitch is remarkably higher than in A's other talk, there is a laugh particle inserted in the word, both vowels are prolonged. Both syllables bear an intonational accent. A's facial and prosodic action together convey strong affect of amusement and surprise. Prosody and face also constitute A's "mitä" not as a repair initiation (see e.g. Schegloff 1979), but as an expression of the speakers stance towards what she has heard. Accordingly, A responds to A's "mitä" not by repeating or paraphrasing what she has said, but by nodding four times in line 35.

By her action, the facial components of which we see in Frames 7-9, A eventually responds to B's invitation to join in the assessment. She does that with a strong display of affects of amusement and surprise. The participants enter into a moment of shared emotion and heightened mutual participation in the assessment activity (cf. Goodwin & Goodwin 1987: 28-33). In Goffmanian terms, this moment also involves a successful movement restoration of the mutual recognition of the projected selves of the participants.

Frame 10 Line 36. A: Ei kau//heet(h)a(h).)

Frame 11 (Line 37. B: h<u>ae</u> //t(h)<u>o</u>lla.)

Frame 12 (Line 41. B: P<u>o</u>ri.//)

The evolvement of B's face is much less dramatic. As pointed out above, she adopted smiling face, with mouth closed, at the end of her story in line 32. During most part of A's "mitä" /"what", B is involved in putting a spoon in her mouth (see frames 7 and 8). After she has removed the spoon at the end of "mitä"/"what", it appears that B's smile is somewhat more intensive than it was before: the corners of her eyes are more wrinkled, and her mouth is longer (frame 9 and 10 as compared to frame 6). In this context, the "intensification" of B's smile is understood as a response to B's facial, prosodic and lexical action.

Goodwin and Goodwin (1987: 33) show how assessments can have a recognizable *peak* or *climax*, during which the interactants' participation in it is most intensive. It appears that lines 34-35, visually represented in frame 7-9, incorporate such peak. Here occurs the dramatic change in A's facial expression. The prosody of her talk is more marked than elsewhere, as the pitch is here clearly higher than in talk that precedes or comes after. However, in terms of words, the assessment has not yet been delivered: the *assessment adjective* (Goodwin & Goodwin 1987:6-7) "kauheeta"/"horrible" that constitutes the core of the *assessment segment* (ibid.) is only produced in line 36. At that point, the participants' facial expression remains rather stable, preserving the features that were established at the beginning of A's "mitä"/"what" in line 34, and the pitch of A's talk has come down, closer to her normal range. Frame 11 shows the facial configuration at the end of the first syllable of "kauheeta"/"horrible".

In overlap with A's assessment adjective, B begins an utterance which is marked as an inference from the story (through turn initial "et"/"so") and which, by reinvoking A's job application as a topic, also ties the story to the talk that preceded it. Through her utterance, which involves a joking advice for A not to apply to the newspaper in question, B indirectly shows that she is in agreement with A's initial line in presentation of self as an unconventional person, thereby adding a new layer to what might be called her corrective action. Through this move in topic and action, B treats the peak of the assessment activity as having been passed.

In the middle part of her utterance in line 37, at the beginning of the Finnish word "ainakaa" (translatable in this context "in any case"), and shortly after A has completed her assessment adjective, B withdraws her gaze from A, thereby dissolving the intensity of the mutual involvement. A's gaze withdrawal follows at the end of "ainakaa"/"in any case": she adopts a "middle distance" gaze in B's direction but below her face. Frame 12 shows the configuration just after A's gaze withdrawal. Thus, by the end of line 37, when the participants have moved verbally to a new action after the assessment, they have also dissolved their mutual visual participation.

Slight smile, however, remains in both participants' faces even after they have withdrawn from the mutual gaze. The continuity of the smiles incorporates the continuity of the participants' affective state, originating in the assessment, and of their affective involvement in the referent of their talk. The mutual withdrawal of gaze brings about de-intensification of this affect (cf. Kendon 1990, 76-81)

The smiles of the participants in frame 11 (along with the laugh token in "t(h)olla" /"t(h)at one") are associated with the new action (joking advice) that B has initiated. However, the smiles in the participants' faces are the "same" smiles that begun as constituents of the assessment activity in lines 32 (for B) and 34 (for A): the smiles did not disappear between the two actions. Therefore, there seems to be a particular *continuity in the parties' facial expression and the affect that it incorporates*: while the verbal action and an aspect of the topic change, the affect, as displayed by the participants' faces, in this case remains the same.

The verbal assessment action is briefly resumed in line 38 through A's exclamatory "ohoh"/"oh no". Right after this, B glances briefly at A and A reciprocates the look. A then (l.39) moves to yet another action, asking where the newspaper appears. Simultaneously with the onset of the question, A adopts "straight face", i.e. ceases to smile. B responds to the A's question in overlap (line 38). During the production of B's answer, the participants once more adopt mutual gaze. While shifting her gaze at A, B also adopts straight face. Thereby, the affective involvement of the participants is finally resolved.² The final non-affective state of mutual monitoring is presented in frame 12.

Summary of the results of the case study

What we have presented here is a case study which as such does not warrant any generalizable conclusions. However, the following hypotheses regarding the uses of face in assessment activity can be presented.
1. It appears that *face is involved in the management of the assessment activity*.
2. Along with words and prosody, *face incorporates the participants' affective involvement in the referent being assessed* (cf. Goodwin & Goodwin 1987, 9). Through their faces in frames 7–11, the participants displayed an affective stance (as "funny" and "surprising") to the referent of their assessment.
3. *Facial displays, and lack of them, also incorporate the participants' momentary affective relation during the assessment activity*. In our example, an embarrassed facial display (frames 2, 3 and 4), and asymmetry of facial display (in frame 6) seemed to incorporate lack of mutual affective involvement between the participants, whereas symmetry in positive facial displays (frames 7-10) seemed to incorporate (restoration of) such involvement.
4. The participants' facial displays are *coordinated with each other, with their gaze, and with the unfolding of their verbal contributions to the interaction*. Positive facial display, like the one in frame 6, in a setting where the participants maintain mutual gaze and where a second position action by a co-participant is due, can serve as an invitation to a corresponding positive display, as an affective component to the second position action, from this co-participant (cf. Goodwin MH 1980; Goodwin 1986; Ruusuvuori 2001). In our example, the relinquishment of the mutual positive facial expression (frame 12) is preceded by mutual withdrawal of gaze (frame 11) and move into a new verbal action.
5. Face seems capable of *extending the temporal boundaries* of the assessment activity. In our example, the smile of one participant adumbrated the assessment activity before the verbal assessment activity was begun (frame 6). The peak of the assessment activity was reached through means of face and prosody (frames 7-9) before the key lexical components of the assessment were delivered (frame 10). The smiles of the participants also maintained their affective involvement in the referent after the verbal assessment had been completed (frame 11). Thus, it appears that the temporal organization of affective involvement, as displayed

---

2 A new spell of affective evaluation follows after a short gap, but the analysis of that is not necessary for the purposes of this paper

Conclusion

Using video recorded data that was analysed through means of conversation analysis, we have in this chapter explored the ways in which facial expression contributes to, and is shaped by, moment-by-moment social interaction. Our point of departure was Bavelas and Chovil's conception of facial expression that focuses on the communicative functions rather than expressive properties of facial displays. We searched to complement their ideas with the methods and research tradition of conversation analysis. In Table two below, we offer a tentative summary of the line of research that this case study might suggest for future work.

Table 2: **Three approaches to facial expression**

	EKMAN ET AL.	CHOVIL & BAVELAS	CA
Key aspect of facial expression	Output of internal psycho-physical state	Communicative resource	Interactional resource
Meaning of face	Key expressions have inherent meanings	Meaning arises from linguistic context	Meaning arises from moment-by-moment interaction process

The difference between the CA-informed approach and the approach of Bavelas & Chovil is in the scale of the analysis. The difference is in the scale of the analysis. It appears that Bavelas and Chovil contextualize facial expressions in "complete" linguistic actions, such as asking questions or giving a personal reaction to what is spoken (see Chovil 1991), whereas our case study, inspired in particular by the earlier work of Goodwin and Goodwin (1987, 1992) sought to contextualize these expressions in the step-by-step unfolding of one particular action, assessment.

The split screen video was a necessary resource for our analysis: without it, the observations reported here would not have been possible. Transcription of the video was a very useful tool during many stages of the analysis. The final analysis and the presentation of the results were greatly aided by framegrab techniques made available in current film editing programs. However, the technology is only one part of the resources that are needed to do video analysis. Our research was informed by the analytical perspective that arises from earlier conversation analytical studies on assessments, from the research tradition of conversation analysis in general, and from the related studies of Bavelas, Chovil, Fridlund and others. This analytical perspective amounts to "mental optics", as it were, which are just as essential as the optics of our video cameras, for observation of social interaction.

References

Atkinson J. M. and J. Heritage (ed.), 1984: *Structures of social action. Studies in conversation analysis.* Cambridge: Cambridge University Press, iv–xvi

Bavelas, J. and N. Chovil, 1997: Faces in Dialogue. In: Russell J.A. and J-M. Fernandez-Dols (ed.) *The Psychology of Facial Expression.* Cambridge: Cambridge University Press, 334–46

Bavelas, J. and N. Chovil, 2000: Visible acts of meaning. An integrated message model of language in face-to-face dialogue. *Journal of Language and Social Psychology* 19:2:163–94

Brown, P. & S. Levinson, 1987: Politeness: Some universals in language usage. Cambridge: Cambridge University Press

Chovil, N., 1991: Discourse-Oriented Facial Displays in Conversation. *Research on Language and Social Interaction* 25: 163–94

Chovil, N., 1997: Facing Others: A Social Communicative Perspective on Facial Displays. In Russell J.A. and J-M. Fernandez-Dols (ed.) *The Psychology of Facial Expression.* Cambridge: Cambridge University Press, 321–33

Darwin, C., 1872: The expression of the emotions in man and animals. London: John Murray

Ekman, P., 1979: About brows: emotional and conversational signals. In: M. von Cranach, K. Foppa, W. Lepenies & D. Ploog (ed.) *Human Ethology.* Cambridge: Cambridge University Press, 169–202

Ekman, P., 2003: *Emotions revealed.* New York: Henry Holt

Ekman, P. & W.V.Friessen, 1978: *The facial action coding system.* Palo Alto, CA: Consulting Psychologists Press

Ekman, P., Sorenson, E.R, W.V. Friesen, 1969: Pan-cultural elements in facial displays of emotion. *Science*, 1964:86-88

Fridlund, A., 1996: 'Facial expressions of emotion' and the delusion of the hermetic self. In R. Harré and W.G. Parrott (ed.) *The emotions. Social, cultural and biological dimensions.* London: Sage, 259–284

Goffman, E., 1955: On face-work: An analysis of ritual elements in social interaction. *Psychiatry: Journal of Interpersonal Relations* 18: 213–31

Goffman, E. 1956. Embarrassment and social organization. *American Journal of Sociology* 62: 264–74

Goodwin, C., 1981: *Conversational Organization: Interaction Between Speakers and Hearers.* New York: Academic Press

Goodwin, C., 1984: Notes on story structure and the organization of participation. In J.M. Atkinson and J. Heritage (ed.) *Structures of social action. Studies in Conversation Analysis.* Cambridge: Cambridge University Press, 225–246

Goodwin, C., 1986: Gesture as a resource for the organization of mutual orientation. *Semiotica* 62(1/2): 29–49

Goodwin, C. and M.H. Goodwin, 1987: Concurrent operations on talk: Notes on the interactive organization of assessments. *IPRA Papers in Pragmatics* 1: 1–54

Goodwin, C. and M.H. Goodwin, 1992: Assessments and the construction of context. In: C. Goodwin & A. Duranti (ed.) *Rethinking context. Language as an interactive phenomenon.* Cambridge: Cambridge University Press, 147–189

Goodwin, M.H., 1980: Processes of mutual monitoring implicated in the production of description sequences. *Sociological Inquiry* 50: 303–317

Heritage, J. 1984. *Garfinkel and ethnomethodology.* Cambridge: Polity

Heritage, J. and G. Raymond, 2005: The terms of agreement: Indexing epistemic authority and subordination in talk-in-interaction. *Social Psychology Quarterly* 68:15–38

Izard, C., 1971: *The face of emotion*. New York: Appleton-Century-Crofts

Kendon, A., 1990. Conducting interaction. Patterns of behavior in focused encounters. Cambridge: Cambridge University Press

Motley, M.T. and C. T. Camden, 1988: Facial expression of emotion: A comparison of posed expressions versus spontaneous expressions in an interpersonal communication setting. *Western Journal of Speech Communication* 52: 1–22

Parinson, B, Fischer, A.H. and Manstead, A.S.R., 2005. *Emotion in social relations. Cultural, group, and interpersonal processes*. New York: Psychology Press

Peräkylä, A., 2004: Conversation analysis. In C. Seale, J. Gubrium, G. Gobo and D. Silverman (ed.) *Qualitative research practice*. London: Sage, 165–179

Pomerantz A., 1984: Agreeing and disagreeing with assessments: some features found in preferred/dispreferred turn shapes. In J.M. Atkinson & J. Heritage (ed.) *Structures of Social Action*. Cambridge: Cambridge University Press, 57–101

Ruusuvuori, J., 2001. Looking means listening: Coordinating displays of engagement in doctor-patient interaction. *Social Science & Medicine* 52: 1093–1108

Schegloff, E.A., 1979: The relevance of repair to syntax-for-conversation. *Syntax and semantics* 12:261–286

Scherer, K.R., 1996: Emotion. In: M. Hewstone, W. Stroebe & G.M. Stephenson (ed.) *Introduction to social psychology*. Oxford: Blackwell

Sorjonen, M.-L., 2001: *Responding in conversation. A study of response particles in Finnish*. Amsterdam: John Benjamins

Monika Wagner-Willi

On the Multidimensional Analysis of Video-Data
Documentary Interpretation of Interaction in Schools[1]

Since the 1980s video-based research has enjoyed an increasing popularity in qualitative social research. This is not only true of sociological research but also for studies in other social science disciplines. Educational science, for example, in particular research into schooling and childhood, uses a video-based approach (see Huhn et al. 2000, Brandt, Krummheuer & Naujok 2001). Despite the broad scope of this method, methodological reflection into video-based research – not only with regard to the specific quality of audiovisual recordings but also with regard to the different ways of interpreting video data – is still in its infancy (see Knoblauch 2000, Wagner-Willi 2001).
In my contribution I will first address some methodological aspects of video analysis and then illustrate the procedural approach of documentary video interpretation using an empirical example taken from my study of schoolchildren's rituals. In conclusion, I will explain the practical uses of this method's multidimensional microanalysis.

Sequential Structure and Simultaneity in Video Data

The current lack of reflection upon video-based research stands in marked contrast to the development of textual interpretative procedures. Since the 1970s they have been consistently elaborated in the course of methodical and methodological reflection – e. g. the narrative interview and narrative analysis created by Fritz Schütze (see 1983, 1987). Up until the present, textual interpretative methods have dominated qualitative research. This predominance can be found in many video-based studies, e. g. in school research, where transcribed verbal communication is *central* to the analysis (see, e. g., Stadler, Benke & Duit 2001).
As Ralf Bohnsack (2003b: 241) makes clear in his critical diagnosis of qualitative methods of picture interpretation, the dominance of textual interpretative procedures relies upon the premise that social reality has to be presented in textual formats in order to gain scientific relevance. The premise is stretched to the extent that the "raw" data must also be in the form of a text, and, indeed, preferably a text created by the subjects of the research themselves. This methodological understanding of scientific knowledge was then drastically taken to be social reality by objective hermeneutics – in the sense that the world is to be understood *as* a text (see Garz & Kraimer 1994).

---

[1] Many thanks to Simon Garner for his great help in translating the text.

Against this background Martina Leber and Ulrich Oevermann (1994: 386) argue, that "the actual sequential structure of all social, psychological and cultural phenomena, objects and events" requires a sequential analysis.

This perspective of social reality as being primarily sequentially structured neglects, however, a further fundamental mode of structuring socio-cultural phenomena, namely, that of simultaneity. This mode is already demonstrable on a textual level, e. g. in transcripts of audio recordings of everyday conversations (see Sacks, Schegloff & Jefferson 1978). In these, notations are used: e. g., to show where verbal utterances overlap each other or to note an expressive activity, such as laughing, that accompanies the words. It is also here, where such audible activities are merely transcribed, that a mode of structuring is discernable, which I would like to term the *interweaving of sequentiality and simultaneity*. Methodologically, that means that a dominant premise of qualitative research – the assumption of a primarily sequential structure of social actions and interactions – must be respectively revised or modified.

The structure of simultaneity varies in its form and intensity depending on the specific situation. In this regard, different levels can be distinguished: (a) the social situation, (b) the interaction, and (c) the actions of individuals.[2] Levels (a) and (b) can merge into one, as, for example, in a therapeutic conversation; however they don't have to. During a school playground break we find the coexistence of a great number of interactions. On the level of interaction (b) we come across bodily, gestural-facial and verbal correlation. The level of individual acting (c) is characterized by bodily-sensual-spatial and verbal coordination. Thus we find simultaneity with regard to coordinated, correlated and coexistant activities. It is based on corporality, materiality, image quality and scenic arrangement – in other words on the *performativity* of social reality (see Wulf, Göhlich & Zirfas 2001).

While the basic model of sequentiality is a successively ordered text, the basic model of simultaneity is a picture. For, as the art historian Max Imdahl (1996: 23) makes clear, it is the "simultaneous structure" that is fundamental to the latter; a "sense-creating contemporaniety".

So in social situations we find a performative process that is characterised by the interweaving of simultaneity and sequentiality. Video is particularly suited to recording this perfomative process. True, this procedure transforms the space into a two dimensional picture, however it retains the iconicity, i. e. the materiality or quality of image, and the simultaneous structure of social situations. A method for analysing video recordings should take account of this particular quality, i.e. it should not only be directed at analysing the sequential but also the simultaneous structure.

---

2 Levels (a) and (b) correspond to Goffman's terms "social situation" and "encounter" (see Goffman 1981).

The Study

In my empirical study of children's rituals in primary school, I was searching for a way to analyse both sequentiality and simultaneity. The procedure was based on the method of documentary interpretation, conceptualized by the sociologist of knowledge Karl Mannheim and developed by Bohnsack. This investigation is embedded in a research project, lead by Christoph Wulf (see Wulf et al. 2001) focussing on rituals in different educational fields and forming part of a bigger interdisciplinary research project (Sonderforschungsbereich), entitled "cultures of performativity" at the Free University Berlin.

The aim of my study was the reconstruction of ritual practises and interaction of 4th to 5th grade schoolchildren, taking place in the classroom during the everyday transition from break to lesson (see Wagner-Willi 2005). These rituals were analysed with regard to their process and their social context of meaning. Thereby, the bodily, material, scenic and, in the sense of Wulf (1998), mimetic shaping of rituals, i.e., their micro-processual performativity was of particular interest.

Metatheoretically, the investigation was referring to Mannheim's (1980) concept of *conjunctive experiential space*. As a fundamental sort of sociality, conjunctive experiential spaces arise where people in the course of similar social experience develop shared forms of acting and shared forms of knowledge. This sort of knowledge is atheoretical and intuitive. Those who belong to the same conjunctive experiential space or (so to speak) cultural milieu *understand* each other *immediately*; they act and interact in *habitual concordance*.

Different from this form of sociality is the *communicative relation*. There, the participants have to *interpret* each other because they don't have a shared basis of experience. We find communicative relations in interaction contexts where people with different conjunctive experience are involved, in particular in institutional settings. While, for example, peer groups at school can be classified as conjunctive experiential spaces, lessons are constituted by a communicative relation context with different institutionalized social roles.

My study was directed towards the *How* of the ritual-interactive forms children show in the transition from break to lesson, a process in which the detachment from the peer group and the assumption of the role-like mode of acting of a schoolchild is expected by the institution. Thereby, the intermediate stage inside the classroom before the lesson starts was of special interest. In the sense of the anthropologist Victor Turner (1969), this intermediate stage can be understood as a *threshold* or *liminal phase*. It seemed to clearly highlight the area of tension between the peer group culture and the institutional order of the school (see Göhlich & Wagner-Willi 2001). Because the focus of the study was to investigate the performativity of rituals, it was appropriate to use a video-based approach.

For the audiovisual recording of the threshold phase between break and lesson in three classes, we used a fixed position for the camera. The camera was positioned so that, as well as the threshold space of the door, a wide field of view of the room was also included. The videotaping was preceded by an explorative phase with participant observation.

Actionism in Classroom

The following analysis centers on scenes from a videotape that was recorded in the classroom of 4th grade schoolchildren, showing a phase in the transition from the first long break to lessons. In the analysis we will focus on two participants: Robert and Roswitha. (Video footage from 18.3.99, 10:26 – 10:32).

Territorial encroachments between Roswitha and Robert
Robert (not wearing his coat) enters the classroom after Andre and Michail. He walks rhythmically, briefly circling his lower arms around each other, to his seat near the door, closely followed by Roswitha (who is wearing her jacket open). As she passes, Roswitha places her hand on his back, pushes his upper body over the desk and presses him onto the desktop. She bends over him and slaps him several times, quickly and hard, on the back. Robert, who in being bent over grasps the thermos flask that is standing on his desk, cries out: "Ah, ah, ah, ah," as Roswitha slaps him. Roswitha straightens up again, thrusts out her chest as she walks, tosses her long hair from side to side and laughs. She turns towards Robert and takes off her jacket. Robert looks at her and holds the bent over pose for a while. Then he straightens up. As she takes off her jacket at her place at the neighbouring desk, Roswitha turns to face Robert again. Robert moves the items on his desk to the side. Then he jumps onto the chair in front of him and draws himself up to his full height. More and more children stream into the classroom. Robert casts his gaze around the classroom as he moves rhythmically again, rolling his hands in small circles around each other, and calls out in a sing song voice: "Ferero Küßchen". Meanwhile Roswitha goes back towards the door again with her jacket in her hand. She approaches Robert and looks at him. Just as she passes his desk, Robert jumps up onto the desktop, then down onto Sirin's (Roswitha's neighbour's) chair, over onto Roswitha's chair, back down onto the floor and runs to the window (on the other side of the room and out of camera view). Roswitha watches Robert's scramble over the desk and chairs and shouts: „Hey". Then she goes to the coat rack and hangs up her jacket. Sirin, who is approaching from the door and taking off her jacket, looks briefly at Robert, bends immediately over her chair and wipes the seat with her hand. Then she finishes taking off her coat and goes to the coat rack.

In the meantime, Roswitha has hung up her coat. (...) While the teacher, followed by Roswitha, steps into the aisle, Robert returns from the window area. When he arrives at Roswitha's seat he skips, supporting himself with a hand on the back of her chair. The teacher walks past Robert. Robert who has moved away from Roswitha's chair, is jostled by Roswitha as she returns. He bangs against Sirin's chair as he tries to support himself on the desktop with his left hand. Roswitha grins broadly. Robert gets up and moves away while Roswitha takes her seat.

(After circa a minute:) Robert turns away from Binol with whom he had been speaking. With one foot on the chair, he leans his upper body over the desk, looks up and calls out loud: "Ferero Küßje, aah".

When Robert, with his dance-like motion, heads for his seat near the door at the beginning of the scene, he is caught up in a pointedly physical interaction by Roswitha. From behind, she bends his upper body over the desk top and slaps him repeatedly on the back. In a mutual interplay with these slaps Robert makes paraverbal noises: "ah ah ah ah", noises that sound joyful rather than upset and that hint at the sexualised meaning of

Image 1: Roswitha slaps Robert on the back

this physical encroachment, an encroachment initiated "from behind" in an "on-top/underneath" position. After Roswitha has finished with Robert, she makes her way to her desk nearby, thrusting out her chest coquettishly, swinging her hair and laughing. Her display gives the impression of being both triumphant and appealing. By provoking intense physical contact in a dominant position, Roswitha has deviated from the traditional gender roles which were most commonly observed in the video recordings. According to these, the offensive initiation of interactions between boys and girls is performed by the male party.

In the continued course of the interaction, Robert reverses the unconventional performance of roles mimetically. At first, with his jump onto his chair, he brings himself into a spatially higher and blatantly territorial position. As at the beginning, he makes a rhythmic dance-like movement again, but this time accompanied by a singing: "Ferero Küßchen" while Roswitha comes towards him. As she passes his desk, he seems to be running away from a further encounter with her. However, his flight includes a provocative territorial encroachment on the two girls' chairs. They show differing reactions: while Sirin immediately turns her attention to cleaning her chair, Roswitha stares at Robert in surprise and expresses displeasure ("Hey"). With his scramble over the desk and chairs Robert intensifies the dramaturgy of the whole scene: the movements become faster and the territorial encroachments more extensive and con-

Image 2: Robert scrambles over the desk and chairs

spicuous. They also include other children, who, as a background foil, highlight the mimetic relationship between Robert and Roswitha.

When Robert returns shortly afterwards, the gestalt of the mutual game with Roswitha is completed. His skipping is accompanied by a renewed territorial encroachment upon Roswitha's chair. Roswitha, who has just got back from the coat rack, then shoves him so that he bangs himself against the desk. She clearly exhibits her enjoyment in doing so with her grin. Roswitha's jostling is a renewed reversal of Robert's territorial encroachment on the chairs. At the same time she makes another physical encroachment. The gestalt of the scene is thus drawn back together both spatially and physically.

Not only a completion of the gestalt but also a sort of epilogue to this reciprocal and interactive entanglement is then offered to the observer: about a minute after it has ended Robert bends his upper body forward over his desk, looks up and says again loudly "Ferero Küßje... aah." Thus he repeats the physical-spatial positioning which Roswitha put him in at the beginning of the scene, and refers – by repeating the brand name of a praline chocolate – to the elements of enjoyment, pleasure, and eroticism that he once again articulates paraverbally as he did during Roswitha's initial encroachment.

The interactive involvement between Roswitha and Robert clearly displays traits of *actionism* in Bohnsack's (2004) sense, that is: a joint spontaneous action; an experimental quest for habitual concordance. These actionist practices present a particular form of dealing with differences in the liminal phase of the transition from break to lesson, and can be described as *conjunctive ritualisation* (Bohnsack 2004). This ritualisation fulfils two functions: 1. the processing of gender differences and 2. the processing of the difference between the rule structure of the peer group and that of lessons.

First this actionism is directed towards the experimental initiation of new relationship structures between the genders. This takes place in a spontaneous game of entanglement with the body and with the space and its inner territorial boundaries. The physical contact and the recurrence and reversal of asymmetrical positioning are just as much elements of this actionist quest as the sexualised gestures, dance movements and utterances.

The liminal phase of the transition from break to lesson is particularly suited to such actionist practices precisely because the conjunctive relationship structure created by the peer group in the break, with its predominantly gender-homogenous alignment (see Thorne 1993, Wagner-Willi 2005: 65ff.), no longer possesses primacy and the communicative disciplinary regulatory structure of the lessons is not yet established. This leads to a highly unstructured situation characterized by simultaneous coexistence and correlation. Here, actionist practices can take place; practices of experimenting with different gender roles, "for fun", spontaneously and without significant risk of ridicule.

Secondly, these actionist practices exhibit a distance-taking from the institutional order with its symbolic and spatial-territorial elements, 'role distance' in Erving Goffman's (1961) sense. The simultaneous execution of the various communicative rituals of getting ready for lessons – for instance hanging up outer clothing on the coat racks and taking one's seat – is dealt with conjunctively. So Roswitha uses the desk top – whose function, in the context of lessons, is for writing on – as the instrument of her physical encroachment on Robert; and by doing so, she simultaneously underlines symbolically that his taking of his seat is a mere compulsory act. Robert, on the other hand, uses the desk and chairs as an assault course and thereby disregards not only their institutional function but also reverses the institutional spatial arrangement of the room – and, on top of that, this is accompanied by an injury to the inner-territorial boundaries of the seating plan. At the same time the institutional ritual order with its micro-ritual sequences is temporarily suspended.

Such actionist practices occur in the social situation of the transition from the habitual structures of the conjunctive experiential space of the peer group, to the institutional communicative sociality of class, whose regulatory structure is distinguished by standardisation and a reduction of bodily-sensual activities. A considerable number of aspects – which Turner has described as *liminal* – unfold here. These include "kicking over of the traces" and experimentation, likewise the game with the symbolic elements of familiarity or the reversal of social positions. Fun, sensuality and pleasure, spontaneity, rhythm and movement are typical performative forms of conjunctive ritualisation in the liminality, ritualisations, that are in a tension with the simultaneously observable rituals of getting ready for lessons.

On the Multidimensionality of Documentary Video-Interpretation

The empirical example demonstrates the multidimensional quality of social reality, a quality which can be grasped by documentary video-interpretation through the dimensions of time and space and the related sequential and simultaneous structure.

As already mentioned, two different social dimensions can be distinguished: on the one hand the *communicative collectivity*, and on the other hand the *conjunctive experiential space*. The communicative context of meaning, as we find it in institutional fields, produces a role-like mode of acting and a generalized, theoretical knowledge, that is abstracted from the different existential backgrounds and milieu-specific experiences of the actors (see Mannheim 1980: 287ff.). In the video clip the communicative dimension is recognizable, where the interactors refer, by their actions, to the institutional order of the school and to their role as schoolchildren.

In contrast to this, conjunctive experiential spaces (e. g., the milieu of a specific peer group) are rooted in biographical commonalities; i. e. in commonalities of socialization and of milieu-specific social experiences. In these experiential spaces we find an immediate, intuitive understanding and habitual concordance among those who belong to them. The everyday conjunctive practices are structured by collective orientation, which is structured by atheoretical, experience-based practical knowledge (see Mannheim 1980, Bohnsack & Nohl 2003, 369f.).

Furthermore, the conjunctive context of meaning itself can be differentiated. Thus it is characterized by an interlocking of different conjunctive dimensions, of different conjunctive experiential spaces. For example in the video clip, the gender dimension is at the centre of the actionist practices. However, following the comparative analysis of interactions of other children in the same class, this dimension is interconnected with the dimension of adolescence. Thus the "little ones", as the bigger children call them, do not show such actionist practices. Rather, they are focused on performing rituals of getting ready for lessons.

Methodologically, the documentary interpretation is founded in an analytic attitude, that turns from the "What" to the "How" of sociocultural phenomenon, and thereby to their performative processes. The What, the immanent meaning of the actions and interactions, is analysed in the first stage of interpretation: the *formulating interpretation* (Bohnsack 2003a). Therefore, the elements of conduct and interaction are described in detail without imputation of motives of acting (i.e. "In-order-to-motives", Schütz 1971: 22ff.). Besides, this stage of interpretation corresponds to the *pre-iconographic description,* the first level of iconology, a method of interpreting works of art, developed by the art-historian Erwin Panofsky (1997: 35f.). The simultaneity is taken into account by describing the physical-spatial organisation and the scenic arrangement of the observed interaction and by analysing simultaneous interactions.[3] The explication of the observed phenomenon has yet to come to such a level of detail that the coordination of the elements of conduct and their embedding in long-term interactive processes, as well as in the social situation itself, don't get lost from sight.

The next stage of interpretation, the *reflecting interpretation*, aims at the conjunctive and communicative dimensions of documentary meaning (Bohnsack 2003a), that is the How of the described social situation, interaction and, if for them relevant, the actions of individuals. Thereby, also the way of handling objects, stylistic props and territories, in other words their symbolism and meaning, is of interest.

A central component of reflecting interpretation is *comparative analysis*, which aims to find homologies as well as contrasts in regard to the conjunctive and communicative

---

3 Due to limitations of space I cannot go into the interactions of other children that took place simultaneously in the video example (see: Wagner-Willi 2005: 300ff.).

dimensions of the observed interactions, according to the principle of *contrast in similarity* ("Kontrast in der Gemeinsamkeit", Bohnsack 2003a: 37). The systematic comparison is effected with regard to the level of the social situation, e. g. in my study the case-external comparison of the video footage of the phase of transition with video footages of lessons. Furthermore the comparison is also made in respect of the level of interaction inside a specific social situation, e. g. the case-internal comparison of video clips of interactions inside the video footage of the phase of transition. In this way it is possible to identify the communicative dimension (of the institution) as well as the different dimensions of conjunctive experiential spaces – peer group culture, gender, adolescence, etc.

As with documentary interpretation in general, video-interpretation, too, pays attention to the dramaturgy and interrelation of the actors by analysing the *organisation* of interaction. The terms of the explication refer to the verbal, bodily, spatial and material aspects, thus to the simultaneous structure of the organisation of interaction. Often its complexity increases through the sequential structure of dramaturgy: e. g. coexistent interactions can increasingly interrelate; individuals can be involved in ongoing interactions etc. Especially dramaturgic climaxes indicate a high intensity of simultaneity. In the case of discourses, Bohnsack (2003a: 86) calls them *focussing metaphors*, in the case of scenic courses of action, Iris Nentwig-Gesemann (2002: 47) terms them *focussing acts*. Focussing acts afford a particular insight into the conjunctive dimensions of habitualized practices.

In conclusion, video analysis offers a way into *multidimensionality*, i.e., in the first place into the multidimensional sequential and simultaneous structure of the microprocessual interactive praxis of social situations. Documentary video-interpretation is focused on analysing both the multidimensional *performative* structure of the observed interactions as well as their different *conjunctive* and *communicative* dimensions.

The methods of text interpretation have achieved a high degree of complexity – up to now at the cost of *neglecting* the simultaneous structure of social situations. A methodologically reflected video-interpretation has the potential to *close* this gap while maintaining the complexity of text-based qualitative research.

References

Bohnsack, R., 2003a: *Rekonstruktive Sozialforschung. Einführung in qualitative Methoden.* (5th edition) Opladen
Bohnsack, R., 2003b: Qualitative Methoden der Bildinterpretation. *Zeitschrift für Erziehungswissenschaft*, 6, 2, 239-256
Bohnsack, R., 2004: Rituale des Aktionismus bei Jugendlichen. In: C. Wulf and J. Zirfas (eds.) *Zur Innovation pädagogischer Rituale. Jugend, Geschlecht und Schule.* (Zeitschrift für Erziehungswissenschaft, 2. Beiheft 2004). Wiesbaden, 81-90
Bohnsack, R. & Nohl, A.-M., 2003: Youth culture as practical innovation. Turkish German youth, 'time out' and the actionisms of breakdance. *European Journal of cultural studies* 6, 3, 366-385

Brandt, B., Krummheuer, G. and Naujok, N., 2001: Zur Methodologie kontextbezogener Theoriebildung im Rahmen von interpretativer Grundschulforschung. In: S. von Aufschnaiter & M. Welzel (eds.) *Nutzung von Videodaten zur Untersuchung von Lehr-Lern-Prozessen. Aktuelle Methoden empirischer pädagogischer Forschung*. Münster, 17-40

Garz, D. & Kraimer, K., (eds.) 1994: *Die Welt als Text. Theorie, Kritik und Praxis der objektiven Hermeneutik*. Frankfurt a. M.

Göhlich, M. & Wagner-Willi, M., 2001: Rituelle Übergänge der Kinder im Schulalltag. Zwischen Peergroups und Unterrichtsgemeinschaft. In: C. Wulf et al.: *Das Soziale als Ritual: Zur performativen Bildung von Gemeinschaften*. Opladen, 119-204

Goffman, E., 1961: *Encounters. Two studies in the sociology of interaction*. Indianapolis

Goffman, E., 1981: *Forms of Talk*. Philadelphia

Huhn, N., Dittricht, G., Dörfler, M. & Schneider, K., 2000: Videografieren als Beobachtungsmethode in der Sozialforschung am Beispiel eines Feldforschungsprojekts zum Konfliktverhalten von Kindern. In: F. Heinzel (ed.) *Methoden der Kindheitsforschung. Ein Überblick über Forschungszugänge zur kindlichen Perspektive*. Weinheim, München, 185-202

Imdahl, M., 1996: *Giotto – Arenafresken. Ikonographie – Ikonologie – Ikonik*. München

Knoblauch, H., 2000: Workplace Studies und Video. Zur Entwicklung der visuellen Ethnographie von Technologie und Arbeit. In: I. Götz und A. Wittel (eds.) *Arbeitskulturen im Umbruch. Zur Ethnographie von Arbeit und Organisation*. Münster, 159-173

Leber, M. and Oevermann, U., 1994: Möglichkeiten der Therapieverlaufs-Analyse in der Objektiven Hermeneutik. Eine exemplarische Analyse der ersten Minuten einer Fokaltherapie aus der Ulmer Textbank ("Der Student"). In: D. Garz and K. Kraimer (eds.) *Die Welt als Text. Theorie, Kritik und Praxis der objektiven Hermeneutik*. Frankfurt a. M., 383-427

Mannheim, K., 1980: *Strukturen des Denkens*. Frankfurt a. M. (orig. 1922-1925, unpublished manuscripts)

Nentwig-Gesemann, I., 2002: Gruppendiskussionen mit Kindern. Die dokumentarische Interpretation von Spielpraxis und Diskursorganisation. *Zeitschrift für Qualitative Bildungs-, Beratungs- und Sozialforschung*, 1, 41-63

Panofsky, E., 1997: *Studien zur Ikonologie. Humanistische Themen in der Kunst der Renaissance*. Köln

Sacks, H., Schegloff, E. A. and Jefferson, G., 1978: A Simplest Systematics for the Organization of Turn Taking for Conversation. In: J. Schenkein (ed.) *Studies in the Organization of Conversational Interaction*. New York, 7-55

Schütz, A., 1971: *Das Problem der sozialen Wirklichkeit. Gesammelte Aufsätze*, vol. 1. Den Haag

Schütze, F., 1983: Biographieforschung und narratives Interview. *Neue Praxis*, 13, 3, 283-293

Schütze, F., 1987: *Das narrative Interview in Interaktionsfeldstudien I*. Studienbrief der Fernuniversität Hagen. Hagen

Stadler, H., Benke, G. and Duit, R., 2001: Gemeinsam oder getrennt? Eine Videostudie zum Verhalten von Mädchen und Buben bei Gruppenarbeiten im Physikunterricht. In: S. von Aufschnaiter & M. Welzel (eds.) *Nutzung von Videodaten zur Untersuchung von Lehr-Lern-Prozessen. Aktuelle Methoden empirischer pädagogischer Forschung*. Münster, 203-218

Thorne, B., 1993: *Gender Play. Girls and Boys in School*. Buckingham

Turner, V., 1969: *The Ritual Process. Structure and Anti-Structure*. New York

Wagner-Willi, M., 2001: Videoanalysen des Schulalltags. Die dokumentarische Interpretation schulischer Übergangsrituale. In: R. Bohnsack & I. Nentwig-Gesemann and A.-M. Nohl. (eds.) *Die dokumentarische Methode und ihre Forschungspraxis*. Opladen, 121-140

Wagner-Willi, M., 2005: *Kinder-Rituale zwischen Vorder- und Hinterbühne. Der Übergang von der Pause zum Unterricht*. Wiesbaden

Wulf, C., 1998: Mimesis in Gesten und Ritualen. *Paragrana. Internationale Zeitschrift für Historische Anthropologie*, 7, 1, 241-263

Wulf, C., Göhlich, M. & Zirfas, J. (eds.), 2001: *Grundlagen des Performativen. Eine Einführung in die Zusammenhänge von Sprache, Macht und Handeln.* Weinheim, München

Wulf, C., Althans, B., Audehm, K., Bausch, C., Göhlich, M., Sting, S., Tervooren, A., Wagner-Willi, M. and Zirfas, J., 2001: *Das Soziale als Ritual: Zur performativen Bildung von Gemeinschaften.* Opladen

Bernt Schnettler

Orchestrating Bullet Lists and Commentaries
A Video Performance Analysis of Computer Supported Presentations

> "Those who present themselves before an audience are said to be 'performers' and to provide a 'performance' – in the peculiar, theatrical sense of the term. Thereby they tacitly claim those platform skills for lack of which an ordinary person thrust upon the stage would flounder hopelessly – an object to light at, embarrassed for, and have massive impatience with. And they tacitly accept judgment in these terms by those who themselves need never be exposed to such appraisal. The clear contrast is to everyday talk..."
>
> (Goffman 1981b: 165f.)

The 'lecture' Goffman analyzed in the text cited above is a specific form of communication: It is a kind of institutionalized performance centred around an orally delivered text, whereby a speaker imparts his views on a certain subject (Goffman 1981b). This centred interaction usually takes place in a public or at least semi-public setting. Lectures are frequently given in academic or political contexts with a certain degree of formality. Although the text seems to be here of crucial importance, Goffman points out that a lecture can not be reduced to the activity of speaking. Instead, the speakers' talk is only one part of a special social situation with a specific configuration. In his view, lectures are social events, comparable to a ritual or a ceremony, somewhere between game and spectacle. Therefore, they are organized by 'auspices' and sometimes supplied with a 'star system'. Goffman's interest lies primarily on working out the specifics of this production format and the different roles of the speaker (as animator, orator and principal). What is of interest here is the fact that presentations are special performances, performances that are *constitutive* for certain institutional contexts: teaching in schools, debates in political parties, lectures in universities and papers given at conferences are at the core of what actually constitutes the shared reality in the respective domains. Consequently, a study of the communicative forms and the performative practices of 'lectures' can be expected to shed some light on how these realities are constructed in and by interaction.

Whereas Goffman could rely on his prodigious faculty to observe what was going on around him, new developments both in technology and methodology provide us (normal gifted social scientists) with a new and extremely powerful instrument for the analysis of action, interaction and social performance. Recent advances in interpretive videoanalysis enable us to study the fine details of such performances and the context they are embedded in. Video is especially apt for capturing and analysing complex social interaction – in particular if it is tied to extensive ethnographic fieldwork and subsequent detailed analysis of the recording collected in 'focussed' ethnographies (Knoblauch 2005).

In the following, I shall give an example of what I call video performance analysis. By this term, I do not refer to the illustrative genre in modern art. Instead, video performance analyses shares widely the methodological principals of other established approaches (represented in the respective articles includes in this book): sequentiality, systematic contrasting, reflexivity, visuality and contextualisation. I specially draw on ethnomethodological video-analysis (Heath 1997, Heath & Hindmarsh 2002, Heath & Luff this volume) and video interaction analysis (Knoblauch 2004). Like any other form of qualitative inquiry, video analysis is without doubt "basically a hermeneutic activity" (Knoblauch this volume: 75). Consequently, videohermeneutics (Raab & Tänzler this volume) provides the necessary complement for an *integrative* interpretation encompassing the various modes of interaction in social situation that take place in and are constructive for a certain culture. There have been video analysis of performances before: public appearances of the Pope (Bergmann, Luckmann & Soeffner 1993), wedding ceremonies (Raab 2002), political speeches (Tänzler 2000) or charismatic religious leaders (Schnettler 2001). These studies explicitly focus on the ritual and symbolic dimension and their constitutive function. In this article, I will apply video performance analysis to another modern ritual, recently called 'presentation'. A presentation is basically what Goffman described as a 'lecture', augmented by the use of modern computer equipment to visualize images on a projection screen. The analysis that follows tries to illuminate some specific 'platform skills' indispensable for the orchestration of simultaneously presented different 'texts' – that is: the orators' speech that goes along with the visually delivered texts and images in such presentations.

Orchestration of computer supported visual presentations

The use of PowerPoint (or other software like Apple Keynote or Star Point) has not only had an enormous impact on public speeches, lectures and the like. It actually has reshaped communication within a whole array of institutions. Today, such computer supported visual presentations are enormously widespread, approximately used 30 million times daily throughout the world (LaPorte, et al. 2002). Within a wide range of contexts, presentations have acquired a fundamental role in formal communication. Frequently, they are employed to transmit some kind of 'knowledge' – or at least something that from a participant's point of view claims to be knowledge. Under this perspective, presentations are paradigmatic for a type of society that in sociological diagnosis has been called "knowledge society" (and, in effect, at least there is a certain temporal proximity in the emergence of the term in social sciences and the proliferation of PowerPoint). A closer look at the actual performance of such presentation, therefore, should contribute to a better understanding of what is at the core of this, as some have claimed, new type of society. Obviously, such a broad socio-diagnostic term is much too big to be captured with the lens of any camera. But what can be observed with video is the actual performance of presentations – a topic which has been completely left out by research thus far, despite of the enormous debate that PowerPoint has raised among critics and defenders.[1]

In general terms, a presentation consists of (1) a speaker – sometimes various – (2) orally delivering a lecture to (3) a co-present audience. The oral communication in situ is accompanied by (4) a series of visual elements like tables, graphs, lists, pictures or even short film sequences that have been designed in advance and are projected simultaneously on screen. Presentation, therefore, takes place in a very complex situation, in which one-sided forms of communication, namely the speaker's talk and the electronically supported visual elements, are intertwined with interactive and face-to-face elements in the co-presence of speaker and audience. Hence, presentations include various layers of communicative activities that are presented at the same time. Therefore, speech, bodily conduct and visualisations on screen have to be orchestrated in a particular way.

By 'orchestration' I mean the interplay between speaker and technological devices which is typical for computer-supported presentations. Such presentations are not constituted only by the speakers' voice or body delivering the lecture. Speakers have other instruments at hand, and their 'platform skills' extends to conducting them properly. The technical devices play an important part. Although we may not think of technology as an autonomous actor (cf. Rammert & Schulz-Schaeffer 2002), like in an orchestra, it is the instruments making the music (some of which may even play their own sound). While music is neither a product of the conductor nor the instruments alone, its overall whole arrangement is *synchronized* by the conductor.

It is of special interest for interaction and communication studies that PowerPoint introduces a new element into speeches: the visualization of text simultaneously delivered with the talk – in a more comfortable, persuading and successful way than could ever be achieved by its technical precursors like overhead transparencies or slide projectors. But despite its importance, there is barely any empirical knowledge about this new communicative form. Although paradigmatic for linking knowledge to visualization, unlike other modern forms of communication (e.g. email, videoconferences etc.), there is astonishingly little research on presentations. The pertinent literature is mainly considered with practical questions such as how to improve them, what visual elements to choose for which purposes, how to avoid slide overload, etc. In addition to this large body of normative, practical guides, there are very few empirical studies, those that exist being mostly concerned with the *effectiveness* of presentations. Their results are more than ambiguous: Comparing psychology undergraduates taught with

---

1 Presentation are blamed for impoverishing communication by visual effects instead of arguments (Nunberg 1999, Clarke 2001) or accused for manipulating our thoughts (Parker 2001). Tufte (2003) even claims presentations responsible for severe errors and catastrophes, including the Columbia disaster or the Gulf war.

classical methods and PowerPoint, Szabo and Hastings found no significant difference in academic achievement between both groups, although they concede "that PowerPoint lecture may benefit recall (or perhaps recognition) from memory" (2000: 187). Rankin and Hoaas (2001) concluded the same for students in economics, whereas Lowry (1999) reports clear improvement and Schultz (1996/1997: 160) "significantly improved level of performance", better evaluations and greater acceptance of the technology. Bartsch & Cobern (2003), on the contrary, even report PowerPoint producing poorer learning results. While these studies mainly draw on standardized instruments like questionnaires and surveys, there is virtually no research on the actual *performance* of presentations in its 'naturally' occurring context (except from Brinkschulte 2004). We do not know how speakers accomplish the task of addressing an audience via a combination of spoken words and computer supported visualizations, what the audience does, how 'knowledge' is transmitted and if this communicative form changes the ways in which knowledge is presented and acquired.

To shed light on these questions, we have been videotaping visual presentations in a variety of different fields over several months, collecting a significant corpus of data. In the analysis that follows I will draw on that corpus. Examining the orchestration of simultaneously delivered visual and oral 'text', I will focus on one typical element of the inner structure of computer supported presentations: bullet lists.

Listing in presentation

Bullet lists figure among the most frequent visual elements in presentation. In this form of visualization, textual elements consisting either of single words or fragments of sentences are organized vertically, sometimes preceded by numbers or iconic elements like hyphens, dots or small pictograms. Obviously, bulleted lists with indented subcategories had already become a common format with the extended use of overhead projectors from the 1970ies onwards. It was the introduction of computer presentation software that facilitated enormously both the preparation and the presentation of such lists. It became easier to add or change items or rearrange their order. Even more important, the computer allows revealing information gradually – a practice that with the overhead slides has to be performed by covering part of the transparency with paper and sliding that paper down as needed, or using overlays to add information gradually. With PowerPoint, bullet lists have become so widespread as to be identified with the genre as a whole.[2] As other studies indicate (cf. Yates & Orlikowski in press: 18), lists are, indeed, the most common form used for most of the slides in computer-

---

2 Main part of the criticism against PowerPoint appoints to the supposed reductionism of bullet list. They are seen as a structural weakness of visual presentations leading to poor decision making (cf. Norvig 2003).

supported visual presentations. Actually, within our corpus, the majority of text-slides show listed items.³

Certainly, lists are used in a broad variety of contexts in daily life: we use shopping-lists or to-do lists as an aid memoir or in order to structure our individual future actions. In technical contexts we know that check-up lists assure correct handling of complex instruments, and accounting lists of numbers are one of the basic techniques for analyzing and organizing data. These listings have clear functions of rationalizing action. PowerPoint lists are a slightly different phenomenon: Unlike the former examples, which are mainly embedded in *individual* action or highly fixed interactive processes, lists used in presentations serve as a visual instrument a speaker may use in addition to his speech. Therefore the critical point to be scrutinized is the simultaneity of the visual appearance with the verbal behaviour of the speaker. The question is: How is the visualization of listed elements coordinated with the speech?

Structure and function of lists in oral communication have been studied extensively by linguist and conversation analysts. As Jefferson (1990) has observed, many lists occur in three part units.⁴ Some idiomatic examples are: "here, there and everywhere", "Peter, Paul and Mary" or "Monday, Tuesday and Thursday". Its simplest form is the triple single, for example: "Das wichtigste is' Kontakte: Kontakte: Kontakte" [*the most important is contacts, contacts, contacts*] (taken from Schnettler 2003: 211), a repetition that may indicate something like muchness or serve to reinforce a statement. Lists can be used as a persuasive rhetorical device. For instance, three-part lists are conventionally treated as strengthening or affirming a broader, overarching position or argument (Hutchby & Wooffitt 1998). Listing is a linguistic resource that also serves other functions in everyday social interaction, like enumerating, giving alternative formulations to approximate an expression or for gradation (as in the first example cited above). Three-part lists are also frequently used to summarize some general class of things. Three parts are enough to indicate that we have more than individual instances on their own but instances standing for something more general. There are lists in oral communication that are closed, whereas open lists end with 'generalized list completers' such as "etcetera" or "that kind of thing". Generalized list completers can take the place of the third item. Frequently, they are acoustically consonant with the prior items. As Selting (2003: 7) has found out, in addition to parallelism in syntax, intonation plays a crucial role for the recognizability of spoken lists in everyday communication. It is the timing and prosody of speech, in particular of accented syllable on the list items for the establishment of a common rhythm that makes listing routinely

---

3 Out of a total of 653 slides analyzed thus far, 171 (out of a total of 238 text-only slides) include bullet lists. The other slides showing combinations of text and images (100) or being image-dominated (250), whereas image-only slides are surprisingly rare (27) in our corpus.

4 Although there might be a preference for even more extensive lists in natural conversation in other cultures, as some examples in Sánchez Ayala (2003: 324, 327) indicate.

recognizable. Sánchez Ayala's (2003) comparative formal analysis of lists in conversations shows that both in Spanish and English the construction has developed a stylized intonation pattern based on the holding of tones by means of lengthening of nuclear syllables, a durable syntactic organization based on parataxis and an almost identical inventory of lexicalized expressions to index the end of a list. Moreover, listing can also serve as an interactional resource (Lerner 1994). Finishing the third part can be perceived as completing a speaker's turn or, in collaborative listings, a short delay after a second item can invite another speaker to take his turn and complete the list. Noticeably, as the examples shown above, items in conversation consist of quite short elements, often composed just of singles word tied together by conjunctions.

These findings, nonetheless, pertain to listing practice in everyday conversations. Therefore, it is convenient to specify the differences of lists in visual presentations: In contrast to listing in oral communication which is a sequentially organized structure shaped by a specific repetitive syntax and prosodic patterns, all items in visualized lists are simultaneously present. Further, we do not really know if the listing practice follows a similar structure, as the speaker orchestrates visually presented signs with spoken comments. In order to distinguish the phenomena in question, I will further refer to the visually presented text as the 'list', whereas the spoken part during the exposition of the corresponding slide will be called the 'commentary'.

Before turning to the examples, we have to distinguish between different types of speakers according to the use they make of the projected images in presentation. *Orators* only use the computer image as a kind of silent, colourful wallpaper in the background. Their commentary on a short four items list may exceed more than a quarter of an hour, without ever turning to or pointing at one of the items that appear on screen. In this case, the audience may recognize the progress of the argumentative (or narrative) sequence, orienting occasionally to the list while listening to the orators, especially when recognizing that a certain utterance matches with some part of what is written on the wall. In the best case, these *keywords* construct a coherent nexus between the two texts. One would be inclined to call this inter-textuality, but the abundance of cases in which there is pure redundancy or even mismatch between the two texts prevent us from that.

Performers do act differently: this type of speaker is making extensive use of and is interacting frequently with both the visualisations on screen and the audience. She or he manipulates, in addition to the manuscript, the laptop or the mouse for quickly switching through the slides and often points to the projection using his hand, a pointing device or his or her whole body in order to mediate between visualization and audience. In general, performers spend less time commenting on a single slide. Consequently, the ratio between list and comment is more equal in the latter, which is elementary to carry out the comparison. Therefore, the analysis restricts to this type.

Let us consider the following example, taken from a small internal information meeting in the custom authorities. Daniel, a specialist, is explaining some novelties concerning the standardization of cereal products in Europe to administration personnel. In the beginning of his speech he gives a brief overview on the market situation and the history of standardization committees in different European countries. At this moment of the speech he proceeds to commentary on the international efforts to harmonize the legal and technical standards of this procedure. Slide 11 (Image 1) shows a title and four fragments of sentences organized in a typical PowerPoint list format. In this case, the title ("Objectives of the CEN/TC") represents the core element to which every listed phrasal fragment is a specification, grammatically connected to the title by elliptical verbal constructions. Transformed into a full sentence, the first point can be unpacked as: 'The (first) objective of CENT/TC is to harmonize national standards', the second as: 'The (second) objective is to create greater involvement of all CEN member countries in standardization work' etc. It is important to note that all listed elements follow a similar grammatical structure: the fragments begin with infinitive verbal constructions that are paralleled as anaphora ("to harmonize…", "to create…", "to develop…", "to improve…"). There are two more characteristics that stand out: Firstly, the text includes the acronyms "CENT/TC" and "CEN". Acronyms are condensed abbreviation including key information central for understanding the meaning of the whole text. They indicate that this information pertains to a very special field. Unlike the other words included in this list, the abbreviations are not part of a commonly understandable lexicon, so that either the speaker will have to uncover their meaning or, in case he will not, we will have to suppose some *special knowledge* that the speaker shares with his audience. Secondly, two other visible elements appear on the slide in addition to the listed items: One is an icon on the left bottom of the slide – a stylized European flag with stars and boldly underlined the word "ZOLL" standing for the German Customs Authority. This icon represents the institution. On the right bottom there are two lines printed in a noticeably smaller letter than the main text. The second line includes the name of the speaker in conjunction with his institutional affiliation, and the line above shows the title and date of the first occasion this presentation was shown originally. Such iconic elements and fixed subtitles, repeated on each slide, are quite common features of computer-supported visual presentations. They have a similar function to what is called 'living columns' in books, which is to orient readers (or in this case: spectators) about the talk they are in and thereby framing the presently visible slide as being part of a larger series. Repeated titles on the top, the bottom or the slides' margins therefore serve as a contextualizing

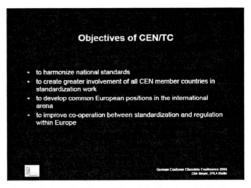

Image 1: A typical PowerPoint slide showing a bullet list

device. However, this contextualizer may not correspond to the actual situation, as in this case: every slide makes reference to the international conference on which Daniel's presentation was originally shown. Such 'misleading' contextualizations also turn out to be common for computer-supported visual presentations being frequently reused by speakers in subsequent talks without updating all of the slides' elements.

Translating visualizations

Certainly, a look at the slide only uncovers the structural aspects of one of the elements that interplay in presentations. Therefore, we will now shift to the commentary. Let us have a look on how this visualization is presented by the speaker. We join the action in the moment when the speaker switches from the previous slide. In extract 1 we can observe how his commentary relates to the visualized list (the arrows indicating the onset of every single listed item):

Extract 1

[... switches to slide 11 ...]
(6.0)

1   Ja, noch einmal die, ↑Ziele dieses Fachausschusses,
    Yes, once again   the   objectives of this expert committee

2   (1.0) ääh, 'nen vorrangiges Ziel is' es zunächst einmal auch
    eh   a prior   aim is   for a start   also

→ 2 die vielen, ↑nationalen Standards,
    the many national standards

3   die in den verschiedenen europäischen Staaten existieren, zu, ↓harmonisieren,
    that in the different   European   countries exist   to harmonize

→ 4 (1.0) und, ääh, 'nen weiteres Ziel is' die stärkere Einbindung,
    and, eh a   another aim is the stronger involvement

5   aller Mitgliedsländer in=die=europäische=Normenarbeit.
    of all member countries in the European work on norms

→ 6 (1.0) ne, es' soll dann weiterhin ein Beitrag geleistet werden,
    no, it shall then further   a contribution be made

7   um die europäischen Positionen auf internationaler Ebene,
    to   the European position   on the international level

8   wie, (eben) bei ISO, der internationalen Organisation für Standardisierung,
    like (precisely) at the ISA, the international organisation for standardization

9   oder auch bei den (Kodex)arbeiten, deutlicher zu formuliern.
    or   also in the works on codex   clearer   to formulate

→ 10 (1.5) ↑und es wird eine enge Zusammenarbeit zwischen Standardisierung
    and   a   tighter cooperation   between standardization

11 und Regulierung angestrebt,
    and regulation   is strived for

→ 12 °'ne,° (1.0) und:äh:, das findet sich dann eben auch wieder, wie ich vorhin sagte,
    well, and   eh that is   found   then just   also again   like I said   before

13 in den Verordnungstexten der E<u>G</u>::, die für uns letztendlich bindend sind=
    in the regulation statuts of the EC, which are for us ultimately obligatory
14 für=unsere=Untersuchungen für=unsere=Gutachten,
    for our   reports   for our   expertises
15 in denen dann=eh Bezug genommen wird auf entsprechende, ↑Standardmethoden,
    in which then eh reference   is made   to corresponding standard methods
16 die also dem jetzigen Stand, von Wissenschaft und Technik, widerspiegeln
    which   the current state   of   science   and technology reflect
(2.0) [... switches to slide 12]

After switching the slide, the speaker takes quite a long pause (6.0). He then restarts with a reference to prior parts of his talk ("Ja, noch einmal..."), and announces what is in effect a vocalization of the title on this slide ("...die, ↑Ziele dieses Fachausschusses", line 1), with a rising intonation on the most important expression. We can easily relate the spoken to the visualized text. Further, we observe that the commentary is not a literal copy of the list, but a transformation of the visualised text into verbal utterance. There are striking differences between both: Whereas the text on the slide is written in English, the speaker translates it in his verbal articulation into German. And he also 'translates', although in a different way, the meaning of the acronym to his audience: The abbreviation "CEN/TC" is spoken out as "this expert committee" and thereby identified as something the audience already knows of. The indexical term relates obviously to their common shared knowledge, so that the speaker is not obliged to further comment on its meaning. And, finally and most important, he 'translates' also syntactically: Whereas the listed items are formulated as (fragments of) final main clauses, the spoken commentary shows a more complex syntactical pattern including inserted subordinated clauses.

In line 2, after a very short pause accompanied by an interjection tag ("ehm") the speaker immediately proceeds to comment on the first item of the list. In articulating that first point, the spoken differs noticeably from the written text: Observe that he explicitly stresses the priority of this first point ("...a prior aim..."); a characteristic that may be expressed in the written text only by its very position on top of the list. In addition, in what he speaks aloud he conveys additional information on this item by specifying that the harmonization of standards is necessary because of the many existing varieties and that this refers to the area of the European countries – both aspects not included in this first item on the slide. Adding of details is a recurrent event, occurring several times within this sequence. The broadest extension is the one given in line 12-16, including aspects which are not present in the visualized text at all.

Throughout the whole commentary, we see these slight variations between what is written and what is said as a recurrent characteristic. In addition, the transcript reveals that the spoken text parallels beautifully the structure of the visualized list: the speaker puts into words every four items, and he verbalizes them in the same order as they appear in the projection. Further, all enunciations are organized in complete sentences. Moreover, the verbalization of each item begins with a slight pause followed by an interjection tag ("...äh, 'nen...", line 2; "und, ääh, nen...", line 4, etc.). Interjections tags (Sanchez Ayala 2003: 339 calls them delay devices) are utterances that mark verbally the separation between the elements of the spoken list and, at the same time, function as continuers linking the former element to the subsequent one. Being a monologue, this speech does not contain turns at talk in a strict sense. During the pause, no one from the audience takes his turn. However, these markers can be identified as operating as a kind of turn that the speaker is giving to himself in changing the footing (Goffman 1981a) from a reader to a commentator of the visualized text. In addition, every spoken item is enclosed in a similar prosodic contour, beginning with a low onset followed by rising intonation and falling to low at the end, similar to the findings of Selting (2003: 58) who suggests that closed lists are often formulated with single sentences and very often show successively downstepped pitch peaks for each item.

In sum, there are clear features of the spoken text that parallel the listing structure of the visualization. Nevertheless, the commentary is not a simple copy of the list on the slide. Therefore, we could hardly conclude the presentation is being directed by the technology or that an 'in-built cognitive' structure of the software imposes itself here. To the contrary, as we can observe, the speaker formulates whole sentences and composes a comprehensive text, quite different from the listed visualized text which consists only of syntactical fragments. Although it parallels the item structure, the structure of the orally delivered text has its own and differing characteristics. Before drawing conclusion on the weak basis of text comparison only, we should, therefore, shift our attention to the speakers' performance; that is the way in which the words are augmented, supported and enacted by bodily conduct, and, especially, gesture and mimic. In order to unveil this specific orchestration, we have to turn to the video data. The performance analysis that follows does not only take advantage of the whole potential of video data. It also tries to accomplish an analysis that surmounts the shortcomings of overspecialized and atomized approaches that cut the data down to slices. We will look at the video considering a somewhat broader problem not only relevant for listing practices but PowerPoint presentations in general. There is a common problem in computer-supported presentations: The equipment – i.e. laptop, beamer and projection screen – is not only a resource for the speaker in order to illustrate his argument. The technical device itself constitutes an additional focus of attention, both for speaker and audience. This may cause the problem of competing foci of attention, foci that may prove difficult to reconcile – as Heath & vom Lehn (2004: 59) observe with respect to a comparable arrangement – and that distract audience and speaker.

Conducting attention

The following sequence shows the beginning of the unit. Daniel stands in front of his audience behind a lectern whereon his manuscript and a mouse to operate the computer lie. After finishing reading the last sentence referring to the preceding slide, there is a long gap in his speech (6.0).

--(6.0)--ja, noch einmal

During this pause, the speaker first looks up from his desk, and then shifts his gaze to the projection wall (image 2), simultaneously turning over the pages of his manuscript. Subsequently, he presses the button on the mouse (image 3), then looks a second time to the screen (image 4) and only after that restarts speaking, facing his audience (image 5). These movements circumscribe the speakers' radius of action and the three different points of attention he is orchestrating while delivering his speech: first, the text of his manuscript, exclusively accessible to him as the speaker, second, the visualization on screen, including text and images both visible to him and to the audience, and, third, the audience itself as co-present persons to which the speaker's talk is addressed. This remarkably complex ecology, further complicated by the several technical devices (mouse, laptop, beamer) that the speakers has to monitor permanently in order to assure proper working, creates a very special situation, different to the one of a classical orator addressing the audience only. This environment produces several competing foci of attention, to which the audience's attention may be drawn. Some of these foci are on the 'front stage' (like the speaker and the screen), whereas some are, at least intended to be, 'back stage', that is hidden to the audience or at the margins of their awareness, like the manuscript (that may have been seen, but generally will not have been read by spectators), or the technical equipment. In the situation where everything is working properly, this arrangement alone implies a quite complex task to manage, leaving aside those (typical) moments when for some reasons of technical breakdown or malfunctioning (of laptop, beamer, mouse or some other device), attention is unintendedly distracted to some aspect that puts itself in the foreground although it should be operating hidden in the background. Hence, what we may call 'conducting attention' is a common problem in computer-supported presentations. As we already noticed before, the speakers' structured talk (e.g. parallelising verbally the visualizations) may be of some guidance for the audience. In addition, as we observe in the following fragment, speakers make use of their gaze, arms and posture in order to conduct the audience through the multi-sensual jungle of a PowerPoint presentation by guiding on a moment by moment basis the attention of the audience.

Consider how Daniel orchestrates bodily conduct and speech in order to conduct the audience's attention. There is a recurrent sequential pattern initiating every single item: First, the speaker looks to his manuscript lying in front of him on the desk, then he turns to the projection, and finally shifts his body to the audience.

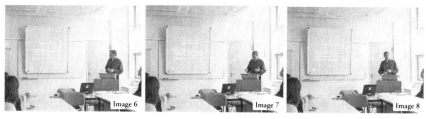

(1.0) und, ääh, 'nen	weiteres Ziel is' die	stärkere Einbindung,
and, eh a	*another aim is the*	*stronger involvement*

Images 6 to 8 show the steps of the typical unfolding of this sequence: First, Daniel is turning his head to the projection (6), then his look goes back down to his manuscript while emphasizing the item's main point with a gesture (7) and subsequently turning his gaze to the audience (8). A similar orchestration is presented for every single item on the list. In coordinating his body shifts, speech, gesture and gaze in this particular way, he not only constructs the item as a distinguishable unit within the list. This repeated configuration also serves to conduct the audience's attention – a fact that can be observed clearly in the person on the right margin, who raises his head in the direction of the screen at the beginning of this sequence, then slightly moving it to the speaker and finally withdrawing it completely towards the end (starting on: ..."aller Mitgliedsländer...", line 5.)

This last observation at least indicates that, although public speeches, lectures presentation and the like have been considered largely as a unilateral communicative situation, we can certainly analyze them under a perspective of interaction. Without any doubt, the degree of interaction may vary to some extent according to spatial circumstances, the number of attendees, the grade of formality etc. Equally, the situation is framed beforehand as asymmetrical. The licence of speaker and hearers do differ quite considerably, as do their participation rights in speech. Nevertheless, as this short extract demonstrates, analyzing this communicative situation in terms of performance unveils the patterns that operate within the presentation as a communicative form that is not restricted only to verbal behaviour. Certainly, the orchestration of visual conduct, body movement and speech only becomes accessible to scrutiny by detailed video analysis.

Conclusion: Performing items in presentation

In this article, I have tried to show how video data can be examined in their synchronous dimension based on methodological principal deriving from ethnomethodological videoanalysis, genre analysis and videohermeneutics. These approaches use preferably naturally occurring data of social situations and subject it to a meticulous sequential analysis that reveals how participants socially organise their actions and activities. The analysis revealed some structural aspects of the inner organization of computer-supported presentation. I described two of the speakers' activities by which he orchestrates his performance: 'translating' and 'conducting attention'. The performance of list items exposed on screen shows some clear correspondence to structural features found by linguists in oral lists, i.e. parallelism in syntax and the role of pauses and intonation which shape the production of items. But in contrast to most of the instances reported in the literature, the listing commentary differs notably in length. Whereas items in spoken lists are often just composed of a single word or short units tied together with conjunctions, comments to visually presented list are usually more extensive utterances.

As central as they may be, items and comments are obviously only one element of what constitutes the communicative genre of computer supported presentations. This form of communication is embedded in a wider context. Therefore, the analysis takes into consideration the ways in which single elements, that are talk, visual conduct and visualizations, are being coordinated by the speaker. It is this special *orchestration* that constitutes the core of computer-supported presentations. As the examples show, the speaker is an *active* participant, accomplishing the complex task of orchestrating speech, bodily conduct, and technological devices in order to deliver his presentation to an audience.

Surely, further details of such presentations have to be examined. But if we ask for a comprehensive interpretation, I would dare to suggest that 'translating' and 'conducting attention' serves a specific purpose, irreducible to a plainly functional aspect. The speaker performs ceremoniously. He is "thrust upon the stage", a stage that confronts him with technical devices only partly domesticable, with competing foci of attention distracting the audience's concentration from him as the central figure. But, although exposed to this situation, he does not "flounder hopelessly". Instead, he manages to re-establish himself as the master of ceremony who is dominating this intricate situation. Thus, we could imagine that translating and conducting attention are elements of a special modern ritual,[5] are forms of presentation oriented to order social behaviour and establish a common world view. It is part of an 'order of rituals' (Soeffner 1996) that re-establishes the individual in the centre of the spotlight, despite all technical force of powerful visualizations.

Acknowledgements

I would like to thank those who generously provided us with access for field research and gave permission to record their visual presentations. This article is based on a paper presented at the ESA Conference in Torun, Poland in September 2005. I am very grateful for valuable comments and suggestions from participants at the confer-

---

5 In a similar vein, Brooks (2004) studies the ritual dimension of presentations.

ence and especially to Hubert Knoblauch and Felix Degenhard, Anika König, Marion Mackert, Sabine Petschke, Frederik Pötzsch, and René Tuma for their support with materials discussed here. I am indebted to Eric Laurier for the English correction. The research project of which this paper is part is funded by the German Research Foundation (DFG) and aims at the reconstruction of the communicative form of computer supported visual presentations. Details of the project can be found on the website: www.praesentationen.tu-berlin.de.

References

Bartsch, R. A. and K. M. Cobern 2003: Effectiveness of PowerPoint presentations in lectures. *Computers & Education*, 41, 1: 77-86

Bergmann, J., T. Luckmann and H.-G. Soeffner, 1993: Erscheinungsformen von Charisma - Zwei Päpste. In: W. Gebhardt, A. Zingerle and M. N. Ebertz (ed.) *Charisma - Theorie, Religion, Politik*. Berlin/New York: 121-155

Brinkschulte, M. 2004: Aspects of influences of teachers' speaking caused by the use of new technologies. A contrastive analysis of different mediated lectures. *unpublished paper, University of Muenster*

Brooks, J., 2004: *Presentations as Rites: Co-presence and Visible Images for Organizing Memory Collectively*. Unpublished Doctoral Dissertation, University of Michigan: Ann Arbor, MI:

Clarke, D. S. 2001: What's the Point? - PowerPoint reduces conversation to simpleminded bullet points. To get your group talking again, try giving one-way presentations the boot. *CIO*, 4, 46-49

Goffman, E., 1981a: Footing. In: (ed.) *Forms of Talk*. Philadelphia: University of Pennsylvania Press, 124-157

Goffman, E., 1981b: The Lecture. In: (ed.) *Forms of Talk*. Philadelphia: University of Pennsylvania Press, 160-196

Heath, C., 1997: The Analysis of Activities in Face to Face Interaction Using Video. In: D. Silverman (ed.) *Qualitative Research. Theory, Method, and Practice*. London: Sage, 183-200

Heath, C. and J. Hindmarsh, 2002: Analysing Interaction: Video, Ethnography and Situated Conduct. In: M. Tim (ed.) *Qualitative Research in Action*. London: Sage, 99-121

Heath, C. and P. Luff this volume: Video Analysis and Organisational Practice.

Heath, C. and D. vom Lehn 2004: Configuring Reception. (Dis-)Regarding the 'Spectator' in Museums and Galleries. *Theory, Culture & Society*, 21, 6: 43-65

Hutchby, I. and R. Wooffitt, 1998: *Conversation Analysis*. Oxford: Blackwell

Jefferson, G., 1990: List construction as a task and resource. In: G. Psathas (ed.) *Interaction Competence*. Lanham, MD: University Press of America, 63-92

Knoblauch, H. 2004: Die Video-Interaktions-Analyse. *sozialer sinn*, 1, 123-138

Knoblauch, H. 2005: Focused Ethnography. *Forum Qualitative Sozialforschung / Forum: Qualitative Social Research [Online Journal]*, 6, 3: Art 44, Available at: http://www.qualitative-research.net/fqs-texte/3-05/05-3-44-e.htm

Knoblauch, H. this volume: Videography. Focused Ethnography and Video Analysis.

LaPorte, R. E., F. Linkov, T. Villasenor, F. Sauer, G. C., M. Lovelekar, E. Shubnikov. and A. Sekikwa 2002: Papyrus to PowerPoint: Metamorphosis of scientific communication. *British Medical Journal*, 325, 1478-1481

Lerner, G. H. 1994: Responsive List Construction: A Conversational Resource for Accomplishing Multifaceted Social Action. Journal of language and social psychology, 13, 1: 20-33

Norvig, P. 2003: PowerPoint: shot with its own bullets. The lancet (London), 362, 9381: 343-344

Nunberg, G. 1999: The Trouble with PowerPoint - The slide presentation is costing us some useful communication tools, like verbs. Fortune, 140, 330-333

Parker, I. I. 2001: Absolute PowerPoint - The software that tells you what to think. The New Yorker, 28.05., 76-87

Raab, J. 2002: 'Der schönste Tag des Lebens' und seine Überhöhung in einem eigenwilligen Medium. Videoanalyse und sozialwissenschaftliche Hermeneutik am Beispiel eines professionellen Hochzeitsvideofilms. sozialer sinn, 3, 469-495

Raab, J. and D. Tänzler, this volume: Video-Hermeneutics. In: H. Knoblauch, B. Schnettler, J. Raab and H.-G. Soeffner (ed.) Video Analysis. Methodology and Methods. Wien, Berlin: Lang,

Rammert, W. and I. Schulz-Schaeffer, 2002: Technik und Handeln. Wenn soziales Handeln sich auf menschliches Verhalten und technische Abläufe verteilt. In: W. Rammert and I. Schulz-Schaeffer (ed.) Können Maschinen denken? Soziologische Beiträge zum Verhältnis von Mensch und Technik. Frankfurt am Main: Campus, 11-64

Rankin, E. L. and D. J. Hoaas 2001: The Use of PowerPoint and Student Performance. Atlantic economic journal, 29, 1: 113

Sánchez Ayala, I. 2003: Constructions as resource for interaction: lists in English and Spanish conversation. Discourse Studies, 5, 3: 323-349

Schnettler, B. 2001: Vision und Performanz. Zur soziolinguistischen Gattungsanalyse fokussierter ethnographischer Daten. sozialer sinn. Zeitschrift für hermeneutische Sozialforschung, 1, 143-163

Schnettler, B., 2003: Sociability. Reconstructing the Ethnotheory of Co-operation. In: A. P. Müller and A. Kieser (ed.) Communication in Organizations. Structures and Practices. Frankfurt a. M.: Lang, 201-218

Schultz, W. C. 1996/1997: Animation with PowerPoint: A Fog Cutter. Journal of Educational Technology Systems, 25, 2: 141-160

Selting, M. 2003: Lists as embedded structures and the prosody of list construction as an interactional resource. InLiSt.Interactive and Linguistic Structures, 35, 1-65

Soeffner, H.-G., 1996: The Order of Rituals. The Interpretation of Everyday Life. New Brunswick: Transaction

Szabo, A. and N. Hastings 2000: Using IT in the undergraduate classroom: should we replace the blackboard with PowerPoint. Computers & Education, 35, 175-187

Tänzler, D. 2000: Das ungewohnte Medium. Hitler und Roosevelt im Film. sozialer sinn. Zeitschrift für hermeneutische Sozialforschung, 1, 93-120

Tufte, E. R., 2003: The Cognitive Stile of PowerPoint. Cheshire, Connecticut: Graphics Press

Yates, J. and W. Orlikowski, in press: The PowerPoint Presentation and its corollaries: How genres shape communicative action in organizations. In: M. Zachry and C. Thralls (ed.) The Cultural Turn: Communicative Practices in Workplaces and the Professions. Amityville: Baywood

Practices of Video Analysis

Elisabeth Mohn
Permanent Work on Gazes
Video Ethnography as an Alternative Methodology

Of all qualitative methods of cultural and social sciences, ethnography[1] is certainly the one that most radically counts on the presence of the researcher. Observations and conversations, encounters and experiences become pertinent sources of an ethnographic approach. Thereby, the ethnographer is not only present and visible in the field, but also remains so in the data collected and in the scientific results. Here, we are dealing with a research genre in which a methodological paradox that proves to be productive replaces the clear division between data collection and interpretation. Neither the field nor the researcher can achieve its individual thick description without the other.

Ethnographic description is linked to the researching gazes which, in turn, are connected with what can be viewed in the field. Discovering/inventing and also completely designing such gaze-entanglements characterizes the creativity and attractiveness of the ethnographic process of knowledge accumulation. In this regard, Video Ethnography indeed turns out to be an ideal procedure to enable one materially to draft, design, and reflect processes of focusing while filming and editing.

A methodology of permanent work on gazes offers the social sciences a dimension of video-analytical work hardly used up to now: the possibility of using focused audiovisual presentations to make social phenomena in the context of possible interpretative patterns sensorially visible.

For this volume, the idea of "linking"[2] video sequences with the text emerged. The three video examples selected deal with gazes into the camera which become data, with audiovisual field-notes which end up in film presentations, and with editing as an

---

1 On the concept of ethnography, see Griesecke (1999), who develops a "productive fictionality in ethnographic research," as well as Amann and Hirschauer (1997), who formulate an ethnographic challenge of empirical research in Sociology.
2 This text is the written revision of a lecture originally held in the form of an audiovisual presentation (Mohn 2004, Video Analysis Conference). With password and title of the example you can see them on http://www.tu-berlin.de/fb7/ifs/soziologie/AllgSoz/publikationen.htm. The video examples are from the project "Youth Culture in the Classroom" (2001-2005), German Research Foundation (DFG). Georg Breidenstein (University Halle-Wittenberg, Zentrum für Schulforschung und Fragen der Lehrerbildung) decided to try out a combination of ethnographic writing and filming in his research team. He engaged a Visual Sociologist (Klaus Amann) and a Visual Anthropologist (Elisabeth Mohn) in order to work on the audiovisual part of the project and mainly to focus on the aspects of bodies (see Video-DVD "Lernkörper", Mohn and Amann, forthcoming 2005).

ethnographic experience. In this way, I hope to focus our attention on the potentials of video-ethnographic practice and its methodological prerequisites.

Seeing and Being Seen

The following examples are from the project "Youth Culture in the Classroom" (2001-2005), German Research Foundation (DFG). Therefore the field I am referring to is the classroom and the entanglements between youth culture and the demands of school. First of all, when you enter the classroom with your camera, you have to find a good position: the window behind you, because of the light, and the young people's faces in front of you, because of sight-lines. Field and medium offer me possible positions in the room and exclude others. When I observe students in class, they are also watching me. Using a camera and determining its position because of the pictures to be produced makes research conspicuous. You can only film when the participants "play along" and interactively deal with the research situation. Students can use the public attention of research, let the filming ethnographer do as he or she pleases or instead direct and guide his or her gazes. Advocates of the "natural situation documentation" may shudder at this point; however, the forms of interaction settle down in the course of entire school days. Direct exchange of glances alternate with phases of allowing insight, in which the fact of observing itself is not a theme. The idea of a "natural situation" and its "natural video data" is connected with the desire for the absence of the researcher in the situation researched and in the data collected. But this is not how ethnography works, since it benefits precisely from this co-presence in the field (cf. Hirschauer and Amann 1997) of the viewer and the viewed and from the interaction between them.

Ethnographic research situations are situations broadened by the ethnographers, and this is what is "quite naturally" revealed in the data collected. Ethnographic research has no problem including forms of data in which the ethnographer is involved in the event being researched; for, what the field is all about is also revealed precisely in moments of such direct encounters. This was demonstrated in an exemplary manner by the anthropologist and filmmaker Barbara Keifenheim in her film

Video Link 1: Gazes into the Camera as Data

Naua Huni (1984). She uses her alien status as a white woman and filmmaker, shows the Cashinahua Indians film images of the industrialized Ruhr region, and thus manages to learn how the Cashinahua see and portray their own culture in confrontation with Whites and their "film drug", which they compare with their own drug experiences.

It all comes down to reflecting on the possible forms of presence in the field. I can easily assume the role of someone interested in joining the lessons. What does this say about school? When do the students start playing with me? What kind of data are the open gazes into the camera? What do I learn about this field when I analyze the disturbance I evoked?

Facing the camera, the students played hide and seek with me. What they did seemed similar to their every day practices in front of their teachers. They used the camera to produce their own little shows or just to interact with me. In one situation, the camera had an influence on a conflict between a teacher and his student, revealing a power context at school. Gazes into the camera reflect important aspects of the field and provide supplementary indications about the web of relationships in which Video Ethnography develops.

Observation and Camerawork

Ethnographic observations are not neutral documents, even if they may employ a documentary rhetoric in their notation. They are produced in the field situation and have an author. Working with notes on observations is different from an "informant ethnography", which handles its data as "hearsay", mainly using conversations and interviews as data. In terms of their data character, observation notes, whether written or filmed, are process-products of continuing work on meaningful viewing and showing. Writing ethnographers would call it work on the "linguistification of the taciturnity of the social" (cf. Hirschauer 2001). When watching and filming, however, the problem of visualizing, rather than verbalizing, meaning emerges. One has to decide what and how to frame with the camera. Designing the moving image articulates the focus of an observation. The camera is used as a "Caméra Stylo" (a picture-pen), which obviously differs from the concept of "taping or recording a situation".

Very much like notebook ethnography, Video Ethnography produces initial formulations, in this case in the form of video sequences embodying focuses of view to be followed up later. Such video notes, audiovisual rather than written field notes, correspond to aspects of the situation and to the ethnographer's sensitivities and selectivity. Their production can be described as a gaze guided while looking for gazes. The methodological paradox typical of ethnography here assumes the form of a simultaneous documentation and visualization in which not only everyday and discipline-specific knowledge, but also professional lack of knowledge with regard to the ethnographic field mutually inspire each other. This contradicts the idea of the video camera as a "microscope of interaction" inasmuch as video sequences here less assume the role of a situation document and are rather identified with the camera-ethnographer's gaze-seeking.

By placing camera shots in the context of an open and seeking production of pictures that nonetheless aims at meaning, focused video sequences emerge whose pictorial information is accessible for reception. With this, then, ethnographic processes of learning, interpreting, understanding, and formulating can be further developed and – somewhat of a novelty for social sciences' usage of video – even audiovisually presented.³ Due to the prevailing rejection of camera angles and editing in sociological video usage, audiovisual presentation and publication of results has hardly been practiced up to now. The possibility of doing so depends on the methodological framework of research. If the camera is used in terms of working on viewing and showing practices, then audiovisual research can just as easily lead to the genre of filmmaking as ethnographic writing leads to the literary genre.

Video Link 2: Audiovisual Field Notes in a Filmic Presentation

From highly selective video sequences maintaining no claim to complete documentation of a situation, focused edited sequences can ultimately emerge which are, for example, able to uncover something about the practices and problems of spending time in school and to present it in a compact interpretative manner. Video Link 2 provides an extreme example of selective camera work. By deciding when filming and editing to focus on the hands of students who raised them to no avail, one aspect of the educational process is documented and simultaneously produced as an observable phenomenon through visualization. In the air of the classroom, the students' raised hands tell about spending time in school. This Video Link is a quote from the video "Stundenweise Schulzeit" [Hours of School Time] (Mohn 2005) from the DVD "Lernkörper" [Learning Body/ Bodies] (Mohn und Amann, forthcoming 2005). "Stundenweise Schulzeit" deals with seven class periods at a comprehensive school and seven class periods at a college-preparatory school. Within 35 minutes each, the camera does not focus on the teachers, but on the "learning bodies" and ignores "the lesson" to focus instead on the complexity of the educational situations, whose "material" is the class period, school time itself. Each of the 14 segments introduces in its

---

3 Since the 1970s, anthropology-ethnology has experienced a regular boom in Visual Anthropology, provoked by new audiovisual recording devices, i.e. lightweight synchronous sound cameras, with fieldwork and film production working hand in hand. In sociology, on the other hand, new technology was placed in the service of conversation-analytical strategies investigating everyday practices on the basis of so-called natural data from natural situations. For this reason, Visual Sociology has for decades abstained from the potential of film portrayals and instead dealt with photography in research processes.

own way various atmospheric accents and micro-themes of the educational everyday world of young students. For presentation of individual class period portraits, the accompanying text provides indices. This part of the DVD methodically demonstrates ethnographic work with the observing camera and film editing.

Selectivity is what makes observations dealing with video material possible. The video editing sequence mentioned above is composed of audiovisual field notes stemming from a second visit to the field. In the sense of circular research, increasingly focused views and pointed research questions emerge from the processing of initial observation notes and then, in application, establish the audiovisual quality of Video Ethnography.

Edited Views and Materials

If Clifford Geertz recommends beginning field research with the question "What the hell is going on here?", then the question "What the hell can be seen here?" is suitable for opening an ethnographic visualization workshop. With the camera, the ethnographer's views were audio visually formatted. On the other hand, the audiovisual "formulation" undergoes intensive work at the digital video editing desk. Video images, with their nonverbal character, are superb in providing the desired attitude of "not yet, not too quickly knowing" towards the meaning-structures in the field.

A team can view the material together, and this provides room and occasion for the verbal in research. The talking and questioning that the video material provokes make explicit the images' information content, and at the same time develop possible focuses for further meaningful processing. In a way, material and research teams focus themselves simultaneously (cf. Fleck 1983).

Since the conception of a natural situation document is of no use in ethnography, there are no processing taboos in refashioning material with the status of audiovisual notes. So why shouldn't we be allowed to revise them? It is not the untouched, unedited document, but the latent production of meaning structures begun in filming which now become the explicit criteria for examining and editing the material. The workshop nature of this phase of research consist of first exploring what still hidden possible interpretations slumber in the material and the viewing thereof without already thinking about a film cut or other audiovisual presentations of results. Editing can be used as a focusing device and interpretative tool in the ethnographic research process.

Audiovisual material is potentially overly complex and requires deliberate reduction to selected perspectives and aspects in order to achieve any interesting observations at all. If sufficient questions have been raised and interests formulated, the material can be dismantled according to the criteria of focus selected, experimentally arranged in different ways, and observed. This process holds potential for discovery and learning.

It is as though we were using paper, pencil, and eraser when we start selecting and defining this sequence instead of another one. We try something, test an idea or a supposition, search for words on the basis of the images and bring in terminology and structure until it becomes clear what indeed is to be shown, said, or written about the phenomenon in question.

The technical procedure of cutting proves to be highly interwoven with the establishment of interpretative frameworks. The definition of a video sequence is neither completely given by the material nor by the filmed situation. Cut during a break in speaking? Or cut after the break in speaking in order to be able to watch the pause? Only the way students gaze while taking a test, or also their heads bent over their papers? And only indicated, or shown in full length? Does this sequence belong in the section on "boredom", or does it show something completely different? Do more differentiated terms force their way into the increasingly inter-medial performance? Also experiences with temporal relations between movements and noises, gestures and words accompany the exploration of the material and train a feeling for the microdimensions of social interaction.

The study of the sequentiality of social practices observed with the camera – here we again face the methodological paradox – only becomes possible in the framework of defined sequences by the ethnographic authors. In short, no observation can be achieved without a gaze.

In audiovisual research, characteristics of scientific cognitive processes materialize cut by cut, become palpable, graspable. Thereby, the production of findings is productively forced and becomes transparent. It becomes accessible for reflection since the audiovisual attempts at formulation become interpreting documents of social practice and are themselves a document of that interpretation.

Participants in one of my workshops on "Focusing Editing" constructed an observation arrangement according to which only those scenes were selected in which students were entering the classroom. For a time, I had rejected these scenes as uninteresting. Now they were picked out, reworked in slow motion, put into a film sequence, and presented without sound, which permitted a unique observation. The expressions on the faces seemed to match perfectly the impression of a funeral procession, an impression produced by means of the distancing method of slow motion. In another case, however, slow motion was a completely unsuitable form of visualization. The indeed shimmering glance of a girl with eyes darting back and forth lost its character in slow motion and thus eliminated further possible observations. Often, using still photos can help us along in interpretation. In a dialogue procedure of questioning and examining, designing a gaze and attempting a visualization, observation and formulation, ethnographic research moves through methodical and methodological shifts in register.[4]

The aim of editing experiments is to raise better questions and develop from them deeper, denser descriptions, whether audiovisual or linguistic/textual. In this way, the

---

[4] Varieties of documenting and methodological register shifts in the ethnographic research process are thoroughly examined in Mohn (2002).

video material can ultimately be cut in an analytically intensifying manner, or, in the next field visit, the camera work can be conducted such that the interpretative frameworks that have been worked out and the chosen camera frames mutually serve each other.

Two years ago, while dealing with the video-footage from first ethnographic observations in the field of school research, I noticed that walking through the classroom is somehow fascinating. Back in the field (2004), I had the opportunity explicitly to focus on these movements with the camera. Video Link 3 is a quote from the video-analytical sequence "Taktik" [Tactic] (Mohn 2005), from the DVD "Lernkörper" (*op. cit.*). As theoretical framework, reference is made to Michel De Certeau (1988). He speaks of tactical practices by means of which consumers become producers in their everyday actions.

In "Taktik", we see students refashioning school discipline in the most diverse ways. A walk through the classroom to the book table becomes a stroll; returning to their desk, a student smashes the book onto a neighbor's desk to make contact with him/her; etc. In sequencing and examining, cutting and ordering the material, the impression arose that the way students coordinated the shift between getting up and sitting down during this "individual study" period created a collective perpetual-motion machine. Whether this video sequence is already able to make visible

Video Link 3: Editing as Ethnographic Experience[6]

"the constantly moving" as the collective production of the "learning body" is something you, as recipients, must decide. Perhaps further video observations are necessary in order to design, or to reject, the image of the perpetual-motion machine.

A Methodology of Gaze-Designs

An ethnographic document or piece of data always relates to a situation as well as to a scientific context. Obviously, there is something fixed on the videotape, but it cannot be separated from the observer's eyes. Suspending the ethnographer's view in data production and replacing it with the camera lens does ethnography a disservice. To rescue ethnography from its subjectivity and selectivity is the same thing as trying to eliminate its basic paradox, its scientific magic potion for life and learning. The productive power of video ethnographic research lies in professional work in and on senses (in both senses of the word).

Video Ethnography not only gives us the opportunity of celebrating the technological capacities of fixation, but also of using moving images to evoke grounded scientific visions corresponding to the audiovisual aspects of cultural and social phenomena. Far from being a research style of representativity, measurement, or proof, Video Ethnography is a soft procedure characterized by gaze-seeking and experimentation, by plausible suggestions and possible views, one whose strength and effectiveness seems to lie precisely in the fact that even well focused pictures can provide material for discussion and provoke a need for communicative validation. It is not the fixation of a fact, but the onward movement of thought which becomes the goal of ethnographic research by means of motion pictures.

Acknowledgments

I would like to express my gratitude to Klaus Amann, Birgit Griesecke, Barbara Keifenheim and Thomas Scheffer for thinking and formulating with me in the revision of this text and special thanks to Richard Gardner for the translation.

References

De Certeau, Michel 1988: *Kunst des Handelns.* Berlin: Merve
Fleck, L. 1983 (1947): Schauen, sehen, wissen. In: L. Schäfer & K. Schnelle (ed.): *Ludwik Fleck. Erfahrung und Tatsache.* Frankfurt am Main: Suhrkamp, 147-174
Geertz, C. 1988: *Works and Lives. The Anthropologist as Author.* Stanford: Polity Press
Griesecke, B. 2001: *Japan dicht beschreiben. Produktive Fiktionalität in der ethnographischen Forschung.* München: Fink
Hirschauer S. & K. Amann (ed.) 1997: *Die Befremdung der eigenen Kultur. Zur ethnographischen Herausforderung soziologischer Empirie.* Frankfurt am Main: Suhrkamp
Hirschauer S. 2001: *Ethnografisches Schreiben und die Schweigsamkeit des Sozialen. Zu einer Methodologie der Beschreibung.* Zeitschrift für Soziologie, 30, 6, 429-451
Keifenheim, B. & P. Deshayes 1984: *Naua Huni. Indianerblick auf die andere Welt* (Film)
Mohn, E. 1997: Paradoxien der Ethnographie. In: J. Berg, H.-O. Hügel & H. Kurzenberger (ed.): *Authentizität als Darstellung.* Medien und Theater Bd. 9. Hildesheim: Universität Hildesheim, 18-42
Mohn, E. 2002: *Filming Culture. Spielarten des Dokumentierens nach der Repräsentationskrise.* Stuttgart: Lucius & Lucius
Mohn, E. und K. Amann forthcoming 2005: *Lernkörper* (Video-DVD)

Eric Laurier & Chris Philo

Natural Problems of Naturalistic Video Data

That *question*

Routinely when we tell other social scientists that we have been filming what people do while they are in cafés[1], we are asked this question (or variations on it): *Doesn't filming change how people behave?* This question appears to raise trouble for the aim of ethnographic filming in cafés to record *naturally occurring* activities, the suspicion being that customers must *react* to the presence of a camcorder, thereby spoiling the 'nautral' record. The camcorder in the café, like the elephant in the kitchen, is unavoidably and very noticeably there. Food made in the kitchen should surely be abandoned wholesale since the elephant's presence contaminates all the cooking done there; and some might therefore conclude that our efforts at videoing should also be abandoned. Certainly an unexpected thing in a familiar place raises questions about its presence there that day, and about how much it will disrupt the workings of that place. The camcorder, though an unusual thing, has a further special status, it is a *recording* device; it is expectedly making a record for some purpose and those that it films may become part of the record. Although they have an agile and nimble trunk, elephants play no part in preparing food in the kitchen nor do they takes notes about the cook's technique. In this sense the camcorder, and the overall project, is more intrusive

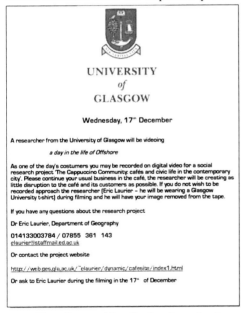

Fig. 1: Poster and flyer distributed at each cafe

---

1 For more details on the café project 'The Cappuccino Community: cafés and civic life in the contemporary city' see: http://web.geog.gla.ac.uk/~elaurier/cafesite/

and disturbing, potentially distracting customers not only by its presence but moreover by topicalising the making and consultation of a visual record. In what follows we want to respond to that question, but we want to go further and expose the grounds of that question.

Producing naturalistic footage

Let us backtrack a little to one of the central methodological aims of the café project: to record, on video, *spontaneous* activities *unsolicited* by the researcher and events *uncontrolled* by any form of lab set up. What was taped during filming in the café would be 'natural' in that sense (Lynch 2002), and from the researcher's side the camcorder had to be handled in ways that allowed things to happen without soliciting those events. New UK university guidelines on informed consent required that customers should be aware of what research was happening in the café, and so posters were put up in the café windows and on the counter, while flyers were put on tables making the presence of the camcorder all the harder to ignore. The posters and flyers contained a brief explanation that the project was 'a day in the life' of the café and alongside the request 'please continue your business as usual' (see figure 1). The question for customers in the café of how to deal with what might be a spontaneous, unsolicited and uncontrolled camcorder[2] thus began to have an answer.

Methodological advice from guides and courses on filming workplaces suggests using *distant* or *wide angle* shots for recording groups of people in public spaces in order not to miss how people respond to one another (Heath 1997, Heath & Hindmarsh 2002). It also suggests, where possible, leaving the camera unattended on a tripod in order to minimise further distraction and disruption to persons in the setting (Barbash & Taylor 1997). A particularly interesting warning comes from Luff (2003) who points out that trying to move the camera to catch an action occurring will always *miss* the beginning of that action, and hence will be an incomplete record. This is because the camera movement would be initiated by the camera operator first noticing the beginning of something, and *then* bringing the camera round to bear on it. MacBeth (1999: 154) points toward just this aspect of looking with the camera when referencing the anthropologists Asch and Chagnon in their filming of women and children crying: "we as viewers of his record, are in the midst of a motivated search, without knowing what could be promised for it, or where". The anthropologists' camera sweeps inelegantly until it finally catches up with a fight *already* in progress. MacBeth is explicating what is entailed in finding something going on with a camera in the

---

2 Putting camcorders where they are not expected can become a mild form of breaching experiment in that they disrupt background routines, and at the same time are recuperated into routine activities remarkably fast.

course of a shot, which is in itself a visual inquiry. Where MacBeth reveals how the camera chases down an event, we decided, following Luff's advice, that we would analyse the spaces of cafés for their promising locations and set the camera up to record what happened in such locations. Figure 2 was a preferred spot in one café, where a sofa and two arm chairs were arranged under a skylight.

Fig. 2: An inquiring look at the device

Having established these café locations, setting up the tripod and camera involved compositional work. With the camera operator's sense of the limited angle of vision, the scene was assessed for what could be filmed and with an orientation to the camera being visible but not positioned in front of a customer's face. A perspective had to be selected in terms of being over the shoulder, from another table, from the passageway and other possibilities that emerged in the analysis of the space of the café for setting up equipment. A set-up would be tried out with the tripod to check whether its legs could be fitted in and the height of the tripod adjusted. Through direct looking and then looking with the camera, the framing was finely adjusted. Once the camera was set-up, as with Lomax and Casey's (1998) study, it was left in that location, although in our case it was simply left recording for up to an hour. The camera would be moved every hour or less to record from other viewpoints and occasionally at the request of customers or staff. Alongside the positioning of the camcorder, the absence of a camera operator at the device was another method by which the presence of the project was minimised. The researcher was nevertheless always a couple of tables away from the camcorder and easily found for those who had queries about the project. With an intendedly low key presence, the camcorder on its tripod was not always immediately seen by customers, and this is what happens in figure 2.

Recognising the un-naturalistic

In his seminal work, Heath (1986) reminds us to turn to the *actual*, rather than imagined, ways in which persons, at the time of filming, witnessably orient, react or respond to the presence of a camera and a microphone. "If we are to make an empirical case for the effects of recording on interaction, then we need to demonstrate an orientation by the participants themselves to the production of their action and activity to some aspect of the recording equipment." (Heath 1986: 176, quoted in Lomax 1998).

What Heath (1986) demonstrated in his study is how a child's shifts in gaze are used to bring a disguised camera's presence into play during a doctor-patient interaction. He shows us that, while the camera is omni-present in the setting, it is by no means omni-relevant. Lomax and Casey (1998) pick up Heath's work to consider the ways in which the video becomes part of the organisation of fieldwork by ethnographers, its introduction, orientation and switching on and off being carried out as integral in displaying sensitivity to what is being put on the (video) record. For their part, the subjects being recorded display an orientation to their status as proper objects of the record, the particular technology of recording in terms of what it makes visible and what it misses, as well as the anticipated preservation of the record for subsequent research. By examining actual instances, as these and other researchers have done, we can move beyond saying simply that there *are* changes, to re-specifying imagined changes as practical matters of witnessable reactions to the presence of a camera. This entails asking about participants producing recognisable actions for the video-record, and also about the viewers' analysis of the video in its scenic intelligibilities as part of record of a particular project in a particular place (Lomax 1998, Jayyusi 1991, MacBeth 1999).

Filming from the spot that produced figure 2, the camera on its tripod was hidden from arriving customers in a corner overlooking a popular coffee table with two sofas under a skylight. Coming round from the counter, the woman with the cap sees the camera early on but does not bring her full scrutiny to bear until she sits down in *frame 2*. Having looked at the camera and worked out that this spot is what it is trained on, she puts her bags down in *frame 3*. She then leans forward to read the flyer on the table in front of her in *frame 4*. It is remarkable that she locates the flyer so quickly. One thing we can note is that the presence of an unattended camera on a tripod raises the expectation of a forthcoming account for its presence, where a pram or an umbrella might not. Objects, in other words, not only carry as part of their category membership of classes of objects (e.g. still cameras, microphones, CCTV) uses to which they can be put, they are also analysed in relation to the place in which they are found. "What is a DV camera doing in my café?" (A question not posed by those in tourist zones, nor amongst trainspotters, nor in a camcorder sales shop etc.) versus "What is an umbrella doing in my café!" Moreover in public spaces objects are analysed by members as potentially belonging to the place or to individuals (e.g. the chairs and tables versus an umbrella).

We can also note that there are *ways of coming into shot:* a camera zooming in on you, a camera operator walking up to you, a camera panning toward you. In this case the woman walks into the shot. Her inquiry then follows as to 'what have I walked into?' People routinely seek to get out of the way of others taking photos or filming if they think they risk being in the way at the wrong moment. They are stepping into the middle of some ongoing work of filming, they look at the direction of the camera, and they follow the projected course of its filming to see what in that scene could be an activity, person or thing worth filming. The classic instance is the tourist couple, where husband snaps wife, and you find yourself walking between the two.³ In his analysis of the observational shot, MacBeth (1999) examines the documentary maker's work as they follow a person through a crowd while walking themselves or search across a scene to find and/lose the scene. What we are seeing here is the member's (in an ethnomethodological sense) inquiry work in entering a scene of recording as to whether or not they are intended objects of the recording.

Fig. 2: Filling the screen of scene A with a close-up of X

In figure 3, when the women move off, the companion in front simply walks by the camera *(frame 1)*, her blue shoulder flashing briefly on the screen. The second woman, while passing close to the camera, stops briefly to wave directly into the camera. The woman's wave tracks from off-screen to mid-screen, the gesture emerging as it does so. Its movement comes to a halt with her face on the right and hand to the left, filling the screen *(frame 3)*. She upgrades her joke-wave at the camera to an exaggerated version of picking her nose, using the distortion of getting too close to the camera to add to this (Katz 1999). She is doing a strategic manipulation of the optics by coming in too close to the lens, in a two-part way. Her appearance is juxtaposed with the existing depth of the scene: we see her joke as a play on the expected distance that persons will maintain from a tripod that is demonstrably recording the café in *general* (as against them in *particular*). What is already involved here is that members are competent in analysis of what a *static* lens will capture in its field of view, and how they should therefore align themselves to it to produce a joke. The *static* camera on its tripod can be looked at and analysed by members, be they out-of-shot or in-shot, as an oriented recording device. So to begin to break down the question, what people *can* do in front of the camera, where this might be a limited repertoire, depends on what the camera's properties are found to be: roving, panning, zooming in on them or fixed. This woman frames herself for the recording device which, in its fixed look, otherwise misses the world that all the other customers are witnessing. In stopping off at the camera, she topicalises the camera for other customers in the café. Its presence is briefly made relevant to the customers as a collective: they look toward the scene she is making and, by smiling, respond to what she is doing.

The joke displays one of the alternative responses to doing what you usually do in the café, which is to fool around in front of the camera. Customers and staff at the cafés made visual jokes on camera with an orientation to their recognisability and reception as such by later viewers of the video, and also in relation to a request for, and ex-

---

3 See Brown et al's (2003) work on practices of tourist photography.

tensive record of, 'appearances as usual' in the café. In making jokes like this, they did not of course contaminate the entire record any more than a joke on a ballot paper spoils the entire election. They created something easily recognised on the record, the sort of artefact that in pursuing naturalistic behaviour would normally be consigned to the digital trash bin for deletion. A simple point here is that there were very few such recognisable acts for our camcorder, though there were plenty of the inquiring looks at the camera that we documented at the beginning of this section. In looking at these un-naturalistic activities, categorised separately in our data set, we have nevertheless looked at aspects of their *natural organisation* (of which more later) and by their recognisability we can anticipate how a dataset can be tidied of the un-naturalistic events and visual inquiries occasioned by the camcorder's presence. Moreover, while they reveal aspects of the café as a place where fun can be poked at officialdom, where there are other customers present as observers (though not observers making a record of the place). Customers can only lark around in limited ways and as a place. However *that* question still looms. What is required now is to excavate the question's grounds.

Ethno-inquiries into video recording

The video ethnography produced a data-set of *naturalistic* or *naturally occurring* customer activities in cafés akin to how many species of social scientists make records of everyday activities in ordinary places. The video data-set is an accountable and expected product of a funded social science research project on the relationship between cafés and civic life. To produce the data-set, the project has been committed to making *recordings* of ordinary life in cafés, even though much of what occurs there is arguably common knowledge. Yet as we have constantly remind ourselves, 'in its seamless familiarity, the world can become difficult to find for the record' (MacBeth 1999: 158) which of course was the launching point for our project. As historians of popular culture warn, the familiar habits and objects of our present are just as ephemeral and perhaps more likely to go unrecorded than the spectacular. Our commitment, then, has been to ensure that these everyday un-noticed ephemera are documented, but that was not our *only* aim in the project. What is a perplexing and confusing element in our café study is that, like Wieder's (1974: 43) ethnography of a half-way house, we are also interested in treating 'the ethnographic occasion as an object of study'. Like other ethnomethodologists, we have an interest in '*naturally organized ordinary activities*' (Garfinkel 1991, quoted in Lynch 2002) whether they be those of laboratory science (Lynch 1985), interpreting ethnography (Wieder 1974), throwing a stick for a dog (Goode forthcoming) or making espresso.

So with our social scientist's shoes on, we transform cafés' daily events via video recording into the video documentary record of certain times and places as stable naturalistic data for the social sciences. What we do not claim is to use reflexivity as a way of taking one step up above, not only everyday activities, but also the methodologies of the social sciences (Lynch 2000). Slipping our social science shoes off, to put our feet on the rough ground of practical reasoning, we walk through the methods of the social sciences and try not to trample through those of other more vernacular experts (i.e. the 'members' of ordinary worlds). This barefoot indifference to the methodological or theoretical warrants of the social sciences arises out of an ethno-archaeological interest in what makes particular practical forms of knowing possible and certain naturally organised ways of inquiring intelligible (Laurier & Philo 2004). A legacy of positivistic research in the social sciences, and indeed also of its critique by qualitative researchers, has been that the term 'natural' continues to be equated with objective and universal (Lynch 2002). Although naturalistic studies do not necessarily pre-suppose a concept of universal nature, they often find themselves critiqued as if they do. Relatedly, when deployed in the social sciences, records of naturalistic activities are inspected and may be dismissed for the distortions, biases and artefacts of that same 'universal' nature that they should be revealing (McHugh, et al. 1974, Raffel 1979). It is thus that Lynch (2002) provides a reminder why *that* question of changed behaviour seems to carry such force when asked by an audience of social scientists. It indexes a series of concerns that form the basis for the evaluation of the worth of a social scientific investigation. "Questions about bias, contamination and representational adequacy inhabit (indeed, they haunt) the practical projects of converting naturally organised ordinary activities (NOOA) into data and reviewing such data in analytical efforts to construct structures of NOOA. The confusion that puzzles, and to some extent entraps ... is a product of a slippage between a praxiological orientation to *naturally organized activities* to a more conventional social scientific effort to analyze *naturally occurring data*." (Lynch 2002: 535).

This is a perfectly acceptable shift to a concern with the quality of the *data*, but what it waylays is an ethnomethodological investigation into *practical reasoning* and the very constitution of that data. How, then, through and as part of naturally organized action, is this naturalistic video data constituted? We have begun to hint at what happens at the time in a reasonably straightforward methodological sense, and we have brought in the problematic of inquiring looks at the camcorder and jokes made for the record. Although the intelligible intentions of these acts are quite different, with only the latter having the record as its target, both still display and betray the presence of the recorder. Raffel (1979: 29) points out that, in making records, while there must be an observer, the good observer should be an 'absent presence'. The unattended camcorder displays a kind of absent presence, although the observer and their subjects are instead beset by the camcorder's particular kind of presence. Those clips that we have been examining are those where the camera has what we might call a *present* presence. The work of making the naturalistic dataset is that they be recognised as such and either dropped on the cutting room floor or categorised separately from the other clips (we labelled them 'un-natural' clips in our corpus).

There is more to video's reconfiguration of social science data because it offers the possibility of a fundamental shift in where, how often, with how many subjects and how long after the activities the observing occurs. With traditional ethnographic written records, the activity of observing may precede and always entails its recording at the time or later in notebooks[4], with entries such as: "*The café is pretty full when two women arrive in café with prams. A guy sitting in the window notices them arrive and offers his table.*"

As Raffel (1979) remarks, there is here no real separation of recording from observing since to observe is to 'take note' of something. Akin to the use of the ethnographer's placement of herself in any setting with her notebook and pen, the placement of the camcorder at the time (and subsequent shifts) are also bound up with what can be observed there and then. That is, as we mentioned earlier, the film-maker surveys the scene to work out where the camcorder could be placed and does it with an orientation to a visibility that is not constant. Moreover, the placement is made with the expectation that events will occur that can be eye-witnessed and recorded from its spot. However, in its preservation of the audible and visible activities of some event when the video recording is re-played during editing, data sessions and seminar presentations, a further occasion arises for observing, and as such finding further things in the video record and, as likely as not, making transliterations from the visual record to textual records. Observation of naturalistic activities, once they are *rendered*, as Garfinkel (1992) would put it, or *transformed*, as Latour (1999) would put it, into video data fundamentally change the work site organisation of social science observation from the ethnographer with her notebook and camera. In this way, its analysis bears strong resemblances to the use of tape recordings of naturally occurring talk that were crucial in the founding of conversation analysis (CA) (Lynch 1997). Where participant-observation is characterised as consisting of many subjects with one observer and many interpreters, the video-record has minimal participation and a potential multitude of observers and interpreters. Observational work is displaced from the fieldsite to the computer or TV screen.

What the video recording provides in the way that it preserves data is seemingly a re-observation of an event's emergence, course and ending. In the practical efforts made to avoid intervening in the events being recorded, to exclude from the naturalistic corpus events that were clearly produced by the presence of an observational device and to preserve the activities 'whole' (e.g. uncut, 'real-time'), the video records hold the promise that the researcher might examine past activities not as *past* but rather as 'formerly present' (Raffel 1979: 129). Like the documentary photographic record, the video record is apparently produced simultaneously with the activity it records, which strengthens its claim as a record produced, then and there, in a way that a textual record which could be

---

4 Video also promises that the fallible ethnographer's memory of what happened which was once supported by the notebook gains further strength through the recordings as an archive of details in one particular place at one particular time.

made at home in another country or hours or years later does not. What Raffel (1979) warns us is that the commitment to recording *all* that happens in an effort not to *forget* the good or, as we would put it here, not to *miss* the surprising details of what and how customers and staff in cafés do what they do, this commitment becomes eventually at best a deferral or at worst an unwillingness of differentiating the good from the bad.

In differentiating the 'bad', in the form of abandoning or separating out clips that display visible reactions to the presence of the camera, observers of the video record let themselves be governed by what is presenting itself. As a form of naturalistic observational science of human action our approach refused to investigate what did *not* appear in the clips. There are all manner of things of course that do not appear and so to proceed otherwise would be opening the doors to bringing up whatever we like as having not appeared. Rather, our empirical grounding manoeuvre was to stick with the video record, examining instead how items recognised as not fitting with the naturalistic corpus were indeed recognisably so. Their 'special' quality lies in members effectively drawing attention to the absent presence of the observer; the ethno-inquiry into the resulting clips is only complete, therefore, once the work of the observer – watching the clips back, complete with suspicious glances at eh camcorder and the odd prank – is also taken into account. Or to put it another way, these brief snatches of data in the overall video-record point to toward a certain incompleteness: unlike the other activities made present in the video recordings, these data are unavoidably and irretrievably and irreplaceably made complete by the presence of the observer. In fact, they are made complete twice over: at the time as 'hailed' by the members and when the observer finally consults the recordings, dividing the 'good' (worthy of further inquiry) and the 'bad' (destined for the cutting room floor but retrieved by us for ethno-inquiry). However thinking along these lines sparks a realisation: yes, the 'good' clips arguably have a completeness arising without the observer's presence, the indifference to the observer allowing them to pass into the central corpus of naturally occurring activities in cafés. Yet what is forgotten is that their completeness is also being found through the oberver's presence in the daily work of analysing video clips and sorting them in the corpus; in that sense ethno-inquiry reveals them being treated identically to the 'bad' clips – it is just that they are put in a different 'pile' and retained for more sustained description in other contexts, answering other research queries. Their completeness too, then, is found through observation and analysis, not through their being self-contained, self-presenting or self-evident.

Returning to *that* question, we can answer it in a video-observational mode: activities that displayed reactions to the camera were excluded from the main data-set. We can answer in an ethnomethodological mode: to produce naturalistic data, the practical reasoning of video recording everyday life is accomplished in the constitutive gap between the absence and presence of the observer in the observational-video setting. Despite the hopes of certain natural sciences for video, there is no way out of the dilemma: the gap is what constitutes the video record. *That* question will always accompany *naturalistic* video in particular because it is the natural question to ask, if a question that can, to adapt a saying of Wittgenstein, lead us like flies back inside the bottle buzzing furiously around its limits.

Bibliography

Barbash, I. and L. Taylor, 1997: *Cross-Cultural Filmmaking*. London: University of California Press
Garfinkel, H. and D. L. Wieder, 1992: Two Incommensurable, Asymmetrically Alternate Technologies of Social Analysis. In: G. Watson and R. M. Seiler (ed.) *Text in Context: Contributions to Ethnomethodology*. London: Sage, 175-206
Goode, D., forthcoming: *Playing with Katie: An account of human-dog play utilizing autoethnography and videography*. New York: City University of New York Press.
Heath, C. and J. Hindmarsh, 2002: Analyzing Interaction: Video, ethnography and situated conduct. In: T. May (ed.) *Qualitative Research in Action*. London: Sage, 99-121
Heath, C., 1986: *Body Movement and Speech in Medical Interaction*. Cambridge: Cambridge University Press
Heath, C., 1997: Analysing work activities in face to face interaction using video. In: D. Silverman (ed.) *Qualitative Methods*. London: Sage, 183-200
Jayyusi, L. 1991: The reflexive nexus: photo-practice and natural history. *Continuum: The Australian Journal of Media & Culture*, 6, 2: http://wwwmcc.murdoch.edu.au/ReadingRoom/6.2/Jayyusi.html
Katz, J., 1999: *How emotions work*. London: University of Chicago Press
Latour, B., 1999: *Pandora's Hope, Essays on the Reality of Science Studies*. London: Harvard University Press
Laurier, E. and C. Philo 2004: Ethno-archaeology and Undefined Investigations. *Environment & Planning : A*, 36,
Lomax, H., & Casey, N. 1998: Recording Social Life: Reflexivity and Video Methodology. *Sociological Research Online*, 3, U3-U32
Luff, P., 2003: *Comments at WIT Meeting*. London
Lynch, M. 2000: Against Reflexivity as an Academic Virtue and Source of Knowledge. *Theory, Culture & Society*, 17, 3: 26-54
Lynch, M. 2002: From naturally occurring data to naturally organized ordinary activities: comment on Speer. *Discourse Studies*, 4, 4: 531-537
Lynch, M., 1985: *Art and Artifact in Laboratory Science, A Study of Shop Work and Shop Talk in a Research Laboratory*. London: Routledge
Lynch, M., 1997: *The Ethnomethodological Foundations of Conversation Analysis*. Cerisy-la-Salle, France: copies available from the author
MacBeth, D., 1999: Glances, trances and their relevance for a visual sociology. In: P. L. Jalbert (ed.) *Media Studies Ethnomethdological Approaches*. Lanham MD: University Presses of America, 135-170
McHugh, P., S. Raffel, D. C. Foss and A. F. Blum, 1974: *On the Beginning of Social Inquiry*. London: Routledge & Kegan Paul
Raffel, S., 1979: *Matters of Fact*. London: Routledge & Kegan Paul
Sacks, H., 1992: *Lectures on Conversation, Vol. 2*. Oxford: Blackwell
Wieder, D. L., 1974: *Language and Social Reality, The Case of Telling the Convict Code*. The Hague: Mouton

Sigrid Schmid

Video Analysis in Qualitative Market Research – from Viscous Reality to Catchy Footage

In qualitative market research, video methods are well on the way to becoming a methodological fad deployed with euphoria and high expectations. This boom in the use of video methods for market research is shaped by two trends: firstly, the strong trend of communicating through visual information (cf. Stephens 1998, Mirzoeff 2001), and, secondly, the growing significance of ethnographic approaches in market research.[1]

With regard to the visualisation trend, it is fair to say that in the business world in particular the verbal forms of communication, namely a text or a talk, have been being largely superseded by combined forms involving visual and verbal or numerical components. Means of visualisation are used everywhere as a back-up for speech and are seen as vehicles with which to pare down information and the time needed to communicate it. The triumphant march of the Powerpoint presentation programme lends elegant expression to this trend that has been assimilated by market research from the word go (Schnettler, this volume). The increasing use of video clips for presenting market research findings is to be seen in this context and primarily demonstrates that success in this field is not only about research competence but also about the competence to stay up to date with communication and presentation requirements. As in the field of social science research (cf. Schnettler, Knoblauch, Raab, this volume), this has become all the more simple in recent years due to falling prices for digital video technology and thanks to the emergence of user-friendly, semi-professional video editing software such as Premiere Pro or Final Cut.

However, beyond the compulsion to use catchy visualisations, the main contribution towards the establishment of video analysis comes from the *ethnographic shift* in qualitative market research that has been apparent for some years now. This shift is a consequence of growing scepticism about the classic survey methods used in qualitative market research, namely the focus group and the interview: their output was increasingly believed to lack everyday relevance, while habitualised and unconscious aspects of product usage and brand selection often remained insufficiently tangible. Moreover, in the face of strong competitive pressure and dwindling spending power, corporate

---

1 The process of becoming established is admittedly already far more advanced in North American market research. Institutes focusing on video analysis and ethnography such as "Ethnographic Insights" or "Context Based Research Group" have been a regular feature of the market for some years now.

market research and marketing departments with years of experience of focus groups behind them felt the need to break new ground in order to generate fresh and profitable product or marketing ideas.² As a result, a new type of research design is finding increasing favour: surveys limited to interviews or focus groups in unnatural studio situations are being supplemented or replaced by research – in whatever form – intended to register the reality of real life and not just *studio* reality.

Against the background of these two trends it is possible to distinguish between two fundamentally different ways of deploying video methods in market research: (1) as a *visualisation tool* to produce material with which to illustrate market research presentations and impart the findings graphically making them easier to take in; and (2) as a *survey instrument* aimed at capturing the full detail of reality and vividly documenting that which remains hidden and unspoken in interviews or group discussions. The specific implications of these two extremely different motivational positions for practical market research are presented below.

Video as a Visualisation Tool

A large part of common market research practice has always consisted of investigating consumers' everyday culture and trying to draw a correlation between this everyday culture and specific consumption habits. Ultimately it is all about exploring a direct connection between lifestyle and consumer behaviour. Up until a few years ago, the classification of consumers according to lifestyle typologies was chiefly the result of large-scale quantitative surveys. Detailed questionnaires were used to find out people's values, shopping habits, socio-demographic data, etc., and from this the most diverse target group typologies were subsequently obtained via segmentation analyses. Quite apart from the accuracy or unreliability of such typologies and lifestyles, these data take communicability no further than what is conveyable by text and figures.

But today's marketing representatives typically seek to get a spontaneous 'feel' for their target group without giving it too much thought. It is most easily for them to understand a typology if they can tie the types back to people they see in and know from their personal everyday life experience. Consequently, additional video surveys are often valued here for their ability to go beyond quantitative figures and interpretations and bring consumer types or target groups to life. After all, it may well be possible to express in coefficients e.g. the fact that a young consumer cultivates a post-materialist lifestyle, but as for the type of person to expect and her preferences regarding concrete items of furnishing, accessories and products against the background of her attitudes and values, all this remains relatively abstract. The coefficient fails to re-

---

2 This particularly applies to major international brand manufacturers in the sector of fast moving consumer goods.

veal that there's a TV set from the seventies standing in her living room, that her kitchen boasts a striking number of eco products by Alnatura, or that her favourite store is the second-hand shop around the corner. But video footage can show this young consumer in her living-room and in her kitchen as she tops a slice of bread with vegan spread. Video is intended to visualise for the client the consumers' everyday aesthetics, including implicit and explicit forms of expression, as determined by lifestyle. One can say that the visualisation of consumers' material expression of lifestyle by means of video methods is therefore the attempt to visualise the network of meanings that lend significant structure to the reality in which they live (cf. Geertz 2000) assuming that these exert a crucial influence on consumption as such.

The fact that this is achieved with the help of ethnography-based video footage is very much in the tradition of an understanding of field research as once defined by Bronislaw Malinowski. From a self-reflexive point of view this means that even when video is used in market research just as a visualisation tool, it allows not only for satisfying clients' wishes in seeking to capture the zeitgeist, but ultimately to flesh out an abstract, empirical skeleton in the best ethnographical tradition (cf. Malinowski 1984 [1922]). Given the video footage manage to provide creatively filmed and edited material of analytical depth, they can convey a holistic picture of complex life worlds of individuals or groups of people. As a rule, the effect on the observer goes then beyond the fast conveyance of information and a paring down of data which are generally expected of visual materials. Added to this is indeed a deeper appreciation of what is depicted (cf. Banks 2001), that certain 'gut feeling for the target group' as the marketer would say. And this is in fact a highly valued feeling in our times of emotional marketing, often leading to confident action-taking such as is barely conceivable based on information communicated in text form.

With regard to the translation into research practice, the production of such video footage intended to illustrate lifestyles tends to be very targeted and the recordings are more a part of the data preparation process than of the survey itself. The content that needs to be taken into account, for example typologies, must be understood before the video camera starts rolling. Therefore, in such cases, it is not so much the video data that constitute the core of the survey and analysis. It is far more a case of understanding the respective life worlds, with their typical everyday aesthetic and lifestyle elements, by means of the in-depth interview and video-free ethnographic research using creative diaries and self-documentation. It is only once the typical elements have been derived from this database that the video survey should begin. To this end, respondents are recruited with close reference to the pre-compiled typologies. Video footage of this kind is ideally filmed by ethnographically trained camera people familiar with the typologies and everyday profiles to be expected. This allows for a video output which is highly consistent with the preceding analyses in terms of the statement made. The aim in working up the video material is not so much to reflect on what the material says in its own right. Instead, the focus is far more on its effect on the recipients. It is important to select footage that the anticipated clientele most probably will interpret in such a way as to allow precisely that holistic understanding and aforementioned gut feeling to set in and be taken for valid. 'Valid' means in this regard 'consistent with the result of the basic analysis'. This calls for very firm control of how the observer might view the material. The scope for interpreting the footage must be limited via comments and labelling, at least at those points where it can't be reduced through selection and editing.

Though such kind of ex-post video visualisation of already developed typologies and segmentations is required from time to time, this kind of video projects is not the core business for video-based market research. The following section now attempts to explain how video material is used in market research as an analytical instrument in the stricter sense.

Video as a Data-Gathering Tool (1) – 'Practices and Routines'

A clear methodological justification for the deployment of video documentation becomes apparent as soon as clients have questions concerning practical activities and/or the products involved therein. Questions of this nature often abound in the context of product development or optimisation. Authentic insights into concrete product usage and everyday practices are seen here as a precondition for sounding out what is required in the way of product optimisation and in order to identify needs early on and thus develop new product ideas.

This results from the belief that people tend to lack a detailed awareness of their everyday actions and generally find it difficult to explicate such expects verbally. A comparison between interview statements and everyday observations for the same person often reveals how people falsely reconstruct their own actions. Experience has shown that verbal survey techniques using a questionnaire, interview or focus group do not generate much interesting information about how he or she actually proceeds in detail when it comes to daily chores and routines. Instead, they merely generate a meagre data base from which product developers are unable to glean very much at all in the way of relevant information. In this respect, video surveys represent a fundamental leap forward in quality, as it is only with the help of visual documentation that a proper database can be created for analytical appraisal of everyday routines that otherwise more or less defy verbalisation.

One can distinguish between three main areas of deployment for video analysis of practices and routines (in connection with product usage): inspiration for new product ideas, further development of existing products, and evaluation of prototypes or new products. For all three areas, the material must be authentic and as natural as possible if it is to contribute towards realistic product development with strong practical relevance. Routines must be filmed in such a way as to demonstrate the underlying unconscious mechanisms taking place; their unreflected nature must not be impaired by the presence of the camera person and the rolling camera. The flow of everyday routines must not be interrupted by intrusive questions. Now, this might seem to imply that the camera person has to remain absolutely passive and is not allowed to pose any questions about what is going on in front of them. Research experience does show, however, that the only way to shed light on this more complex, non-standardised situation is via tried and tested ethnographic techniques: the aim at all times is to create an atmosphere of relaxed trust, in which the respondent is able to forget that certain statements and/or modes of behaviour may be desirable or of interest as opposed to undesirable and uninteresting. It is a fact that the presence of the camera person and camera may disturb an everyday routine sequence. Being a real person of flesh and blood, the camera person often proves to be more of a disturbance here than the camera. Despite the camera person remaining silent throughout, respondents constantly feel called upon to demonstrate reciprocity. As a rule, it is only veteran filmers who manage to prevent this, people who are wrapped up in their role and who are so concentrated on their film work and the camera, both inwardly and in their non-verbal communication, that they really do almost merge with the camera (cf. Grimshaw 2001). Speaking from experience, this effect is not always the case with video ethnographers or film interviewers. And so it happens time and again that, when visited, respondents are put off their stride by the consistently silent presence of these people to such an extent that they don't (are unable to) keep up the unreflected flow of an everyday activity. The lack of any reaction on the part of the filmer is so disconcerting to respondents that they grind to a halt, over-complicate or indeed over-simplify the everyday tasks at hand. Enforced silence is not expedient in such situations. Instead, the ethnographer behind the camera must react naturally to the situation, namely by directing attention away from the video documentation via trivial, relaxing chat. Here it has proved more helpful to talk about things not related to the main topic rather than asking about the activity in progress. In a situation like this, asking about what the person is doing generally leads to a sense of uncertainty or to processes of pseudo-rationalisation, thus annulling the 'routine' situation. Nevertheless, in order to really learn whether there is anything conscious about certain hand movements and activities, and whether an action involves minor considerations and conscious decisions, it is best to finish with a reconfrontation interview, in which film material is shown and during which the respondent should comment on his or her own actions.

If the task is to provide video footage to help generate inspirations for new products or product versions at an early stage in product development, then a relatively broad approach is usually selected. The camera focus here is on the detailed steps involved in – more or less common – everyday practices: cleaning the windows, colouring one's hair, washing the car, cleaning the bathroom, tidying the kitchen, ironing, cooking lunch on weekdays, baking cakes, and suchlike. In cases like this, it is a question of learning from the video material the different routines that arise, the practical everyday solutions that people come up with, and the forms of product usage involved. In such projects, the there is sometimes a limit imposed on the material by means of a narrowly defined sample. The analysis and selection of video footage is a consequence of the research objective. Since the video material desired as output from such studies is generally used for creative product development workshops, it is often also the nature of the event and the workshop programme that influences analysis. Experience shows that the interesting and inspiring aspect of such workshops as far as product development is concerned is video footage showing what are popularly known as 'wow effects' instead of the standardised uniformity of unspectacular everyday routines that can make for hard going. Such 'wow effects' include all the traps and mishaps involved in everyday tasks, and particularly the individual tricks and everyday processes of adaptation and compensation that people resort to when handling products in order to ensure a hitch-free daily existence. This analytical work resulting in wow effects on the side of the observer is often not simple, since many people's daily tasks and chores are frequently very mundane and the individual tricks and coping strategies so subtle as to be incapable of triggering any kind of wow effect. It generally calls for painstaking appraisal of the material to develop interpretations that can serve as an inspiration for product developers, most of whom are technically oriented and scientifically trained.

Video analysis is of course also used to optimise existing products or to evaluate how new products function. In the case of those products where practical usage and handling play an important role, video recordings can provide valuable insights. For instance, a housewife may at most be able to say that despite having followed all the steps given in the instructions, the new dream dish from the oven still didn't turn out right. Here, the video recording can show how she carried out the instructions in practice, or how she devised her very own methods of preparation, and where difficulties may have arisen that now call for optimisation.

Video as a Data-Gathering Tool (2) – 'Authentic Everyday Insights'

In market research, video-analysis lends itself not only to relatively narrowly defined concrete activities and product usage, but also serve to obtain a broader insight into people's lifestyles and everyday realities. Here again, the assumption is that people are hard pressed to describe their everyday life with its wealth of detail, its everyday heterogeneity and viscosity, and especially the habitual, unconscious aspects of life. Nonetheless, it can definitely be of interest to market research clients to gain a grasp of all this. They may be keen to understand the structures through which advertising and products are received, or how products become embedded in everyday logics and everyday emotions. And it is of course often all about tracking down the unreflected and inexpressible little highs and lows of everyday life, the emotional significance of which, as advertising and marketing have long realised, can often be greater than the person concerned is actually aware of.

Video-based ethnographic insights into everyday life are not to be confused with the video illustrations described at the outset, in which the video material serves not so much to generate knowledge as to illustrate analytical findings from preceding surveys based on other methods. Studies intended to generate authentic everyday insights, on the other hand, are conducted with a fundamentally different concern in mind. They have less to do with obtaining a holistic understanding of consumer types or target groups and instead seek to obtain insights into life worlds, which are possible only via intimate contact and the meticulous documentation of reality – an almost voyeuristic procedure. The aim here is to produce video material that can serve as a starting point for analysis. This has implications both for the survey methodology and for evaluation.

Even the collection of data is fundamentally different. Here an attempt is made to portray the coincidental and heterogeneous character of natural reality. The fact that we are not talking here about concrete, scheduled activities means that considerable time has to be allowed for the survey. The minimum – for an average family household – is generally one weekday and one weekend day, although a full week at least is preferable. The filming is done with cameras permanently installed in the rooms of interest; this often means the kitchen or living-room. In most cases, several cameras have to be used in order to capture every point in a room where actions take place. All this calls for technically sophisticated set-ups, firstly to avoid intrusive wiring that would considerably hamper everyday life, and secondly to be able to save the quantities of data generated. The sound quality is often particularly difficult to manage, since the rooms in question are frequently those in which several people talk from different directions. In fact the need for location scouting is quite common, in order to clarify whether a potential respondent's premises are suitable, or what needs taking into account when setting up the cameras. There are some who may wonder whether all this effort is warranted by the output. Is it actually possible to obtain *authentic* insights into people's everyday life in this way? From experience the answer has to be yes and one example from a study on the emotional everyday moments experienced by dog owners with their darling pets would seem to verify this. For the video observation – planned for a weekend and two weekdays – rooms were chosen in which interaction with the dog was likely: the kitchen (as the feeding place) and a second main room named by respondents and in which they spent time with their dog, usually the living room. The aim was to document the everyday interaction between dog-owner and dog to include all the non-verbal signs of emotion and involvement. What form does the morning petting ritual at the breakfast table take, what happens as the impatient animal waits in excited anticipation for its titbit, how does its master react to the food bowl that has been licked clean? In an interview, the majority of dog owners would not think of such moments at all and would at best describe in plain terms: "The first thing I do in the mornings is to feed the dog in the kitchen. I put half a tin into his bowl. I give him a dog biscuit maybe once or twice a day." Only a video observation over several days is capable of shedding light on things like the interactive rituals that actually take place during the morning feed. For instance, in one case, as the video shows, a lady dog-owner sets down the bowl filled with dog food in the same way every morning. She then turns to the task of making breakfast. And each morning, the dog pads up, examines the food in its bowl, turns away with bowed head, lies down in the doorway and waits. The dog owner notices this and asks: "So you don't like that?" The dog looks at her attentively and then glances over to the food cupboard. "So you'd like something tasty on top?" The observer – and probably the dog-owner too – sees the dog positively nod its head. "Then I'll see if I got something for you." Now she takes some cheese out of the food cupboard, which, as transpired in the interview, she had bought especially for the dog. "Look, we've found something delicious for you." The dog approaches enthusiastically: "That's much more to your liking, isn't it". The dog watches her every move. As the owner goes over to the bowl, he marches alongside her so that both arrive at the same time. As the dog begins to eat, the owner kneels beside him and tickles his tummy and back. "Happy now, aren't you. That's more like it." It becomes clear that the dog is part of having a good start to the day. The interaction with the dog distracts the owner from the less enjoyable daily chore of making breakfast and enriches this everyday routine. Spoiling the dog also takes on the character of vicarious satisfaction. The need for something tasty, evidently all too understandable for the dog's owner ("That's more like it."), is something that she herself indulges in less generously, as concomitant interview and ethnography showed. She is more than willing to allow her dog something that she doesn't or can't grant herself.

Only the 24-h video recording[3] is able to shed light on the unconscious side of these kinds of interactive rituals – whether with pets or between human beings. For instance, the lady in question had mentioned prior to the video recording that she only ever gave human food as an extra when she felt like pampering her dog as a special favour. On being confronted with the video recordings, she was amazed and amused at her own behaviour.

Immobile recordings of this kind are ideally supplemented by focused concomitant ethnographical sessions. In view of the need to gain a holistic experience of and become 'submerged' in the respondent's life world, which is often impossible due to lack of time, these focused ethnographic sessions represent a good compromise. They are an adequate means of setting in context the stationary recordings (cf. Knoblauch 2001). Additional mobile recordings of, say, the overall living environment and the social environment, are also helpful; their meaning is brought out via the interaction between video ethnographer and respondent ('participatory cinema', cf. Mac Dougall 1995).

Audiovisual recordings of authentic everyday situations are appreciated by advertising and marketing people for providing them with inspirational material from which to create emotionally charged marketing and communication measures of everyday relevance. Knowing what the consumer's everyday life is like makes it possible to devise messages of relevance to this consumer. Product developers also use such insights into

---

3 As a rule, cameras fitted with motion detection are used; these register movement and then start recording automatically.

latent needs in order to develop ideas for new products: Would it be worth considering a dog food that offers greater scope to satisfy the blatant need for interaction with the dog? How can such rituals be used in order to enhance the identification potential or the aspirational character of advertising?

The Art of Evaluation and Representation: Ending up with catchy footage

When clients go for a research design which includes video recordings they expect to get the research results presented in forms of video footage. Therefore, finding people who are prepared to be filmed in their bathroom or living-room or who agree to a 24-h video recording over several days is the simpler exercise compared to that of evaluating the material gleaned in this way. That is the key challenge facing the market researcher when it comes to video analysis.

Given the *ethnographic shift* mentioned at the outset that has successfully led many corporate market research and marketing departments to appreciate the relevance of the inexpressible but extremely interesting aspects of consumers' everyday life, video analysis now sees itself confronted with high expectations. In a curtailed version of the ethnographic message, the assumption is that the video peephole into consumers' everyday reality creates per se a kind of transparency, and that sheer insight into routines, rituals, latent patterns and emotions can clarify virtually anything that might be of relevance for consumer behaviour. It generally goes without saying for clients that the practices captured on film and video films of everyday life will offer spontaneously obvious insights. However, as repeatedly shown in the evaluation phases, this is by no means the case. Natural reality is in fact unbearably slow, viscous, and monotonous. Just suppose one wants to document and analyse a family's everyday TV usage and degree of attentiveness when viewing: they sit in front of the TV set for hours on end, and this almost every day. Video data hence make for extremely hard going, constituting a mass of material that first has to be dealt with. Genuinely useful insights certainly don't leap out at the untrained observer. They are virtually never obvious at first glance, but have to be extracted from hours and hours of consumers' everyday life. If we stick to the example of our family: what are the reactions to commercials during a cosy evening in front of the television, and how does mother react when watching afternoon TV while doing the ironing? In order to answer these questions and come up with a relevant, valid statement on, say, the effect of advertising or people's receptiveness when consuming media, one needs to begin by applying a trained eye to the process of hermeneutic data evaluation, followed by the key second step of a creative, interpretive approach in accessing the material. After all, the point of the exercise is always to find (invent) a story for any one sequence that conveys its relevance vis-à-vis the needs of the client. This is particularly important if one considers that the isolated everyday routine of a single person does not always provide meaningful insights; instead, the relevant insight doesn't become apparent until a comparative or contrasting framework is introduced, for example the TV family compared to a one-member household.

The bottom line is that routine, time-consuming reality has to be pared down to moments that within a span of 30–120 seconds bring over the underlying aspects of everyday life. The teasing out of this 'condensate' takes place during an involved process of filtration. It is all about selecting the crucial, meaningful minutes from dozens and sometimes hundreds of hours worth of material. On the one hand this involves a substantiated interpretation of the visual data including all forms of non-verbal communication and the imagery of the immediate physical surroundings. A grasp of visual ethnology is indispensable here. On the other hand, weighting and targeted selection of sequences also plays a decisive role. They must eventually provide a conclusive picture that satisfies the validation needs of market research. A sure instinct for the right selection is vital here, since experience has shown that the untrained observer rapidly becomes overwhelmed by the somewhat unspectacular slowness of reality. It takes considerably more effort for an untrained eye to pick out interesting aspects than for someone who has been dealing with the material for days or weeks. Virtually the only way to avoid disappointment is to ensure a meaningful deployment of dramaturgy and visual stylistic devices. Support from specialists in the field of video editing and media production is indispensable here. Experience has shown that it is only through their professional preparation of the material that the exciting aspects of routine everyday life come to light, even for the – methodologically speaking – amateur observer. However, this preparation must be preceded by an analysis of the material, with the subsequent interpretations being creatively implemented in close collaboration between analyst and creative.

The more that market research studies deploy video methods for the purpose of presenting illustrative results that get straight to the point, the greater the need for the allotted time and budget to be shifted from data collection to evaluation and presentation.

Summary Outlook

For some years now, video technology has been growing more flexible, more mobile and cheaper to use. This means that market research is at last able to document and present for analysis aspects of consumer behaviour that were only recorded approximately in the past: the authentic reality of everyday practices, routines and product usage that are so self-evident and unconscious that no consumer can talk satisfactorily about them. Regarding the methods, similar to scientific social research, one is taking new approaches that go beyond established dogmas and taboos of traditional ethnography and visual anthropology (cf. Knoblauch 2004), always in search of best practice. On the one hand this means significant progress for qualitative market research, however, it does not per se promise any added value for the client. Only when the material which in its authenticity is outright refractory is edited in a way that makes the relevant aspects obvious also for non-experts does this method fulfil its purpose in market research – to satisfy customer requirements.

The fact that, as with much ethnographic research (cf. Knoblauch 2001), this is only possible by exploiting and preparing the material using what could be called a naturalistic approach actually sheds a light on the limited ability of the average recipient to understand and interpret complex visual information.

Acknowledgements

I would like to thank Rene Kaufmann for contributed ideas and ongoing discussion and Maxine Demharter for her help with the translation.

References

Banks, M., 2001: *Visual Methods in Social Research*. London: Sage
Geertz, C., 2000: *The interpretation of cultures*. New York: Basic Books
Grimshaw, A. 2001: *The ethnographer's eye: Ways of seeing in anthropology*. Cambridge: University Press
Kaufmann, R. and S. Schmid, 2005: Film ab! Neue Videomethoden in der qualitativen Marktforschung. *Research & Results*, 6, 20-23
Knoblauch, H., 2005: Focused Ethnography, *Forum Qualitative Sozialforschung / Forum: Qualitative Social Research [Online Journal]*, 6, 3: Art 44, Available at: http://www.qualitative-research.net/fqs-texte/3-05/05-3-44-e.htm
Knoblauch, H., 2004: Die Video-Interaktions-Analyse. *sozialer sinn. Zeitschrift für hermeneutische Sozialforschung*, 1, 123-138
Knoblauch, H., Schnettler, B., & Raab, J. (this volume): Video-Analysis. Methodological Aspects of Interpretive Audiovisual Analysis in Social Research
Mac Dougall, D., 1995: Beyond observational cinema. In: Hockings, P. (ed) *Principles of Visual Anthropology* (2nd edition). Berlin/New York: De Gruyter, 115-132
Mac Dougall, D., 1978: Ethnographic Film: failure and promises. *Annual Review of Anthropology* 7, 405-425
Malinowski, B., 1984 [1922]: *Argonauts of the Western Pacific*. Illinois: Waveland Press
Mirzoeff, N., 1999: *An introduction to visual culture*. New York: Routledge
Schmid, S., 2005: Fokussierte Ethnographie – Der neue Königsweg in der qualitativen Marktforschung? *Planung und Analyse*, 6, forthcoming
Schnettler, B. 2001: Vision und Performanz. Zur soziolinguistischen Gattungsanalyse fokussierter ethnographischer Daten. *sozialer sinn. Zeitschrift für hermeneutische Sozialforschung*, 1, 143-163
Schnettler, B. (this volume): Bullet Lists and Commentaries. A Video Performance Analysis of Computer Supported Presentations
Stephens, M., 1998: *The rise of the image and the fall of the word*. Oxford: University Press

Epilogue

Hans-Georg Soeffner

Visual Sociology on the Basis of 'Visual Concentration'

Trust in Words – Distrust in Images

The Humanities and the Social Sciences have a long history of association with the written word – and in fact, this association has for the most part been voluntary – (see Goody 1981), in the course of which the introduction of the phonetic alphabet signified a new 'qualitative jump' in the evolution of human language use (Goody & Watt 1981). Not only did the phonetic alphabet emancipate itself from the analogue relationship between written symbol and 'the world of things' by making a recognizably random relationship between the sign and the signified the basic principle of written language, but it also represented the first attempt to reconstruct through transcription the series of sounds produced in the process of speech. In this way, written language refers in an explicit fashion to spoken language, or, to put it more pointedly, in the practice of written language, spoken language continually employs itself as the primary point of reference (Soeffner 1989: 81). It is above all due to this state of affairs that the relationship between "text and image, image and text" (Harms 1990) has taken on a totally new dimension, albeit only recently and with maintained emphasis on spoken and written language as the points of reference, because it requires of those doing the interpreting to discover the dissonances between textual and image media and to take them into account.

Although it may appear trivial, we should recall in this context that, in our culture – and not only in ours –, the communicative form, the creative energy, and the ability to convey the narrative and truth of images was not subject to even the slightest mistrust over many hundreds of years. Indeed, images were regarded as guarantors for the conveyance of tradition, of beliefs, and of knowledge, even when they were not associated with text. The stained-glass windows, frescos and paintings in our churches and cathedrals are mute evidence of this, just as is the trust the educational theorists of the early modern age (see for example the '*orbis pictus*' of Amos Comenius and the murals on the city walls of the "City of the Sun" in Tommaso Campanella's work of the same name) held in the ability of images to convey 'true knowledge'. Furthermore, conventions in 'allegory', of iconography and of the principles of image construction put semantic systems and syntactical rules at the disposal of the visually-oriented societies of this period, making it relatively simple to arrive at an intersubjective process for decoding these images (see Gombrich 1986). Mistrust of images' alleged multivalence could only arise in an era in which the written word and text had become the guarantors of intersubjectivity and of 'objectivity'. This was the case because, through the increasing fixation on texts that had to be read, not only had the ability to decode images been lost along the way, but also because we have become relatively blind to the multiple meanings or even the ambivalences held within texts.

The German Research Society (DFG) symposium, the results of which are presented in the previously mentioned anthology under Wolfgang Harms' editorship, has demonstrated very clearly how speech-dependent representation, interpretation, and scholarly analysis still is, even today, despite the wealth of images available to us and the great respect with which images are approached by their interpreters (above all in the arts). In addition, it reminds us of to which great extent our ability to conduct autonomous pictorial reconstructions of social worlds, to interpret, and to analyze them are subject to distrust. We have no trouble acknowledging the role images play as implements in the traditional *ars memorativa*, similarly in the spirit of the use they found in Amos Comenius' 'orbis pictus' – as a didactic instrument. As for the rest, we prefer to cite Brecht: "A photograph of the Krupp works or of the A.E.G. factory reveals next to nothing about these institutions" (Mazzoni 1990: 448). When it comes to documentary photography, we still doubt the "ability of an image to accurately represent reality" (loc. cit.) – these are the terms in which the symposium discussed Alexander Graf Sternbock-Fermor's autobiographical study ("Ein Leben als Bergarbeiter", 1921) and the Association for Social Policy's early twentieth-century photographic documentation of life in Berlin's tenement courtyards. The authors come to the conclusion that photography "can only be effective in association with texts" (Mazzoni 1990: 450). – By way of an aside, the suggestion that this statement contains is all too often abused to propagandistic ends (see Rutschky 1993), as when appropriately manipulative commentaries are associated with photographs. Satirical photomontage also draws on this principle, as exemplified in the works of John Heartfield.

Nevertheless, we find in the essay collection edited by Harms – still representative as it is for the discussion of the text-image or image-text issue – theoretical and methodological considerations that reflect the thrust of our research. For one thing, it offers an analysis of visual habits that have been altered through the increasing influence of the visual media on our perception (loc. cit: 450), in other words of the growing powers of both production *and* interpretation recipients (who often use cameras themselves) have developed in respect to new visual media. Of additional interest is Aron Kibédi Varga's (1990) attempt – despite his efforts to establish analogies to classical rhetoric, which he himself sees critically – to provide means for seeing "visual argumentation and visual narrativity" as autonomous discourses independent of text. We also find a designation of the difference in how the human eye on the one hand "visually sizes up" written texts (which our eyes must follow letter for letter) and images on the other (which permit our eyes to "wander" more freely) (cf. Huber 1990b: 401). In fact, textual analysts are thus now discovering something in the field of the psychology of perception has long been acknowledged as fact in that they are taking the range of different mechanisms into consideration that determine how we perceive the world around us.

However, the debates on the relationship between text and image and image and text we touch on in this context, as well as related specific questions ("What makes it possible for us to conduct a terminological interpretation of images and how can we distinguish correct from fallacious interpretations?" Huber 1990a: 399), although they have been conducted, sometimes in quite intensive form, by archaeologists, art historians, historians, and media studies specialists, have only been dealt with in a peripheral manner in the field of sociology. This seems astonishing for a number of reasons, for sociology is and will continue to be – despite its well-developed survey techniques and the resulting understandable preference for conducting surveys – an observational science, *as well*. The 'translation' of data gained through observation into textual protocols or of visual recordings into transcripts in the form of language is part of the daily business of sociological field research. What is more, at a very early point in our discipline's development, one of its 'classical thinkers', Georg Simmel, noted that societies, or at least urban societies, are conglomerations of observers, for "compared with those in small towns", the comings and goings in large cities demonstrate "an immeasurable dominance of seeing others as opposed to hearing them" (Simmel 1992 [1908]: 727). Thus, sociology retains this function as the process of observing and interpreting observers (Goffman 1959, 1961, 1963, 1967)

This fact calls for us to draw consequences for both the development of sociological theory as well as in the context of methodology and methods of empirical social research. On the basis of protosociological essays, for example the "Anthropology of the Senses" ("Anthropologie der Sinne", Plessner 1970) or a "Phenomenology of Perception" (Merleau-Ponty 1966), we need to develop concepts for a sociology of the senses. The interaction and the mutual complementation ('synesthesia') of the senses should come into consideration, as well as the phenomenon that "each sense has its own 'world'" (cf. Merleau-Ponty 1966: 260ff).

What we plan to investigate within the context of this theoretical problematic is of relatively modest scope. Human powers of vision, observation, and the observation of observers has – and in this we concur with the above-mentioned authors – always been accompanied by processes of interpretation and understanding that imbue the senses with "sense", provide a foundation for all perceptions through "constructions of the first order" (Schütz 1971), and continually generate everyday, pre-sociological and, yes, visual forms of typification (cf. Frey 1999). We intend to employ this everyday potential for visual typification towards a methodologically controlled, only slightly visual "construction of the second order" (Schütz 1971, cf. also Soeffner 1989: 126ff): towards a *'photographic visual concentration'* of those everyday visual typologies that people apply to themselves, their surroundings, and their fellow human beings. In doing so, we have opted – following the example set by August Sander – for the eye and "its world" (Merleau-Ponty 1966) of visual typologies. Texts that interpret or accompany the image, or have been attached to it as an afterthought have been – with the exception of certain limited and separately represented information (see below) –

consciously left out. The visual concentration is meant to interpret itself, supported by sequences of images alone, resulting in a 'language of imagery'.

Interpreting Images through Images

Along with the way our glance sizes an image up (see above) – entirely different to how we read texts – a number of other structural characteristics must be taken into consideration which make the processes of composition and reading written texts (but also a few of the basic principles of spoken language) different from visual perception. Each 'participating' observer, or an observer sitting behind a one-way mirror, is aware of the problems that arise when we attempt to set down protocols of our observations in writing. Even before we start to search for the 'right semantics' for the actions, gestures, bodily and facial expressions, articles of clothing, etc. we observe, we are faced with the dilemma that total and simultaneous perceptions must be brought into a succession of written thoughts. Language constructs temporal sequences which we did not perceive or in place of other ones we did perceive. In addition, the temporal sequences created by the structures of language

suggest a corresponding causal sequence: Starting with occurrences that were originally simultaneous, we arrive at a 'first this', 'then that', which can easily lead to a 'because this first', 'therefore later that'. In short, the period of time in which the perception occurred is transformed into written language and reading time of another nature. Although the 'ethereal' quality of what one perceives at a given moment is given lasting form, thereby attaining the goal of discursivity, the new semantic and syntactic systems of linguistic order nevertheless function according to laws of their own, with their own finalities, causalities, images, and typologies. All of these, in turn, come together to take effect on the 'original perception' as it is reflected in our memories. They color and transform our memories, at least insofar as we do not have access to Proust's madeleine experience and its evidentiality.

The goal of bringing time to a halt that lies at the core of the methodology underlying 'visual photographic concentration' – as opposed to the case of snapshots – is, in view of the dilemma of how to transform images into text, initially intended to establish a visual discursivity. With this we mean making

it possible to arrive at a continually renewable, visual sizing-up of an image that reconstructs the construction of what is being observed. In a second step, sequences of images (on the selection and the sequencing of images, see obove) are produced so as to ensure that the result of this visual interpretation can be assessed and the visual typologies represented in these images are recognizable.

Of course the procedure for 'visual photographic concentration' we are suggesting does not preclude a linguistic interpretation at a later date. Nonetheless, our primary aim is – in the strict sense of a visual sociology – to approach the representation of society through visual means within the context of a *methodologically controlled descriptively and analytically 'self-sufficient' methodology and method* and to test this construct by means of our planned case study in the form of a pilot study. In other words, using the procedure we have suggested, we intend to not only document elements of social life that have already been visualized, but in addition to make them 'readable' as images. Images and sequences of images are, or so we assume, when it comes down to it just as multivalent and characterized by fillable gaps (Iser 1970) as are texts. Nonetheless, they can be, at least when conceived of as methodologically controlled constructs, subjected to systematic and objectifiable analysis in the same manner as are written texts – in our case, even before the linguistic interpretation sets in.

Precursors and Role-Models

Walker Evans' and James Agee's photo-essay *Let Us Now Praise Famous Men* (1989 [engl. orig.: 1939]) represents an exception in the relationship it establishes between image and text. In their work, the authors attempt to establish a balanced relationship between text and photos. "Photographs are not illustrative. They and the text are coequal, mutually independent, and fully collaborative." (Agee cited in Mitchell 1994: 290). Walker Evans's photos are presented in the first part of the books, completely separate from the text and also lacking any kind of explanatory textual gloss as to when and where the photos were taken. In the second part, Agee's text is presented, which however does not make direct reference to the photos in the first part. This unusual form of presentation makes the photos along with the text into coequal elements of a final product. The photos appear as independent vessels of information that do not require any further reference in the text.

A final photographic product of this sort does not come about through taking simple, quick snapshots of 'subjects' encountered in the field. As commissioned representatives of the Farm Security Administration, James Agee and Walker Evans lived with these people over longer periods of time before they started gradually to take pictures of some of them. We have already referred to the similarity of their project to ethnological procedure. A closer look at the photography of August Sander, who was active in Germany at the beginning of the 20th century, evidences how the medium can not only be employed as an instrument for the collection of data, but also for analysis and representation.

August Sander represents an exception among the photographers of the early 20th century. In his photographic work *Menschen des 20. Jahrhunderts* ("People of the Twentieth Century"), he demonstrated his ability to profit from the documentary and analytic potential of photography in a manner that can even today be regarded as groundbreaking for photographic ethnography, as "an example of photography as science" (Sontag 1999: 61). August Sanders' 'sociological' work consists of portrait photographs which he then arranged in files. The particular order of the photographs was intended to reflect the stratification of society as Sanders perceived and interpreted it at the time. His books of photographs contains – in contrast to Walker Evans' and James Agee's photo essay – no further text commentary other than cursory information on the profession or status of the person depicted. The order of the images as he chose it comments itself, thereby replacing textual references.

However, not only the order in which the photographs are presented is 'sociological' and 'analytical', the photos themselves have this characteristic, for they are consciously created social scientific constructs, Sander's constructs of reality. He did not merely take these 'objects'' picture, as when taking a snapshot (cf. Berger undated: 36ff). Instead, his pictures were the product of a dialogue between the photographer and his models. Sander was able to convince people to "'design' an image of themselves before the camera, to make known their expectations of society through the use of clothing, body-language and gestures, to demonstrate social self-understanding" (Keller 1994: 39). In this way, his portrait arrangements are analytical (self-)representations. In this process, the models' self-interpretation and that of the photographer, or in other words the situation created in the process of making the photograph, converge within the photograph.

Sanders' photographs record typical and, in this sense, representative poses. In contrast to the conventional strategy of portraiture that amounts to a beautification of the represented person, i.e. also to presenting the observer with an illusion in the service of aesthetics or the dominant taste of a given era, in Sanders' case it is the transparency of the relationship between photographer, model, and audience that is decisive. Sanders attempts to maintain transparency and honesty in this "dialogue between the photographer, the model, and the audience by interfering in this both suspect and familiar threesome through various means in order to create an 'alienating' distance" (Keller 1980/1994: 39). In addition, he extends the scope of his portraits to include scenic elements, i.e. through including local color, which Keller (loc. cit: 40) has termed the "narrative tendency" in Sanders' photographs.

In the same way that we attempt to capture an informant's self-representation at the verbal level in an 'open' interview, Sanders succeeded in capturing these self-representations in the form of images with a single photograph. The decisive aspect is that the photograph is a cooperative product, a product of interaction, to which process the photographer or ethnographer contribute to the same extent as does the 'informant' and that this cooperative construction, or rather reconstruction of a construction, conducted by the ethnographer/photographer remains obvious and plausible for the observer.

As a result of his approach – at its core a theory of social classes – Bourdieu is interested in demonstrating how through photography "class-determined values can be transmitted without any instruction whatsoever" (Bourdieu 1981[1965]: 54). In doing so, he is above all concerned with analyzing "the social uses of photography" (see subtitle) to show how the mechanisms of distinction and the various forms habitus takes on within a given society can be disclosed through observation of the interplay between "class differences and classes consciously differentiating themselves from one another" (loc. cit: 58 ff). This is an entirely legitimate, albeit very limited, perspective on this allegedly 'illegitimate' art form. It is a perspective that leads to the following apodictical, even then outdated, statement: "In short, photography can be regarded as a form of art, but it can never be anything more than an art form of the second order" (loc. cit: 76).

If we remove the class-theory blinders from this text (yet without forgetting the topic they are caught up in), thereby widening our perspective on it, Bourdieu's observations offer a wide range of productive thoughts towards the conceptualization of a 'visual sociology'. He, too, takes up his analysis with an insight how society is molded by or is dependent upon photography's topics, typifications, and means of representation. To this extent, photography, as an 'average person's art form', is capable not only of revealing the "aesthetics of the 'common people'" (loc. cit: 18); furthermore, the interviews conducted by the working group around Bourdieu demonstrate how deeply the visual habits, the representational and typificational repertoires associated with photography are anchored in respondents' consciousness and how 'rule-directed' both the processes of production as well as the interpretation of photography are. As a result, 'family photography as a rite of household cult practice' (loc. cit: 31) and, moreover, 'the ritual character of photography' (loc. cit: 32) are disclosed. One element of this is the principle of 'frontality', a specific form of (self-)expression in which the photographic subject presents him- or herself for the photographic instrument and the 'image-maker'. Bourdieu believes, and it seems at least to be plausible, that frontality "is linked to deeply-rooted cultural values": "It is a manner of honor that we approach the camera in the same fashion as we approach a person we respect and whose respect we expect in return." (loc. cit: 94). This part of Bourdieu's argumentation demonstrates remarkable similarity to Goffman's thoughts on the production, retaining, and defense of a personal "image" and the ritual practices associated with this undertaking (cf. Goffman 1967: 25).

Photography's ritual character does not only bring into balance social tension or the ambiguity of social 'rites of passage', but also – as Bourdieu accurately observed – the relationship between the momentum of an action and the 'expected' gesture in the photographic image: "To the extent that something in the way of action is depicted in the photo, it is as a result forever 'immovable' and removed out of time. It is – and the words reflect this condition exactly – the harmony or the balance of an eternal gesture" (Bourdieu 1981[1965]: 88). Such significant gestures that are recognizable as such for both their producer as well as the recipient can only be constructed "because the way in which society employs photography is determined by the conscious selection of categories that organize familiar ways of seeing the world from among the full extent of its possible uses" (loc. cit). It is this both implicit (H.-G. S.) as well as 'conscious' selection that leads us to conclude that "photographic images can be considered as exact and objective reflections of reality" (loc. cit).

Bourdieu acknowledges, and this links him to our approach, the mutual effects of implicitly known and used typologies and the attempt of those depicted in the photographs to appear 'natural'. This results in that "faked naturalness" and that "theatrical expression" (loc. cit: 92) that lay photographers and their 'victims' create together. In this cooperation, both parties strive for the mutual achievement of an aesthetic, form-giving, and form-retaining imbuing of significance (*Überhöhung*), for the representation of a temporally limited yet lasting social identity. – One can be 'captured' by a coincidentally successful snapshot, while in an 'arranged' photograph one desires to be 'well captured'. Thus, it is particularly valid for photographic portraits – but above and beyond them also for each 'shot' that forms the captured image and fills it with meaning – that in photography, "an art-form [articulates itself; H.-G.S.] that imitates art" (loc. cit: 85). This art-form makes conscious use of the 'core image's' embeddedness in specific surroundings, which in turn is given its own construction principles through a 'strong world of symbols' (see loc cit: 48). This is a principle of construction in which the "logic of mutual acts of enhanced signification of the person and his surroundings" (loc cit: 49) find expression.

These tactics aiming at elevation or exaltation, recognizably aesthetically determined, that are inherent to photography serve to explain how we come to perceive photography as a 'surpassing moment' (Boltanski 1981: 158) that in turn appears to refer both to the photographer's intention and to that of the recipient that the (aestheticizing) construction that is the image "coincide with an intention that can be concretely formulated" (Bourdieu 1981[1965]: 104). It is through 'normal' photography's implicit, but at the same time very strong regularity and through the stasis of the recipient's expectations inextricably linked to this regularity that it becomes possible to break these rules in a conscious and intentional fashion, to generate irritations and, through these, to refer to the – otherwise common – impact of these implicit rules. The excess contained within the 'surpassing moment' is now consciously organized in a manner other than usual. In this way, explicit reference is made to the principles of construction otherwise implicitly in effect; this procedure appeals to the recipient to become an interpreter. When Man Ray termed himself a "fautographe" (Chamboredon 1981: 195), he was – in the same sense as our considerations – referring to the intentional implementation of the violation of rules and the irritations that this practice is bound to bring about.

In the collection of essays edited by Bourdieu, Luc Boltanski introduces another aspect of importance to our approach (Boltanski 1981: 137 ff). He refers to the sterility that is structurally preprogrammed in photography and the resulting problem effecting above all press photographers of the necessity of selecting of the 'best', 'most accurate', 'most typical' photograph for 'a' topic, 'an' event or 'a' situation, from among a total of up to 600 or 700 'shots'. We make systematic use of this problematic as presented by Boltanski in our approach by, in contrast to press photographers, documenting the serial nature of photographs referring to one theme or one object. In this way, we hope to make plausible and 'visually explicable' through this sequence of images the selection of the one image that for us represents the depicted social world in a 'sufficiently meaningful' manner. Thus, sequentiality, as one of photography's principles of construction, is both put to use for and 'disclosed' before the interpreter.

All in all, our reading of Bourdieu, running as it does a bit against the grain, unearths those principles that we seek to employ towards the legitimate use of this so-called 'illegitimate art-form' for our conception of a 'visual sociology'. Quite like Bourdieu, we are convinced that photography's implicit catalogue of rules and its 'interpretation of the world' can be made explicit and that the everyday knowledge of its 'semantics', codes, and syntactic rules make it possible to read images in not only a plausible fashion, but moreover in a manner that is to a great extent anchored in intersubjective perception. This can be achieved at that point at which the catalogue of rules is made explicitly and systematically accessible through images, sequences of images, and the visually plausible selection of images, in other words through the interpretation of images by means of images. In other words, we undertake the methodic visualization of Roland Barthes' insight that "photography is not just perceived", but rather "read"; "it is associated more or less consciously by the public that consumes it with a traditional array of signs: and each sign has as its precondition a code, and it is our task to decode this code (or its connotation)" (Barthes, cited in Boltanski 1981: 153).

Conclusion

At the center of our project stands the central issue of whether a 'image-through-image-interpretation', without reference to written text and language, on the basis of a 'visual concentration' is possible. It is this very *possibility*, the potential for a 'visual sociology' that by and large sustains itself through the "power of the image" (Frey 1999) that we intend to assess systematically. This assessment includes as a matter of course the possibility that the procedure be corrected and that the limits of the fundamental idea be made visible. From our perspective, the most intriguing aspect lies in realizing a very old idea, namely that images in and of themselves convey 'true knowledge' and can interpret the world without having to conform to the bounds of language, that this old idea can be thus conceived in a *pure, exaggerated form* and can be 'tested' to see how of what use it might be to sociology as a observational science.

If it is true that, as Roland Barthes maintained, "(p)hotography cannot simply be perceived", but is "read" in accordance with a code of imagery that must be decoded, then this means that the 'implicit set of rules of the photographic process' (Bourdieu [1965]1981) creates 'interpretations of the world' that rely on semantics, codes, and interrelated signs located within imagery. In short, the trivial realization that photography and photographs represent interpretations must be expanded to include the insight that these interpretations occur *in accordance with a catalogue of rules* and on their own achieve typicalizing concentrations of perceptions that not only 'project' the latter 'into the image', but also make them readable through the specific representation in a medium, i.e. *establish them on a new, medially conveyed level accessible to observation and interpretation (a new order)*.

Bourdieu's reference to the high symbolic value of photography, his insistence on the existence of recognizable principles of construction and the introduction of heightened meaning, in other words photographic processes of concentration, supports our hypothesis that a *thick description through images* can be achieved, which, *analogous* to Geertz' linguistic 'thick description', makes visible the symbolic order in which people move through their respective social worlds and milieus through their actions and interpretations. I can entirely concur with the thesis that just as 'thick description' requires prior interpretation, so too does 'thick description of images', the 'visual photographic concentration' assumes the presence of a catalogue of interpretative rules of the kind that is implicitly part of photography's structure and has always been put to use by photographers – *but rather than in language, in the images' codes*. What is more, the procedure we are suggesting by no means excludes a post hoc linguistic interpretation *and* validation, variation or falsification of what we have achieved.

Finally, the visual project is explicitly characterized as an "interactive project": *together* with our photographic subjects, we will construct that scenario in which – with reference to the 'adequate meaning' (Weber 1976 [1972]) we wish to achieve – the principles of construction valid in the social order we are representing are most 'ideally' concentrated. *This* act of construction comes to be through the dialogue we enter into with our photographic subjects. However, at the decisive moment, it is the photographer who is looking through the viewfinder. To put it more pointedly, one could say that the way the scenario is realized (constructed) is a product of interaction – the *construction of the moment*, the moments, and the shots are, to the contrary, the work of the person doing the perceiving, selecting and 'shooting' – the photographer. The photographer makes a decision through her choice of how to frame the image ... and interprets the scene at the moment she presses the shutter. *In the process of collecting the series* in which the specific situations, manners of action, etc. are represented through a categorization in types, the photographic subjects once again make an equal contribution to the process, just as they do when that image is chosen which appears to offer the greatest 'degree of concentration' and that constitutes the fruition of the organization and the construction of the series as an instrument of interpretation and instruction. The question of "who is really constructing whom?" can be answered in the following three steps of our procedure: (1) the 'setting' (scene) is the product of interaction; (2) the choice of how the moment in which the images are shot is the 'construction' of the photographer; (3) the series and its 'concentrated core' are selected through a process of shared construction between the photographer and the photographic subjects.

Acknowledgments

The photos in this article were taken by Sybilla Tinapp.

References

Agee, J. & W. Evans, 1989 [engl. orig.: 1939]: *Preisen will ich die großen Männer: drei Pächterfamilien.* München
Berger, J., undated: *Das Leben der Bilder oder die Kunst des Sehens.* Berlin
Boltanski, L., 1981: Die Rhetorik des Bildes. In: P. Bourdieu et al. (ed.) *Eine illegitime Kunst. Die sozialen Gebrauchsweisen der Photographie.* Frankfurt am Main: 137-163
Bourdieu, P. et. al., 1981[1965]: *Eine illegitime Kunst. Die sozialen Gebrauchsweisen der Photographie.* Frankfurt am Main
Chamboredon, J. C., 1981: Mechanische, unkultivierte Kunst. In: P. Bourdieu, L. Boltanski, Castel, J. C. Chamboredon, Lagneau & Schnapper (ed.) *Eine illegitime Kunst. Die sozialen Gebrauchsweisen der Photographie.* Frankfurt am Main: 185-202
Frey, S., 1999: Die Macht des Bildes. Der Einfluß der nonverbalen Kommunikation auf *Kultur und Politik.* Bern, Göttingen, Toronto, Seattle
Goffman, E., 1959: *The presentation of self in everyday life.* Garden City
Goffman, E., 1961: *Behavior in Public Places. Notes on the social organization of gatherings.* New York
Goffman, E., 1963: *Stigma.* New York
Goffman, E., 1967: *Interaction Ritual. Essays on Face-to-Face Behavior.* New York
Gombrich, E. H., 1986: *Bild und Auge.* Stuttgart
Goody, J. (ed.) 1981: *Literalität in traditionalen Gesellschaften.* Frankfurt am Main
Goody, J. and J. Watt, 1981: Konsequenzen der Literalität. In: J. Goody (ed.) *Literalität in traditionalen Gesellschaften.* Frankfurt am Main: 45-104
Harms, W. (ed.) 1990: *Text und Bild, Bild und Text. DFG-Symposion 1988.* Stuttgart
Huber, H. D., 1990: Die Sprache der Bilder und die Bilder der Sprache: Sprachanalytische Anmerkungen zu Baruchellos 'La Correspondence'. In: W. Harms (ed.) *Text und Bild, Bild und Text. DFG-Symposion 1988.* Stuttgart: 399-413
Iser, W., 1970: *Die Appellstruktur der Texte. Unbestimmtheit als Wirkungsbedingung literarischer Prosa.* Konstanz
Jäger, G. & Mazzoni, I. D., 1990: Bibliographie zur Geschichte von Text-Bild-Beziehungen. In: W. Harms (ed.) *Text und Bild, Bild und Text. DFG-Symposion 1988.* Stuttgart: 475-508
Keller, U., 1994: Sander und die Portraitphotographie. In: A. Sander (ed.) *Menschen des 20. Jahrhunderts: Portraitphotographien von 1892-1952* (edited by Gunther Sander). München: 11-18
Merleau-Ponty, M., 1966: *Phänomenologie der Wahrnehmung.* Berlin
Mitchell, W. J. T., 1994: *Picture Theory: Essays on Verbal and Visual Representation.* Chicago, London
Plessner, H., 1970: *Anthropologie der Sinne.* Frankfurt am Main
Rutschky, M., 1993: Foto mit Unterschrift. Über ein unsichtbares Genre. In: B. Naumann (ed.) *Vom Doppelleben der Bilder. Bildmedien und ihre Texte.* München: 15-28
Schütz, A., 1971: *Gesammelte Aufsätze* (Vol.1). Den Haag
Simmel, G., 1992 [1908]: Exkurs über die Soziologie der Sinne. In: G. Simmel (ed.) Soziologie. *Untersuchungen über die Formen der Vergesellschaftung, vol. 11* (edited by Otthein Rammstedt). Frankfurt am Main: 722-742
Soeffner, H.-G., 1989: *Auslegung des Alltags - Der Alltag der Auslegung. Zur wissenssoziologischen Konzeption einer sozialwissenschaftlichen Hermeneutik.* Frankfurt am Main

Sontag, S., 1999: *Über Fotografie (11th edition)*. Frankfurt am Main
Varga, A. K., 1990: Visuelle Argumentation und visuelle Narrativität. In: W. Harms (ed.) *Text und Bild, Bild und Text. DFG-Symposion 1988*. Stuttgart: 356-367
Weber, M., 1976 [1972]: *Wirtschaft und Gesellschaft. Grundriss der verstehenden Soziologie.* Tübingen

Contributors

Hubert Knoblauch, Professor of sociology at the Technical University of Berlin. Email: hubert.knoblauch@tu-berlin.de

Eric Laurier, Senior research fellow at the University of Edinburgh. Email: eric.laurier@ed.ac.uk

Dirk vom Lehn, Dr., Researcher at the Work, Technology and Interaction Unit, King's College London. Email: dirk.vom_lehn@kcl.ac.uk

Thomas Luckmann, Dr., Prof. emeritus at the University of Constance

Paul Luff, Dr., Reader at King's College London. Email: paul.luff@kcl.ac.uk

Elisabeth Mohn, Dr. phil., Visual Anthropologist, researcher, writer, filmmaker, lecturer (freelance), Berlin. Email: e.mohn@onlinehome.de

Lorenza Mondada, Dr., Professor of linguistics at the University of Lyon and Laboratoire ICAR (CNRS). Email: Lorenza.Mondada@univ-lyon2.fr

Anssi Peräkylä, Dr., Professor of sociology at the University of Helsinki, Department of Sociology. Email: anssi.perakyla@helsinki.fi

Chris Philo, Professor at the University of Glasgow. Email: cphilo@geo.gla.ac.uk

Christian Heath, Dr., Professor of Sociology at King's College London. Email: christian.heath@kcl.ac.uk

Jürgen Raab, Dr. rec. soc., Lecturer at Konstanz University. Email: juergen.raab@uni-konstanz.de

Johanna Ruusuvuori, Dr., Assistant professor of social psychology at the University of Tampere, Department of Sociology and Social Psychology. Email: johanna.ruusuvuor@uta.fi

Cornelius Schubert, Researcher at the Technical University of Berlin, Department of Sociology. Email: cornelius.schubert@tu-berlin.de

Sigrid Schmid, Unit Director of GIM Vision, the video and ethnography department of the Gesellschaft für Innovative Marktforschung. Email: s.schmid@g-i-m.com

Bernt Schnettler, Dr. phil., Assistant at the Technical University Berlin, Department of Sociology. Email: bernt.schnettler@tu-berlin.de

Hans-Georg Soeffner, Dr., Professor of Sociology at the University of Constance. Email: hans-georg.soeffner@uni-konstanz.de

Dirk Tänzler, Dr. phil., Private Lecturer at Konstanz University. Email: dirk.taenzler@uni-konstanz.de

Monika Wagner-Willi, Dr., Researcher at the University of Zürich, Institute for Special Education. Email: wagner@isp.unizh.ch